Idea Makers and Idea Brokers in High-Technology Entrepreneurship

Fee vs. Equity Compensation
for Intellectual Venture Capitalists

ELIAS G. CARAYANNIS
and TODD L. JUNEAU

Westport, Connecticut
London

Library of Congress Cataloging-in-Publication Data

Carayannis, Elias G.
   Idea makers and idea brokers in high-technology entrepreneurship : fee vs. equity
compensation for intellectual venture capitalists / Elias G. Carayannis and Todd L. Juneau.
      p.   cm.
   Includes bibliographical references and index.
   ISBN 1-56720-456-2 (alk. paper)
   1. New business enterprises—Management. 2. High technology
industries—Management. 3. Entrepreneurship. I. Juneau, Todd L., 1966– II. Title.
HD62.5.C369   2003
658.1—dc21   2002069697

British Library Cataloguing in Publication Data is available.

Library of Congress Catalog Card Number: 2002069697
ISBN: 1-56720-456-2

First published in 2003

Praeger Publishers, 88 Post Road West, Westport, CT 06881
An imprint of Greenwood Publishing Group, Inc.
www.praeger.com

Printed in the United States of America

The paper used in this book complies with the
Permanent Paper Standard issued by the National
Information Standards Organization (Z39.48–1984).

10 9 8 7 6 5 4 3 2 1

To George E. Carayannis, Esq. and Dr. Maria G. Carayannis

To Cheryl, Eric and Kevin Juneau

To McDonald Stewart and James Stewart

Contents

Part III: Insights from Practice and Lessons Learned in IVC

Preface: Uses of This Book

Entrepreneurs often need the expert advice of professional service providers (consultants, attorneys, public relations, recruiters, etc.) to develop successful business strategies and their start-up firms. These providers are in essence trading their intellect for monetary compensation. For start-up firms, there is a potential impediment in their current relationship with professional service providers in that these relationships are arm's-length, contractual agreements, while the service required may actually be very strategic and organic to the success of the start-up.[1]

Also, the entrepreneur often lacks the resources needed to pay these providers the market rate for that expertise. The alternative is for the entrepreneur to depend on "middlemen" (such as incubators or venture capitalists or VCs) to arrange access to this expertise—for which the entrepreneur pays a heavy price by sacrificing substantial amounts of equity.

A *potential* solution to this dilemma is the use of equity-based compensation for professional knowledge providers. Instead of the fee-based approach, where the professional service provider bills the client based on time and effort, the equity-based approach pays the provider with a share of ownership in the client, i.e., stocks, options, bonds, etc., which can then be converted to cash at a later date (e.g., through an initial public offering or IPO).

---

[1] Some parties want an arm's-length transaction; one does not always want a marriage. However, this decision should not be trust-based, but cost-based since trust is never a negotiable item and must always be present between counselor and client.

This model of compensation is already used by a small number of firms that specialize in serving high-technology start-ups. Notable examples (profiled in this book) include law firms (Venture Law Group and Wilson, Sonsini in Silicon Valley), management consultants (recent "incubators" and "venture funds" established by Accenture and McKinsey & Company) and even information technology service providers (PSINet and EDS).

Why are these firms adopting the equity-based approach instead of the traditional fee-based approach? This book argues that the equity-based approach reengineers the relationship between professional services and entrepreneurs:

- It encourages the "expert" to understand the fundamental business of the start-up client.
- It improves the alignment between the interests of the expert and those of the client.
- It allows the client to pay for services when cash reserves are low.
- It reduces the ultimate cost of such services by avoiding the use of a financial middleman allowing start-ups to be "direct" with their service providers.

Most important, the equity-based approach transforms professional service firms into *intellectual venture capitalists or IVC*: with a substantial stake in the success of the new venture, professional service providers and entrepreneurs become active partners in crafting a successful business strategy and invest in the new venture their intellectual capital in the form of specialized value-adding professional services.

In explaining the mechanism of this new approach, this book presents a conceptual framework, field practices, and multiple case studies that demonstrate the full range of benefits and risks generated by the intellectual venture capitalist approach. Therefore, this book should be of significant interest to entrepreneurs and service providers (such as lawyers, accountants, management consultants, and others), who can use the model presented to craft contractual relationships which create win-win opportunities through proper integration of business strategy for a start-up with advice provided by professional service firms. Such an approach would allow a firm to better align the interests and knowledge of service providers and their entrepreneurial clients via the equity-based compensation model.

Moreover, to illustrate the benefits, drawbacks, and nuances of the equity-based approach, and the transformation of professional service firms to intellectual venture capitalists, this book includes detailed case studies on how this approach was used primarily by service providers (such as intellectual property law firms) in their work with high-technology start-ups. While most books aimed at entrepreneurs focus solely on how to get financing (primarily from venture capitalists), this book attempts to show how other business partners are critical to start-up success. It should be of interest to entrepreneurs looking for strategies to improve their chances for business success, professional service providers who target the start-up market, as well as students and researchers of the entrepreneur and the entrepreneurship phenomenon who could benefit from the case studies by deriving a more comprehensive perspective of the process and dynamics of calculated risk-taking.

In this context, this book should be useful for the growing number of undergraduate and graduate university courses on entrepreneurship, where it can be used to teach potential entrepreneurs ways to leverage their relationships with professional service organizations. While other books focus on a more unilateral thematic approach, such as informing entrepreneurs about intellectual property, or advising lawyers on how to manage their client relationships, *this book aims to bridge the gap in perception and understanding between professional service firms and start-up ventures, thus outlining the concept and practice of the intellectual venture capitalist.*

Acknowledgments

We would like to thank the numerous sources for our work. Their time, interest, and insights in our work are greatly appreciated.

We would also like to thank our families. Their patience, understanding, and support have been a key success factor for this project

Finally, we would like to thank Gary Nath and Nath & Associates for their support as well as Jeffrey Alexander for his assistance in researching and compiling an earlier part of this manuscript.

Part I:

The Intellectual Venture Capitalist as Concept and Practice

Chapter 1

Introduction:
Intellectual Venture Capital for
Entrepreneurship

> "It has become clear that the way to riches is not through collecting
> fees but through acquiring successful equity stakes," said Michael
> Hall, a partner in the Silicon Valley office of law firm Latham &
> Watkins. "Many professionals will not take on new engagements
> without getting the opportunity to acquire meaningful equity stakes."[2]

Almost any entrepreneur who launches a new venture, and in particular a high-
technology venture, encounters situations requiring the counsel and expertise of
professional service providers. Available and critical services include various
types of attorneys (specializing in intellectual property, labor and employment
law, corporate transactions, and other topics), consultants (for business and
technology assistance), public relations specialists, recruiters, and so on.
Unfortunately, the services of these outside experts are often quite expensive.
Some entrepreneurs might argue that some professional service providers are
almost mercenary in their tendency to charge the maximum billable rate that the

---

[2] "The Cutting Edge: Focus on Technology; More firms are willing to work for stock options," *Los Angeles Times*, 24 January 2000, Davan Maharaj, staff writer.

market will bear (this may have resulted in some entrepreneurs lumping their venture capitalists in with their lawyers, resulting in the pejorative derivative "vulture capitalists").

> Upon entering the gates of Heaven, St. Peter remarked how the young the recently deceased attorney looked for a man of 84 years. The attorney responded: Oh, you must have been looking at my billable hours, I'm only 42, can I go back to work now? (Anonymous)

Cash-poor technology companies which ask their lawyers, accountants, and other consultants to accept stock or stock options as payment for services combined with a volatile equities market have focused greater attention on the practice of accepting stock in lieu of their full fees or other traditional forms of compensation.   While the volatility of the market for small technology companies clearly illustrates the risk to both entrepreneurs and professional service providers inherent in this approach, the boom in Internet stocks during the late 1990s at least raised the awareness of both sides as to the potential mutual benefits of equity-for-service arrangements.   Even before the Internet bubble market, a small number of law firms (such as the Venture Law Group in Silicon Valley) demonstrated the viability of this model.

As background for the high technology area which spawned these practices, an introduction to the business implications of intellectual property rights (IPR) protection is provided, covering the risks and opportunities inherent in pursuing or failing to pursue various IPR strategies.   Throughout the book, several case studies drawn from the authors' experience with a number of global product and service industries are used to illustrate stories of success and failure in high-technology venturing and the role of the intellectual venture capitalists. Critical success and failure factors are specifically identified and linked with a discussion of the *fee-based compensation model*, in which intellectual venture capitalists are paid strictly based on time and labor, versus *value-based compensation* in such forms as stock options and/or bonuses that mature after the successful public launch of an enterprise.

An integration of the threads of insight derived from the case studies concludes the book with a composite case study that will consist of a set of key questions and possible answers.

MOTIVATION: WHY CHOOSE THE EQUITY-BASED APPROACH?

In view of the volatility of high-technology stocks, it seems somewhat unreasonable for professional service firms to accept equity in start-up firms in lieu of the fees they would normally earn for their services. At the same time, since entrepreneurs want to protect the valuation of their start-ups, they tend to be reluctant to hand out equity or stock warrants to all comers. Given these conditions, the issue of using equity as compensation for professional service providers appears to be illogical.

At the same time, these arrangements do exist, and became much more common in the late 1990s although they have been around for several decades.[3] Venture Law Group, a law firm specializing in start-up work, was founded in 1990[4] and adopted the equity-for-service approach as its standard practice for compensation.[5] Since then, other law firms joined in using this form of compensation, and the practice later spread to other service providers, including architects, business consultants, industrial designers, and executive recruiters. John Nesheim, author of the popular how-to book entitled *High Tech Startup*, notes that his research reveals numerous prospectuses for initial public offerings (IPOs) where the start-up firm's attorney had a personal share of ownership, or where the attorney's firm had taken equity through a trust or fund established for that purpose.[6]

The key to reconciling expectations and reality is in understanding how the traditional fee-for-service billing arrangement between clients and service providers can be inappropriate in a start-up situation. Most professional service firms, especially law firms, charge very high rates per hour for their services. Nesheim states that when using attorneys who assist start-ups in negotiations with venture capitalists, chief executive officers (CEOs) "should expect a fee in the range of thousands of dollars."[7] In addition to start-up attorneys, entrepreneurs commonly require the services of patent counsel, public relations firms, human resource consultants, recruiting firms, and general business consultants. To obtain the services of the most qualified of these service providers can consume the start-up's much-needed pool of seed capital and increase substantially its "burn rate" of capital, which is an even more ominous portent for potential future investors, thus boosting the venture's cost of capital.

The result is a potentially dysfunctional relationship between the entrepreneur and these critical service providers. In a conventional fee-for-service arrangement, the professional service provider is typically motivated by the need to maximize billable hours and collect higher fees.[8] This is particularly true in a law-firm setting, where associates are expected to generate enough revenue to support the compensation for the law firm partners. As a result, the advice and services given may not serve the long-term needs of the client. The entrepreneur, naturally, wants access to the service provider's expertise at minimal cost.

While the advice and services of these outside service providers are often critical to the success of the start-up, entrepreneurs may feel as though service fees are obliterating the resources of their ventures. On the other hand, attempts to economize on fees may be perceived by professional service firms as a ploy

---

[3] The Cooley Godward law firm first introduced the practice in 1963.

[4] The Venture Law Group is a spin-off from Wilson Soncini when there was a disagreement over how much risk to take among that firm's partners.

[5] Susan Ornstein, "Lawyers Need Equity, Too," *The Industry Standard*, 3 April 2000.

[6] John L. Nesheim, *High Tech Startup* (Saratoga, CA: The Free Press, p. 101).

[7] Ibid.

[8] An exception is the case of in-house lawyers who do not bill hours; however, it is rare for start-ups to have in-house lawyers.

by entrepreneurs to get something for nothing. Entrepreneurs often find that their ability to use the best-qualified service provider is limited, in order to preserve capital. Moreover, and since successful entrepreneurs understand that finding and using the best-qualified service providers are essential to the viability of the start-up, they are generally forced to accept the services while putting off payment for as long as possible. The risk here is that the service provider also has a business to run and may stop working or, worse, may sue the start-up to recover the debt for services already rendered.

The equity-for-service model provides a way around this potential business-related conflict of interests by creating incentives that better align the goals of the two parties. By compensating the service provider partially in equity or debt, the service provider gains a stake in the *long-term success* of the venture, rather than an individual, short-term task or engagement. The emphasis of this structure is on maintaining a mutually beneficial relationship between the entrepreneur and the professional service firm. This may result in a legal conflict of interest as we will later further explore. Although this underscores that there is no panacea, it also shows that there may always be room for improvement in managing and maximizing the usefulness of a start-up's business partners and everyone's return on investment. The resolution and even the prevention of such conflicts of interest (COI) may be achieved through a strong foundation of trust that of course is not always easy to attain or maintain:

> It was Silicon Valley law firms that in the late 1990s started investing in client companies. The practice spread north and south, and remains primarily a West Coast phenomenon. The practice drew attention for a couple of reasons. For one, some of the Silicon Valley firms were reaping impressive gains from the investments, at least on paper. Portland law firms came to the party rather late, and didn't strike much gold before valuations started to tank in the spring of 2000. But the equity stakes also drew criticism. Some observers questioned the ethics of lawyers or law firms becoming part-owners of their clients. In such cases, the reasoning went, the lawyers might be tempted to advise the client to pursue strategies most likely to boost the value of the equity investment, rather than those actions that were more objectively in the best interests of the client: "One way to combat that is to actually [invest in] more of your clients," said Mike McArthur-Phillips, a partner with Davis Wright Tremaine. "That diversifies the equity holdings, much like diversifying your personal portfolio—you don't lay awake at night worrying about that one holding," he said. Also, the total amount of equity the law firms are accepting in any one year is on the order of 1 percent of their annual revenue—enough to make the client's performance "fun to watch," as Campbell[9] put it, but not enough to cause anxiety.

---

[9]Robert Goldfield, *"Law Firms Continuing with Equity Investments,"* Business Journal of Portland, 16 March 2001

Another reason to adopt the equity-for-service model is to attain cost savings, as new ventures tend to face serious financial hurdles ("growing pains" or cash flow crunches), overshadowing their initial problems. For example, in the biotech area, after a start-up has poured $100,000 into developing a patent portfolio, the next step becomes more challenging as shown in Table 1.1.

Table 1.1
Clinical Trials Costs/Timing

Phase	Overall Risk Overcome	Time to Complete	Cost per Subject	Number of Subjects
Preclinical	10%	n/a	n/a	n/a
Phase 1	20%	0.5-1.0 years	$8-$15,000	20-80
Phase 2	30%	1.5 years	$8-$15,000	100-300
Phase 3	67%	3.5 years	$4-$7,000	1,000-5,000

50% of clinical trial costs are returned as tax credits.

Animal Studies to Support Clinical Trials

Phase 1	$500,000
Phase 2	$1 million
Phase 3	$1.5 million

FDA APPROVAL

$300,000 for Prescription Drug User Fee Act II fee
$500,000 to $1.5 million for preparing and filing New Drug Approval application

Case Study to Highlight Expense—ACMED
Payoff: $1 billion = $100 million/year for 10 years

Phase	Number of Subjects	Cost per Subject	Total Cost	Cost of Animal Studies to Support Phase
Phase 1	60	$15,000	$900,000	n/a
Phase 2	200	$15,000	$3 million	$1 million
Phase 3	2000	$7,500	$15 million	$1.5 million

FDA approval $1.6 million
Total Costs $23 million
Source: Adapted from *Biotechnology*, 2001.

Fortunately, it should be noted that even these costs can be alleviated to a degree via the Equity-for-Service approach, since a large portion of Food and Drug Administration (FDA) approval costs involve fees for clinical trials, expert consultants, and attorneys, many of which are willing to consider such an approach.

THE INTELLECTUAL VENTURE CAPITALIST: A NEW PERSPECTIVE ON PROFESSIONAL SERVICES FOR START-UP FIRMS

In view of their adopting a "skin in the game" risk-based approach, professional service providers who specialize in serving start-up ventures undertake the role of an intellectual venture capitalist (IVC). As introduced, the professional is a partner in the new venture, contributing expertise, wisdom, and resources (such as contacts) that are critical to the success of the start-up and not just a supplier of services. Accordingly, the compensation for an intellectual venture capitalist differs substantially from the traditional *fee-for-service model* prevalent in professional services. Instead of simply billing a client for a rough estimate of the time and effort expended, the IVC takes compensation in the form of equity ownership in the new venture (the *equity-for-service model*). However, this also changes the relationship between the professional service provider and the entrepreneur, creating an active partnership towards the success of the new venture in place of the traditional client-provider relationship.

For the purposes of this book, *intellectual venture capital is the specialized knowledge, expertise, know-how, networking, and goodwill that each of these stakeholders, including the entrepreneur, brings to the table.* By definition, such capital may include but is not limited to financing, ideas, knowledge management, and business or technological processes that facilitate everything from launch to production to marketing and selling. The providers of intellectual venture capital may include but are not limited to angel investors, accountants, patent attorneys, consultants, executive recruiters, and public relations specialists. To illustrate the new relationship, this book will provide cases that focus on the interaction between intellectual property (IP) attorneys and entrepreneurs. Arguments and examples are also presented that show how this model applies to other knowledge-based service providers who work with entrepreneurs as well as some of the factors to be considered when working out an arrangement. This provides both breadth, covering a range of client companies (across technologies, industries, and size) working with a range of knowledge providers, as well as depth, exploring the implications of this model for entrepreneurs and their outside legal counsel.

The prevailing model for contracts between knowledge-based service providers and entrepreneurs uses fee-based compensation, where the entrepreneur pays for advice as it is dispensed rather than after it has been implemented, other than following a policy of late payment to retain the possibility of refusing to pay for a particular work product.

Thus, the professional expert assumes little of the risk inherent in acting on that advice. The reengineering of the relationship between the entrepreneur and the IP attorney towards a more evenly balanced configuration of the risk/reward frontier requires an equity-based model. In this approach, the IP attorney takes payment in the form of equity in the start-up. The professional then receives payment at the time the equity is sold, thus tying compensation to the successful execution of strategy based in part on the advice of the attorney. This compensation model is already being used by a few law firms, such as the Venture Law Group and Wilson, Sonsini in Silicon Valley.

One example shows how this model has benefits for both the start-up firm and the professional service provider. The senior partner of an established patent law firm in Washington, DC, agreed to represent a small company for the preparation, filing and licensing of patents covering its proprietary technology. The partner incurred over $100,000 in legal fees and expenses in filing, and obtaining a portfolio of U.S. and foreign patent rights. Unfortunately, the company could not pay these expenses. Having no real alternative to writing off this business loss, the partner agreed to take a percentage of the company. The partner became a member of the board of the firm and contributed significantly to the strategic direction of the company. After years of effort to find a partner for the technology and payment of additional government filing fees and legal fees out of his own pocket, the lawyer helped to arrange the sale of the firm, which will net the law firm approximately $500,000. This is a *500 percent return* on investment (ROI) over a four-year period. The senior partner commented that albeit bumpy this is the road that he would clearly like to follow as much as possible instead of using only the fee-based approach for similar clients.

THE EQUITY-FOR-SERVICE APPROACH: AN OVERVIEW

In the equity-for-service approach, a service provider takes at least part of his or her compensation in the form of an equity-backed instrument rather than a simple payment. The instrument can be actual shares of stock, or some derivative such as stock options, warrants, or other variations. The actual monetary compensation therefore occurs when the security is liquidated (for example, when the venture holds its initial public offering or goes public). Therefore, this is a delayed compensation strategy. It differs from a contingency fee arrangement (where the payment is made upon achieving a specific goal or outcome) in that the amount of the compensation can vary considerably based on the specific circumstances of the venture, and that the basis of value for the compensation is the financial performance of the venture, not the rates set by the service provider. The mechanics of the relationship, then, are the exchange of expertise and advice from the professional service provider for partial ownership in the *future* financial success of the client venture. In a game-theoretic analysis, the equity-for-service arrangement introduces the *shadow of the future* into the relationship between professional and client. As noted by one business consultant, professional service firms would like to establish ground-floor relationships with "the next Microsoft." In return, entrepreneurs would like access to the best available advice, although they may not have the cash to acquire that advice through normal channels. The emphasis here is on the *long-term* relationship between the two firms and their principals, not a specific contractual obligation. This arrangement can have some secondary benefits to the parties involved, through the structure of the equity-for-service arrangement.

To the extent that the entrepreneur avoids the need for cash to pay professional service providers, the venture is able to preserve its capital for investment directly in the business. This could, in turn, reduce the pressure to raise additional funding from venture capitalists prior to IPO. Experienced entrepreneurs are well aware that an investment from a venture capital firm comes with strings attached. Venture capitalists can use their ownership and financing to increase the pressure on management and to take control of the direction of the company. In some cases, founders of firms have been forced out due to disputes with venture capital investors. Venture capitalists have earned, in some cases, the reputation of being a necessary evil.

The equity-for-service approach also transforms the professional services provider, since the act of becoming an investor rather than simply a service provider requires greater attention to the client. The equity-for-service approach requires professionals who know the market and the business world, or at least how to research the market. This shifts their emphasis towards more of a business consulting role in addition to any other specialty they offer.

PROFESSIONAL SERVICE FIRMS AS SUPPLIERS OF INTELLECTUAL VENTURE CAPITAL

The equity-for-service approach may be more appropriate than the fee-for-service model in today's knowledge age with all the risks ("known unknowns"), uncertainties ("unknown unknowns") as well as opportunities. The challenge facing service providers and entrepreneurs in the start-up market is how to quantify and value intangibles (e.g., knowledge, know-how, IPR, etc.). Through the IPO, the stock market values and monetizes intangibles by discounting all the future risks and rewards to the present, including the future value-added of the professional services rendered (hence the dictum that the value of a publicly traded stock is the net present value (NPV) of its future cash flows). This approach also shows how to bundle the intangibles into a relationship (how to ensure that service providers fully apply their expertise to the client relationship, instead of simply marketing expertise). By aligning incentives with long-term success, the arrangement protects against the classical problem of moral hazard in a contractual relationship. That is, by assigning compensation based on long-term financial results, the entrepreneur can ensure that the service provider will not either sell the venture services that it does not need, or fail to deliver the services needed to ensure success. However, this introduces the potential challenge that an attorney does not exercise independence of judgment that a cash transaction might provide.

With the equity-for-service approach, the service provider and the entrepreneur no longer enjoy an arm's-length relationship . Success depends on the mutual understanding of motivation (client and professional). For some professional services, the provider may not be well-attuned to the realities of the marketplace where the entrepreneur operates. The equity-for-service approach guarantees that the professional service provider gains a better understanding of what it takes for the entrepreneur to compete and succeed.

The term "intellectual venture capital" reflects the effective value of the intangible assets that outside professionals add to a new venture. *By monetizing their expertise as equity, professional service providers reflect their contribution to the success of the venture as an investment rather than a cost and it is in this manner that they become venture capitalists and specifically intellectual venture capitalists as compared to service providers.* Conventional venture capitalists already contribute expertise to their investment ventures, by providing opportunities to network with other firms, serving on venture boards, and by guiding a venture's CEO through the start-up process. Professional service providers serve in a similar capacity, and should have their value recognized in a similar fashion—through partial ownership of the venture rather than as an expense on the income statement.

What are the types of intellectual capital supplied by professional service firms? The expertise which start-ups use from outside providers can take many forms:

- Legal expertise in how to structure, operate, and maintain a business
- Management expertise on how to formulate and execute strategies
- Human resources expertise on how to identify and recruit key talent
- Marketing expertise on how to position and publicize the venture's place in the market
- Design and manufacturing expertise on how to shape the products offered by the venture

By converting this expertise into equity across a range of clients, the professional service provider can build a *portfolio* of intellectual capital investments across multiple ventures. In this way, professionals leverage their expertise as financial options building a *risk management* mechanism for maximizing potential returns through the diversification of those investments.

MANAGING INTELLECTUAL CAPITAL IN VENTURE FIRMS

Intellectual capital management is typically viewed as a concern limited to large organizations that have the resources available to measure and track all intangible assets. Although entrepreneurs are hard-pressed for the time and expertise to manage intellectual capital as a conscious activity, they manage their intangible resources implicitly as part of building a start-up firm. After all, since most start-up firms lack much in the way of tangible assets such as financial resources, their intellectual capital constitutes the substantial majority of the strategic assets of such firms. Venture capitalists commonly judge the strength and potential of a start-up by what its intangible assets are—namely, the business record, experience, expertise, and know-how of the management team (human and organizational capital), the connections and networking of the management team with current and potential customers, suppliers, complementors, and strategic partners (social capital); and its patents and other intellectual property instruments such as copyrights, trademarks, and trade secrets (intellectual capital).

One could argue that the core competence of a start-up firm is derived primarily from its ability to manage its intellectual capital, both that of the founder-owners as well as that of its partners and service providers, namely, its intellectual venture capital. In order to grow beyond the start-up stage, a new business venture must be able to compete effectively against entrenched incumbents in the market through superior innovation. New entrants can challenge incumbents by introducing disruptive technologies" which transform market competences from strengths into weaknesses.[10] These entrants must be able to develop a defensible and proprietary capability in a disruptive technology, or else that technology could be co-opted by incumbents. Therefore, start-up firms must have a strong and reasoned strategy for accumulating and protecting intellectual capital, using both legal means (such as patenting or copyright) and managerial competence (through the development and protection of trade secrets—e.g., customer lists, vendor lists, suppliers, information on making the product, selling the product, packaging the product, delivering the product, meeting customers, landing a new customer account, and information on competitors).

Intellectual capital management encompasses more than intellectual property or technologies; it also involves strategies to acquire and utilize specific skills and expertise in a cost-effective and efficient manner. A normal mode of operation for start-up firms is to access such intellectual capital from outside sources, such as professional service firms. In particular, most start-ups cannot commit the resources to maintaining in-house counsel (unless legal knowledge is a critical aspect of the start-up's business). Therefore, it is natural for a start-up to use outside counsel for most legal matters, including employment agreements, corporate transactions, and intellectual property issues. In fact, the degree of outsourcing in an early-stage start-up company can be extremely high. Many firms choose to outsource a range of activities, such as financial management (for example, by "renting" a chief financial officer through a placement service), industrial design, manufacturing, product testing, and software development. In extreme cases, the only intellectual capital retained inside the start-up firm is the core proprietary technology (if any) used to build the company's products, and the firm's business strategy and business models. At least during the start-up phase, most other necessary skills and expertise are needed only for short, defined periods of time (thus removing the

---

[10]Clayton Christensen, *The Innovator's Dilemma* (Boston: Harvard Business School Press, 1999).

need to have such skills available internally) and/or are readily available on the open market from professional service firms.

CHALLENGES TO THE INTELLECTUAL VENTURE CAPITAL APPROACH

The use of the equity-for-service model brings new challenges to the relationship between the entrepreneur and outside professionals. These new challenges may require a shift in how those relationships are structured and managed. While these challenges will be discussed in more detail throughout this book, here is a summary of some major issues and concerns:

- Conflict of interest (COI). If the professional service providers have an equity stake in the venture, will they work to maximize personal return or to benefit all stakeholders in the venture? How independent can they be in practice?
- Securities law and regulation. Securities laws constrain the ability of "insiders" to liquidate their holdings in a venture (for instance, the "lock-up" period after an IPO, namely the time—typically six months—after an IPO during which the owners of equity can not liquidate it to avoid excessive post-IPO stock price volatility). Will these constraints limit the conversion of expertise into actual profits for the service provider?
- Incentives within the professional service firm. If employees in the firm take personal holdings in their clients, will they continue to work for the benefit of the firm or instead work only to maximize personal wealth? Will employees with less valuable clients grow envious or resentful of more successful employees?
- Risk management. Since the professional service provider is only one factor in the success of the firm, what happens to that professional's value if the venture fails due to external factors?
- How does a service provider make an informed investment when the prospectus is still a twinkle in the eye of the CEO?

One unintended consequence of the intellectual venture capital approach to professional services could be that professional services become collateralized and securitized. In effect, professional service providers could trade the stock options or other equity instruments gained through their services on a secondary market. This is analogous to the marketplaces" for professional services now operating on the Internet. Sites such as Guru.com offer a matchmaking service which helps firms to identify providers of outside consulting expertise, and then charge customers a finder's fee for arranging the contract between service providers and companies. Another unintended consequence may reside in tying the health of the legal industry to the stock market. This would not seem to pose a problem in a bull market. However, during a bear market or a prolonged downturn, start-ups may not only have trouble finding funding but they may even have trouble finding law firms financially strong enough to take a risk on a start-up via an equity-for-service deal. Such a trend has risks and downsides as the ones discussed above, however, it can also play an instrumental role in rationalizing the process of resource allocation to new ventures leading to an increasingly frictionless knowledge economy. Part of this rationalization process may be the start-up hibernation mode:

> With venture-capital spending in a deep freeze, dozens of entrepreneurs stranded in the technology recession are choosing an alternative only slightly preferable to death: hibernation. While innumerable start-ups have met their maker, jettisoning staffs and selling off the Aeron chairs, a hard-headed handful are crawling back into their garages, bedrooms and basements until, they hope, the arrival of better days. Some of the same entrepreneurs who were raising millions of dollars a couple of years ago, when starting a company seemed easy, now find themselves making daily sacrifices to keep their dreams alive.[11]

---

[11] *Wall Street Journal*, 2001.

Chapter 2

Challenges and Opportunities in Working with Start-ups

> Heidrick executives say their equity billing program is a common-sense reaction to recent trends in the job market where more executives are leaving well-established firms to accept lower salaries—but stock options—in start-ups and smaller companies: "It no longer made any sense for us to accept only cash compensation because that was artificially low," said Stephen Unger, managing partner of Heidrick's media, entertainment and interactive content practice. "Now, if a prospective client doesn't want to make up the shortfall with stock options, our preference is to avoid doing work for these kinds of companies in favor of others who are aligned with our interests."[12]

Start-up companies face special difficulties in their attempts to contract out for legal services. The most obvious problem is that most entrepreneurs do not have unlimited resources to spend on lawyers. The best law firms charge clients hourly fees that could often deplete a start-up's cash reserves before the business gets off the ground. Given the high cost of legal expertise (for example, a qualified patent attorney will often charge several hundreds of dollars per hour

---

[12] "The Cutting Edge: Focus on Technology; More firms are willing to work for stock options," *Los Angeles Times*, 24 January, 2000, Davan Maharaj, staff writer.

spent on a client's case), entrepreneurs may feel as if they are being "bled dry" by lawyers' bills. Entrepreneurs are often in need of a solution by which they can obtain critical legal expertise, but not at the typical rates billed by most lawyers. It would not be unheard of to spend (and bill) 50 to 100 hours just having introductory meetings and planning the developmental needs of a start-up before anything tangible gets accomplished. Firms doing a high volume of technology work may prepare incorporation papers in 20 minutes regardless of the charge to the client.

The inherent friction between lawyers and entrepreneurs involves more than money, however. The typical personality traits found in the legal profession are often diametrically opposed to those of the average entrepreneur. Where lawyers see risks entrepreneurs see opportunities and that is exactly why they are so complementary to each other. Lawyers are expected to be primarily risk-averse and conservative, as it is their job to advise clients on how to avoid unnecessary exposure to potential legal and business problems. Lawyers who join large law practices are perhaps particularly risk-averse, as they may decide that joining a law firm is a more certain and stable career path compared to working in a small practice or as an in-house counsel at a corporation.

In contrast, entrepreneurs are of course tolerant of risk, even embracing it as a character trait. The founders of a start-up company invest much of their personal commitment, as well as time and effort, into their ventures. This makes entrepreneurs also extremely goal-oriented. Therefore, entrepreneurs are more likely than most business executives to resent any limits on their actions or any delays in achieving their business objectives.

This contrast in style sets up a natural conflict, which could easily undermine the business relationship between an entrepreneur and his or her lawyer. The entrepreneur will tend to be someone who wants to accomplish a goal at almost any cost. The entrepreneur has a personal investment (physical and psychological) in the start-up, and therefore views anyone who appears to impede the success of that start-up as a threat. A lawyer by nature and profession will tend to advise the entrepreneur that certain courses of action are not feasible, or that the business will need to slow down to ensure that all legal protections are established and regulatory requirements are observed. While this advice may be perfectly valid and reasonable for any given situation, resentment and mistrust may result if entrepreneurs continuously push to pursue certain objectives and their lawyers constantly require them to reconsider or change the start-up's strategy. One path to overcome such mistrust is to find a way to ensure that lawyers' interests are aligned with the entrepreneurs', while still enabling both parties to achieve their objectives for personal and professional success. In this way, an increasingly strong foundation of trust in the form of social capital serves to enhance and empower a business relationship and leverage intellectual capital (see Figure 2.1).

Figure 2 .1
Processes Linking Knowledge Sharing, Learning, and Social Capital

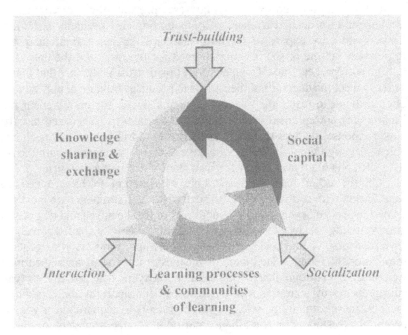

Source: Adapted from Carayannis & Alexander (1999).

LAW FIRMS WORKING WITH START-UPS: THE ENTREPRENEUR'S PERSPECTIVE

> After I got pulled into start-ups, I had a real hard time for three months, but then it clicked....This is where I want to focus the rest of my career. The energy, the level of desperation, and the excitement can't be matched. Everyone is unified and moving in the same direction.[13]

Entrepreneurs have a strong tendency to view attorneys with suspicion, even considering them a necessary evil. The reality of the business environment requires legal counsel for any significant business undertaking. New businesses face many dangers from external forces, including competitors, regulatory authorities, technical difficulties, and the vagaries of customer demands. Most start-ups are built on a business plan with relatively low tolerances for failure, so a challenge which delays the development of the venture presents a potentially devastating problem for a start-up during its initial phase of existence.

---

[13] Lunar Design CEO, April 1999.

Typical comments of entrepreneurs who are dissatisfied with their outside counsel focus on the attitude that lawyers exist mainly TO tell entrepreneurs what they cannot do, or that lawyers prevent the entrepreneur from implementing a desired strategy. Compounding this problem is the fact that lawyers are very expensive for most start-ups, so the entrepreneur gets the impression that he or she is being charged for the time that the lawyer uses to tell the entrepreneur "no." Compounding this distrust is the fact that lawyers, in order to meet the demands of their firms to produce "billable hours" of work, are often difficult to reach and may not be responsive to the entrepreneur's needs. Finally, any entrepreneur who engages a moderate- to large-sized law firm for outside counsel realizes that these law firms tend to focus on larger clients who able to pay high monthly fees or who have a retainer agreement with the firm, so the start-up is often overlooked or given short shrift by the law firm.

On the other hand, it is possible for lawyers to have a constructive relationship with start-up clients. In such cases, entrepreneurs are most satisfied when lawyers go beyond the traditional role of legal counsel and demonstrate an understanding of business realities and also show a real appreciation of entrepreneurs' visions and goals for the start-up. Lawyers who generate the impression of being a facilitator of business rather than an impediment are welcomed by entrepreneurs. In addition, lawyers can prove their value to entrepreneurs by acting as a resource for other important contacts within the local business community, referring entrepreneurs to acquaintances who may be potential investors, strategic alliance partners, service providers, or customers. The dilemma for entrepreneurs is that the lawyers with the best assortment of contacts are almost always in very high demand and must charge high billing rates to justify the time spent on any particular client.

One critical point to consider is that not all entrepreneurs are the same. They may have very different motivations and backgrounds, and these differences tend to lead to very different approaches to dealing with outside counsel. Radosevich mentions one way to differentiate entrepreneurs: "(1) inventor-entrepreneurs who are or were...employees and who actively seek to commercialize their own inventions, and (2) surrogate-entrepreneurs who are not the inventors but who acquire rights to" technology developed by others."[14] The "surrogate-entrepreneurs" in many cases are more experienced businessmen who use technology as a vehicle to purse a perceived business opportunity. These entrepreneurs may have a better appreciation of the need for legal advice during a start-up's early existence, and therefore may assign high value to the advice and time of a good attorney. In contrast, entrepreneurs who are primarily engineers or technical professionals may have less familiarity with the business world, and have more of their energy and experience invested in their particular technology. These technical entrepreneurs often do not understand that technical merit is not the sole determinant of a venture's success, and therefore assign lower value to the legal realities brought up by an outside counsel.

---

[14] R. Radosevich, "Technological Entrepreneurship," *International Journal of Technology Management*, December 1995, pp. 250-265.

LAW FIRMS WORKING WITH START-UPS: THE ATTORNEY'S PERSPECTIVE

We're not merchant bankers, we're not venture capitalists, but the law firm is changing its business model.[15]

There are two types of attorneys who work with corporations: *in-house lawyers* and *lawyers in private practice*. Start-up corporations do not commonly have in-house counsel and so a very different role between an attorney for a start-up and an attorney for a public or mature private corporation exists.

The Issue of Trust

Most people think of lawyers as courtroom-trained, ready-to-sue litigators. In fact, most lawyers never see the inside of a courtroom after moot court competition in law school since 99 percent of lawsuits settle before they ever get to court. This is not to say that there aren't a lot of lawyers who do litigation; they do, it's just that they do all the paperwork and fact-finding for litigation and eventually one or the other party sees where it is headed and decides it is less expensive to settle than to keep paying the lawyers. Start-up lawyers not only do not have a litigator's view of the world, which typically involves demolition of wrongful structures and redistribution of errant wealth, but instead *view themselves as construction workers who erect corporate structures around dreams and technologies*. This is not to say they are naive, but merely that they prefer to be a different sort of journeyman. Thus, it is always interesting when start-up lawyers first meet entrepreneurs since lawyer know that entrepreneurs probably don't trust them, hate having to ask for advice, and probably have had a bad experience or two with another member of the profession. And yet, they come asking for advice of some sort.

Using the Right Tool for the Job

Most lawyers who work with start-ups have a specialty: patent lawyers, corporate lawyers, securities lawyers, employment lawyers, and lawyers having a niche in a particular regulatory area such as telecommunications, food and drug, environmental protection, and so on. Most lawyers in this area have another advanced degree besides law. Absent an already existing relationship with a lawyer, many entrepreneurs seem to start their legal odyssey with either patent lawyers or law firms that are known to specialize in start-ups. Invariably, when a start-up initiates a relationship with a law firm, the entrepreneur frequently expects their first lawyer to be able to do it all. This almost always leads to false starts. General-practice firms frequently dispense horrible advice on topics such as patents or trademarks, patent lawyers frequently try to do incorporations or securities, and "technology firms" frequently contain only one

---

[15] Steve Babson, Chairman, Stoel Rivers, March 2001.

star player. A better model would be to think of specialists in the medical profession, or of just using the right tool for the particular project.

Billing Issues

The next place an entrepreneur may stumble is by placing undue emphasis on cost. In fact, the issue of billing for time, experience, and expertise seems never to be questioned for certain unfathomable specialties like valuations or tax law. However, entrepreneurs frequently attempt to haggle or be overly concerned about cost with their start-up lawyers instead of focusing on the issues at hand for the new organization. The main downside is that the message this gives to the lawyers is that the entrepreneur is gripped by fear and does not believe the organization will make it over the goal line. At a minimum, this will put the idea into the lawyer's mind that the start-up is not an "A" client since they won't be around very long anyway. In fact, a start-up needs "A" work and "A" service just as much as, if not more than, an established concern, since there is very little room for error in these arenas.

A recommended approach would be to ask for a free initial consultation to check the chemistry and trust level. Ask for a fee schedule, a list of representative clients, biographies of each attorney who will work on your files, and the probable point attorney who will be assigned to you. Then, if possible, provide a fairly large up-front payment to immediately establish the relationship (enough to cover a meeting of a few hours with multiple attorneys) and have a daylong meeting to set forth a detailed plan. Then request the lawyer to set forth, free of charge, in a detailed quote with as many flat fee charges as possible, the exact cost for each item on the to-do list.

At this point, entrepreneurs frequently do not know how they want to be billed or how the lawyer should handle communications with them and forwarding of correspondence. Of course, law firms will bill, communicate, and write letters their way if no direction is given. This also happens to be the most expensive way. A recommended approach is to delineate how the billing will be done. Should bills be sent monthly or by project? Project billing allows an entrepreneur to see the bill attached to the item completed. Monthly billing makes the company office manager much happier by managing cash-flow expectations. In an equity-for-services arrangement there may be no incentive to monitor billing or it may be agreed to be completely ignored; however, these records are surely going to be kept by the law firm in case it is needed to prove their entitlement to the amount of stock received or to show what happened on what date to avoid a claim of malpractice, should the attorneys bring a lawsuit against the entrepreneur later. Accordingly, it is recommended to ask for these records since they are being collected anyway. Another area of the relationship which is frequently ignored is how the inevitable "urgent communications" will be conducted, and how letters containing "items for immediate client action" will be differentiated from the "for your records" type of reporting.

Although these items seem rather unimportant to an entrepreneur, billing and communication problems are the biggest source of problems in a lawyer-client relationship and have a direct effect on the amount of equity a law firm may demand.

Different Perspectives

It is important to understand the psychological difference between lawyers and entrepreneurs. One saying has it that "lawyers look at the world and see problems, entrepreneurs look, and see opportunities." To illustrate, it is important to understand how a lawyer is trained and views the world. On one level, lawyers are taught to split the world of decisions into "business decisions" and "legal decisions." Business decisions are those relating to the level of risk to accept and allocation of resources and are outside the province of legal training and expertise. Generally, these are decisions that lawyers are not trained to make and many lawyers believe they should only be made by businesspeople. Thus, lawyers can only provide input on these decisions after many years of experience or where the lawyer has special training in business.

Legal decisions are about which is the best strategy or mechanism given the particular set of facts, about which consequences may attach to a particular set of client activities. These are decisions that a lawyer feels obligated to make for a client since it involves the lawyer's expertise and are not areas clients should be involved in. Crossing this line is a trust issue.

For start-ups, the main difference with established clients is that most start-ups come to expect their lawyer to make risk and resource decisions for them, whereas companies with an in-house lawyer only want the lawyers to provide them with the options available in a particular circumstance and the consequences of choosing a particular course of action. Of course, this makes start-ups a much more exciting client than established companies, where questions and requests for analysis seem to come out of a black box. In a start-up, there is much more need for a lawyer to provide business and legal guidance from the very start.

This do-it-all approach may be convenient for the entrepreneur, but it also has a serious cost in later consequences. A poor foundation will eventually lead to the entire structure falling down. Accordingly, entrepreneurs who attempt to stretch their lawyers beyond their professional limit and expertise are risking the entire enterprise. Thus, it is worth taking the time to understand exactly why particular lawyers think they have the qualifications to do the job.

Communication and Listening

Another problem that lawyers frequently have with entrepreneurs is that the self-confidence it takes to venture into the unknown is frequently the weakness which causes the entrepreneur to ask for the lawyer's advice, only to turn around and not follow it. It is essential that entrepreneurs learn to "listen with their life" when their counselors are speaking. In this same vein, it is important for lawyers to be proactive with their entrepreneur-clients such that no situation ever turns into an "I told you so." Entrepreneurs must make sure that lawyers understand that it is not only necessary but encouraged that if a lawyer sees something wrong happening, a telephone call and vigorous questioning must take place. Honesty and clear communications are key to success.

A specialized problem with entrepreneurs also occurs in patent law, which does not occur in any other area. This is the problem of the entrepreneurs' expectations relating to the manufacture, marketing, and commercialization of inventions. For some reason, many start-up inventors expect patent lawyers to assist them with these manufacturing of the invention. Patent lawyers, on the other hand, are engineers or scientists themselves and hold law degrees. They generally have no idea how to make, market, sell, or finance the inventions and thus there is a serious disconnect. This disconnect is resolved only in rare cases by patent lawyers who have a lot of experience and are adept at business themselves. Some of the technology firms attempt to satisfy part of this by offering entrepreneurs the services of "the partner with the golden Rolodex." He or she is usually quite expensive and is rarely seen, in the wild or in captivity. Many of these law firm partners have an extensive network, which can facilitate licensing and financing. However, manufacturing and marketing contacts or advice are almost never available to the entrepreneur. This understood, an entrepreneur would do well to understand what things lawyers can do and cannot do.

Dispute Resolution

Last, one area which inevitably comes up in law is a lawsuit between a lawyer and a former client; usually for nonpayment, overcharging, or neglect. Entrepreneurs would do well to know what type of firm they retain. Some firms believe that to sue a client is to invite a malpractice claim. Other firms believe that to be in business is to be in a lawsuit, so protect yourself from deadbeat clients and sue away. Of course, this is a definite consideration for a start-up—it is one thing to have a $900+ per-hour attorney firm on your side, it is quite another when they are sitting on the other side of the table. A recommended approach is to ask the local bar association to arbitrate the problem and find a solution. This is not only preferable but it is essential since start-ups generally can ill-afford any sort of litigation. Although litigation can be a strategic tool, it can prove prohibitively expensive for a start-up.

The working relationship aside, it is important to note that lawyers and entrepreneurs get a similar thrill when embarking on a new project. However, the roles between them can be as different as night and day. Most CEOs have a pretty good idea that to start up a company will require a lot of money, hard work, perseverance, and luck and that their role in this venture will require them to wear many hats. Entrepreneurs soon learn firsthand that the combination of visionary, fund-raiser, salesperson, manager, decision maker, and referee, is a delicate balancing act which tests every last shred of a nerve. In contrast, a lawyer has a day job. An entrepreneurs' business is much like "other people's children" to some lawyers, in the that lawyer may teach them or coach them or guide them but borrowing the car or an organ donation is out of the question.

This sharply contrasts with the deep commitment entrepreneurs have to their venture and for whom no sacrifice is too great.

Lawyers on Board

This is not to say that lawyers who work for start-ups are not committed, but it is different and it must be both pointed out and understood. The lawyer who is actually going to engage in any sort of equity-for-services arrangement is already a maverick in the legal profession. These topics are not taught in law school, or if they are taught, it is only from the viewpoint of problem and not opportunity (e.g., the poor lawyer who ran afoul of the ethics enforcers, or bar counsel, and lost license, position, and a fortune in legal bills from his defense lawyers). This maverick now comes in two forms: the "Rainmaker" and the Head of the Law Firm's Investment Committee (or some similarly named committee). This is the person who chooses to invest.

As a premise, the idea that lawyers would give their clients money is, well, fall-out-of-your-chair funny. Everyone knows that lawyers *collect* money, they don't *give it back*. Well, we're not in Kansas anymore and some of the rules have changed. With two main forces at work, some firms do give their clients money, some trade stock for services, some do a combination of the two. The two main forces driving this are (1) the new firms, i.e. West coast firms, were trying to compete with the profitable old, East coast firms, and (2) the race to keep up with sky-rocketing associate compensation.

West vs. East

Without getting into too much detail, in order to stay afloat the West Coast firms had to come up with a way to make profits like the East Coast firms. The East Coast firms had traditionally profitable areas such as banking, financing, and the like, which put pressure on the West Coast firms to raise salaries and bonuses to keep their employees and partners. Using technology companies as their base, a few of them developed a methodology whereby they could create an investment fund through partner contributions and invest a modest amount in selected clients (e.g., $50,000), alongside a venture round. They would make this investment in a handful of companies every year and would use the principle of diversification to spread their risk out. This meant right-sizing one's expectations about return on investment and expecting to do no better than the venture capitalists (VCs). Typically, VCs expect five times return within five years. This is not greed, however, it is necessity in the high-risk world of VCs in order to survive. VCs understand that out of ten investments, five will be a complete loss. Of the remaining five, two will return the money invested, two will return the money invested plus a small profit, and one will be a screaming success. Better understood with numbers, an example would look like this: $10 million invested in ten companies. $5 million lost, and it is not only OK, but it is expected. $1 million kept for five years and returned from each of two companies. This is expected. $2 million returned from each of two companies after five years. Last, $52 million returned from one company. Eventually, some technology companies make it big and, at an appropriate time, the law firms would sell their equity at great profit. This profit would then be used for distributions to the partners who contributed to the original investment fund, and for paying bonus money to their associate attorneys in order to keep them from leaving for an in-house position with a client or at a competitive firm.

Law Firm Business

It is important to understand, briefly, the juicy details of how the business side of law firms works in order to understand how the equity-for-service model came about in the legal arena and how it is operated. The first thing to understand is that each law firm is organized and operated differently. This surprises most people, probably because they expect that setting up a law firm and running it is mostly a function of standardized forms and procedures. This is not the case. Yes, there are standard forms but lawyers don't use them verbatim. Yes, each law firm is a business providing legal services, and thus is subject to the same pressures as every other service providing business and this should provide a standardizing force. But it should be understood that the agreements that set up law firms are partnerships or limited liability partnerships (LLP) or limited liability corporations, (LLC), and they are all agreements which are tailored to what the partners choose and what the local bar association allows.

Each state bar association has its own set of rules, particularly as to billing practices, conflicts of interest, and form of organization. For example, lawyers are forbidden from being partners with non-lawyers in Illinois. However, the District of Columbia allows for lawyers to be partners with non-lawyers where the firm's sole purpose is to practice law and the non-lawyers abide by D.C. ethics rules [D.C. Rule 5.4(b)]. Another example concerns billing. Some states require lawyers to provide clients with a written statement of how the attorney charges for work performed. Although commonly misperceived even by its lawyers, the District of Columbia does not require a written retainer agreement unless the legal services are contingency fee work or for a new client who does not fully understand the hourly billing basis.[16]

Compliance with Ethics Rules

The three biggest ethical areas, which drive the lawyers' investing behaviors are (1) conflicts of interest relating to taking positions adverse to a client's interest; (2) the prohibition against entering into a business transaction with a client; and (3) the prohibition against taking an unreasonable fee.

The details of how these requirements are fulfilled are set forth in chapter 6, but suffice it to say that every Equity-for-Service arrangement must have a

---

[16] Private communication with Barry Cohen of Crowell & Moring.

written agreement between lawyer and client setting forth the exact details of the agreement. Not to do so is to invite disaster; it may also be unethical in some circumstances.

Another situation where ethical requirements modify the investing behavior concerns, for example, the form of the law firm organization. The choice of the type of form a firm had to use was always easy to remember in the old days: a partnership. All law firms had to be partnerships in many jurisdictions. They were not allowed to be corporations, since the ethics rules thought that by allowing firms to be corporations it would unnecessarily prevent liability from attaching personally to a lawyer, and therefore service and ethical compliance would be better by not allowing the form. Recently, the choices have been expanded in just about all state jurisdictions. Some firms remain partnerships for historical reasons. Some firms are now professional corporation (PC), limited liability partnership (LLP) or limited liability corporation (LLC) These organizations can have the flow-through aspects for income of partnerships and the liability protection of corporations. Interestingly, the previous decision for lawyers was to choose the amount of risk to take—that is vicarious liability. Now, the decision also includes how to maintain flow-through tax advantages and avoid double-taxation. Some states even explicitly required law firms to be of a certain structure (e.g., law firms were not allowed to be LLC). However, many of these rules have been changed as bar associations have become more comfortable with allowing various forms and checking malfeasance through other means. Some of the other changes involved a change in Internal Revenue Service (IRS) rules, the so-called Check the Box Regulations which replaced the Kintner Regulations in 1997. These rules essentially state that firms are allowed to decide for themselves how they would like to be taxed (Checking the Box), making sure that they maintain enough of the look and feel of the stated organizational structure to avoid prompting the IRS to recharacterize them and levy taxes based upon corporate double-taxation rules. A good discussion of the details of these issues may be found in *Law Firm Partnership Agreements*.[17]

You Are Not in Kansas Anymore

The result of these ethical requirements and organizational limitations is that most of the partners currently in law firms today were all trained at a time when the business of running a law firm did not consist of much more than fairly simple operations. For example, an entire firm would consist of hanging out a shingle, attracting clients, performing the services (e.g., drafting or filing documents), getting the bills mailed out, making sure that the bills were paid and the checks were deposited, paying staff and attorneys, and splitting the remainder among the partners at a yearly office retreat. Clients looked to these firms for arm's length advice, not a marriage.

In contrast, today's law firm marketing and advertising budgets run into the millions of dollars. Document production has gone beyond the paperless office

---

[17] By N. Corwin and J. Ciampi (New York: Law Journal Seminars-Press, 1998).

and into external networks, or extranets, which offer clients a Web-based legal experience where general background advice is available for free, documents are co-produced by client and lawyer in real time and filed electronically, and due dates are available to a client for download by synching their Personal Digital Assistant (PDA) with the Web-page the attorney generated for this project which contains a calendaring feature. Young attorneys do not stay at any one firm for more than a few years before moving on the next highest bidder or to a client. Large firms are merging with larger firms to minimize administrative costs and keep up with ever-increasing associate attorney salaries and partner bonuses, and small firms are struggling to make payroll each month because of the competition. It is in this environment of competition that a potential new form of client-lawyer arrangement was born.

Much like the variability of firm structures, equity-for-service arrangements can be set up in many different ways. One of the original methods involved inadvertently doing work for an insolvent company and then trying to recapture the fees by taking stock. Many firms have unwittingly done this with little or no success. One of the problems this raises, is who is going to pay the tax on the "phantom" income and who is going to cover out-of-pocket costs associated with doing the work in the first place.

Another method involves taking stock as payment for the opportunity cost of deferring the actual payment of legal fees. This is a great bonus to the firm and a very flattering and expensive gift from the client, but if the amount of the stock is rather small the ill effects of over-diluting the start-up's stock can be avoided. The effect of this on the structure and management of the firm is no different than the example above. The problem arises like this. The stock is usually not redeemable until the company goes public, or has some other qualified "liquidity event" where investors are allowed to sell. Nonetheless, who fronts the money for the associates who are doing the work? Was there an election to pay taxes on the present value? And who pays these?

Another method is to estimate the amount of legal services needed within a given time, such as the first year, and to take this amount in stock. Of course, these and other variations are explained in greater detail. The management and operations concerns apply to this example as in the previous two.

CASE STUDY: THE TWO PERCENT SOLUTION—PRE- AND POST- INTERNET BUBBLE

Historically, name brand law firms in Silicon Valley have been known to tell start-up clients: give us two (2) percent equity in order to complete a start-up's corporate legal services[18]:

Twelve years ago, taking equity in a client was of sufficiently dubious propriety to spark a debate over whether the ethics code permitted it. Ten years

---

[18]David Schellhase, "Rethinking the Equity Equation." *The Recorder*, 23 February 2000, p. 5.

ago, Wilson Sonsini Goodrich & Rosati was the only firm that did it. And then four years ago, Venture Law Group was founded on the principle that equity is everything. Today, one prominent law firm is considering doubling its standard corporate rates for clients who refuse to part with an equity stake. If this firm goes ahead with this fee structure, others will no doubt follow suit.

Before the onset of the Internet bubble, Silicon Valley firms struggled to compete with their East Coast counterparts. Out of necessity they took start-up companies as clients. However, start-ups do not have the resources to pay these firms. As the debts mounted between these law firms and their client start-up corporations, it became apparent that billing a cashless entity had only one outcome, namely default on the start-up's debts and massive write-offs within the law firms accounting system.

Accordingly, a creative solution to carrying this level of debt was discovered: the ability of law firms to leverage the large amount of deal flow from the start-ups combined with taking an "equity kicker" (equity participation incentive), provided these firms with the means to get at least one success story out of a multitude of failures. In this way, a single IPO (Initial Public Offering) of a start-up company could literally fund an entire year's worth of equity venturing (namely providing services to start-ups that end up not being able to pay).

As these law firms were able to capitalize on some very large successes, their name and reputation grew. One result of this was that these so-called name brand law firms who had developed close working relationships with venture capital firms became able to command equity for the privilege of being represented by these brand name law firms[19]:

> But what the client really buys with two percent of its equity isn't legal services, but the hottest commodity in the Valley: a network of contacts among providers of private equity capital.

Thus, the two percent rule evolved from a mechanism of subsidizing new pools of clients to a gatekeeper mechanism in order to attract only the best clients. Discussions with the lawyers within these firms who manage these equity programs reveal that the two percent rule had an additional aspect—namely, preserving a number of shares of a start-up company for later venture rounds.

In particular, it was discovered among the law firms and start-ups that if too much equity had been given away prior to venture capital funding, the venture capitalists were not interested or would demand that everybody would reduce their equity holdings as a concession to commit venture capital funds. The basis of this is that venture capitalists generally prefer to obtain a majority or at least super-minority of the shares of a start-up in order to control their investment.

---

[19]Ibid.

Chapter 3

Developing Win-Win Relationships:
The Equity-for-Service Model

Numerous authors are moving away from traditional ideas about the basis of firms' competitive advantages, such as superior strategic formulation by top managers, and towards a view which emphasizes the internal resources of the firm (see, for example, Barney, 1991). Recent works focus in particular on knowledge creation (Nonaka and Takeuchi, 1995) as the source of a given firm's unique and inimitable advantage. To be more specific, the firm's advantage is a function of the specialized knowledge held by its employees, the ability of the firm's management and other organizational routines to access that knowledge, and the integration of that knowledge into action (Grant, 1991). We focus on the significance of knowledge economics and "co-opetitive" dynamics in understanding the role and potential of electronic commerce in an increasingly globalized and electronically based economy.

KNOWLEDGE ECONOMICS IN A POSTCAPITALIST GLOBAL ECONOMY

Knowledge remains an infuriatingly vague subject to write about—let alone sell. Telling a reasonably effective company that it should focus on "knowledge creation" is rather like telling an orchestra that it should concentrate on "music making."[20]

On the macroeconomic scale, knowledge is the focus of analysis of the "new" dynamics of the global economy. In an era of globalized, highly mobile financial capital, multinational corporations can essentially "arbitrage" across national borders to find the best firms to integrate into their mode of production (leading to *knowledge arbitrage* and *strategic serendipity* opportunities; [Carayannis, 2001a, 2001b, 2002a, 2002b, 2002c]). Reich (1991: 111) writes that in the new "global web" of enterprise, "power and wealth flow to groups that have accumulated the most valuable skills in problem-solving, problem-identifying, and strategic brokering." Drucker (1991) claims that this globalization of enterprise and economic transactions is transforming the world economy from capitalism to a postcapitalist society.

CAPITALISM AND POSTCAPITALISM

Our plan is to lead the public with new products rather than ask them what kind of products they want. The public does not know what is possible, but we do. So instead of doing a lot of market research, we refine our thinking on a product and its use and try to create a market for it by educating and communicating with the public.[21]

In a capitalist society, wealth flows to those who control the flow of financial capital. In the early days of manufacturing, the capital requirements of production facilities were modest, allowing the accumulation of physical capital to be financed internally by the increased production afforded by factory methods (Rosenberg and Birdzell, 1985: 166). But as the technologies of production grew more sophisticated and their resource demands increased, economies of scale emerged. This placed greater emphasis on the ability of enterprises to access financial capital. Also, as noted by Chandler (1977), the rise of an entirely new class of industry, namely communications and transportation firms, required distributed facilities and closely coordinated operations. Financial management skills became crucial to the development of these enterprises. The development of public capital markets increased the range of tools and the breadth of skills which managers could use to acquire financing. This has led to the rise of financial markets of such tremendous sophistication that humans can navigate these environments only with the aid of computers. In turn, managers are concerned that their actions are now dictated by financial forces beyond their control; they are no longer able to channel financial capital, but instead are beholden to its demands.

In postcapitalist economics, wealth flows not to those who control financial capital, but to those who can acquire and direct intellectual capital. Since financial capital is now widely available across the world, effective money

---

[20] *The Economist*, 10 May 1997, pp. 12-15.
[21] Akio Morita, Chairman, Sony Corporation.

management is only one skill necessary to the success of firms. The increased velocity of commerce (especially electronic commerce) and competition demands multifaceted expertise from a firm. In fact, the changes in the world economy are placing requirements of skills and resources that often exceed those of a single enterprise, necessitating the formation of multiple alliances to ensure that the members of each alliance can marshal the intellectual capabilities to deal with the complexities of their environment. Only through the judicious and experienced application of knowledge can firms hope to outperform their counterparts and achieve sustained competitive advantage.

The postcapitalist knowledge-based economy operates with dynamics which differ radically from those assumed by neoclassical economics. First, unlike other forms of capital, intellectual capital is not only unevenly distributed, but it tends to grow without physical limits. A firm which captures and exercises unique knowledge capabilities will tend to attract more expert employees, thus exhibiting "increasing returns to scale." According to Arthur (1996), this dynamic leads to a new form of economics, namely knowledge economics, that is very different from traditional, process-oriented economics. He notes that "they call for different management techniques, strategies, and codes of government regulation" (p. 101).

Second, in traditional economics, free markets are the purest form of economic organization, and competition between diverse enterprises provides the "invisible hand" which Adam Smith (1776) claimed would guide market participants to mutual gains through trade. However, free market efficiency is predicated on numerous stylized assumptions, including perfect information symmetry provided by price signals. We now know that prices do not perfectly capture all information relevant to a transaction, leading in some cases to the use of bureaucratic organizations to conduct transactions (Williamson and Masten, 1985). Since information is often not distributed symmetrically, knowledge (which is based upon information) is also concentrated unevenly. Therefore, in knowledge-based markets, pure competition may not result in the most efficient solution. A direct corollary is that while a lack of competition is assumed to be a market failure in traditional economics, it may be an optimal solution in certain situations in knowledge-based economics.

Third, the forms of organization in knowledge-based economies differ from those in traditional markets. Chandler (1977) shows how mass production and mass distribution required a level of coordination best handled by bureaucratic mechanisms within the firm. Transaction cost economics, as described in Williamson and Masten (1985), suggests that the "visible hand of management," in Chandler's terminology, will supercede the "invisible hand" of the market when the dimensions of the transactions, such as asset specificity, transaction duration or recurrence, complexity, and measurement problems, create a situation where internal coordination and control can govern those transactions more efficiently than market mechanisms (Milgrom and Roberts, 1992: 30). A key assumption of transaction cost economics is that individual opportunism will require coercive control and monitoring to ensure economic efficiency in such transactions (Ghoshal and Moran, 1996). If opportunism is not assumed in all cases, or if opportunism is exercised along a continuum instead of assumed as an absolute, it is possible for other forms of organization to emerge, including internal markets (Halal, 1996) and hybrid organizations.

GAME THEORY, CO-OPETITION, STRATEGIC INFLECTION POINTS, AND STRATEGIC CAPABILITY OPTIONS

> You can not overtake the runner in front of you by following in his footsteps.[22]

> The essence of firm is the set of relationships among its stakeholders and between itself and other firms....The most important objectives of commercial relationships are cooperation (the joint activity toward a shared goal), coordination (the need for mutually consistent responses), and differentiation (the avoidance of mutually incompatible activities). Game theory is a helpful way of describing these relationships. So although the discussion of cooperation begins from the familiar business problem of achieving success in a joint venture, we go on to explain how that issue can be described by the most famous of all games—the Prisoner's Dilemma. The objectives of coordination and differentiation are represented by the Battle of the Sexes and the Game of Chicken, respectively. I also describe the paradox of commitment—how it is possible to gain by limiting one's own options.[23]

By taking a game theoretic approach to strategy, Brandenburger and Nalebuff (1996) derive one alternative to pure competition as the basis for interfirm relations. They begin by noting that the concept of rationality, which underpins both traditional economics and the "bounded rationality" of transaction cost economics, is never absolute. For example, "two people can both be rational and yet evaluate the same outcome quite differently" (p. 60). They discuss the concept of allocentrism: evaluating a multiplayer game from the points of view of all the players. Brandenburger and Nalebuff (1996: 39) describe co-opetition as "a duality in every relationship—the simultaneous elements of cooperation and competition. War and peace. Co-opetition." Instead of viewing all players as competitors, this approach can reveal that some opponents are in fact "complementors", who may add value to others. By focusing on turning apparent zero-sum situations into positive-sum games, Brandenburger and Nalebuff argue that firms should pursue a strategy of co-opetition, combining cooperation and competition depending on the exact situation to achieve the greatest gainsharing among all players. Co-opetition is exercised through the formation of value nets, where the firm interacts with suppliers, customers, competitors, and complementors to maximize its own added value, in turn raising the returns to the other players in the net. Co-opeting occurs when you collaborate with your rivals and compete with your partners in

---

[22] Mao Tse-tung in (Kay, 1995).
[23] Kay (1995).

pursuit of win-win market player/stakeholder configurations (Carayannis and Alexander, 1998). There is a need for cooperation—to encourage individual persons to pursue a common goal against the contrary pressures of their own interests. There is also the problem of coordination. It often is important so that everyone does the same thing, even though precisely what it is that everyone does is not important at all. But there is also a need for differentiation. Although all different aspects of an activity need to be covered by an organization, if all firms in a market adopt similar strategies, the outcome is unlikely to be profitable for any of them (Kay, 1995).

> In an industry, a strategic inflection point is when the balance of forces shifts from the old structure, from the old ways of doing business and the old ways of competing to the new. Before the strategic inflection point, the industry simply was more like the old. After it, it is more like the new. It is a point where the curve has subtly but profoundly changed, never to change back again. It is very difficult to tell when an strategic inflection point occurs even in retrospect. And it is even harder to tell while going through one. People who experience one develop a sense of it being an inflection point at different times. (Grove, 1996)

The concept of creating strategic technological capability options implies that by investing in given technologies, firms create opportunities or options for themselves, to make still additional investments in the future. The idea is more commonly understood in terms of "staying on the learning curve": machine tool companies that adopted numerically controlled production technology in the early 1970s, found it easier to switch to integrated computer-based manufacturing a decade later; these firms developed capability options, which could be exercised to reduce the cost of adopting subsequent, more advanced technology vintages. In this context, the capabilities developed in the first technology transition facilitated a subsequent transition to the more advanced technology. This implies that part of the benefit of the original investment was the capability to work with automated processing equipment, a capability that translated more easily into the adoption of Computer Integrated Manufacturing (CIM) technology in the 1980s (Carayannis, Preston, & Awerbuch, 1996).

TRUST AND ECONOMIC TRANSACTIONS

Another focus of the recent economic analysis is the concept of trust. The rise of modern managerial capitalism from the old regime of family enterprise is viewed as a watershed in the move from craft production to mass production. These new companies were able to replace family ties with purely economic loyalties. Many economic historians argue that "how these loyalties were created....we cannot know for sure" (Rosenberg and Birdzell, 1985: 124). One possibility is that these firms grew from military units who developed mutual loyalty in battle (Rosenberg and Birdzell, 1985: 125). But larger social forces seem to be at work to lead to the rise of entire economic systems based on economic loyalty. In particular, economists are now exploring the idea of "social capital," the ability of people to cooperate towards a common goal beyond purely financial motives.

To form and lead the kinds of hybrid, cooperative organizational forms described above, companies must command substantial social capital. Clearly, just as knowledge is the lever of intellectual capital, trust is the lever of social capital. Fukuyama (1995) defines trust as "the expectation that arises within a community of regular, honest, and cooperative behavior, based on commonly shared norms, on the part of other members of that community" (p. 26). He attributes the development of shared norms to social activities such as religion. Thus, the economic development of various societies is the result of social development which determines whether a given society is "high-trust" (such as the United States) or "low-trust" (such as China), with high-trust societies more likely to adopt advanced forms of economic organization.

KNOWLEDGE EXCHANGE AS THE BASIS OF COOPERATION

Fukuyama ignores the development of global webs of enterprises, where entities from different societies coordinate and cooperate in individual action toward common goals. Such international alliances have increased in the past two decades. These groups themselves must be based on some kind of trust, although their members do not share common social backgrounds. We argue that building trust in such networks requires the sharing of intellectual capital to build social capital. In other words, knowledge exchange forms the foundation for trust in corporate alliances, linking intellectual capital with social capital.

Knowledge has certain characteristics which make it very distinct from other media of exchange, such as financial capital or physical capital (e.g., land). Knowledge can be transferred between firms or individuals, like other forms of currency. But unlike money and land, knowledge, once transferred, is held by both the donor and the recipient. Hence, knowledge is not transferred in a formal sense; it is shared. The act of sharing knowledge allows both parties to utilize that knowledge independent of the other. Knowledge sharing, then, is by nature a positive-sum game; neither party is deprived of knowledge by engaging in sharing. However, knowledge sharing may lead to a zero-sum game if one party is better able to use that knowledge in a market situation than the other. For example, if a firm "reverse engineers" the products of a competitor, and then introduces an improved model onto the market, it can profit abnormally from the unintentional "sharing" of its competitor's knowledge. Intellectual property laws are intended to protect firms against the unintended appropriation of knowledge by outsiders. But since firms are notoriously "leaky" when it comes to knowledge, such legal protections are of limited value.

Given that firms are unable to protect their knowledge absolutely, they may be able to preempt the misappropriation of their knowledge by sharing it with their competitors. This, in turn, can create the expectation that the competitor will in turn share its knowledge with the donor firm. Thus, knowledge becomes an object of barter between firms towards the development of a new form of economic relationship. The equal exchange of knowledge constitutes a quid pro quo which, in turn, reinforces a growing trust between the parties to that transaction. As long as the knowledge exchanged between the firms is perceived by the recipients to be of equal value, trust can be built. In contrast, many alliances and joint ventures fail because the participants are either unwilling to share knowledge, on the faulty assumption that they are "parting with" that expertise, or because the parties are unable to attain a mutually agreeable arrangement for the sharing of knowledge ex ante and the division ex post of the intellectual assets resulting from cooperation.

Knowledge exchange does not rule out downstream competition between two firms. Again, knowledge is simply the foundation of intellectual capital, not its equal. Possession of knowledge is one thing; its application and control is much more significant. Hence, firms may be willing to cooperate to share and develop jointly "generic knowledge," which they then apply in their unique ways in differentiated products on the market. The availability of that pool of generic knowledge adds value to the products of both firms, yet still allows them the freedom to compete with each other at the market level.

THE DYNAMICS OF KNOWLEDGE-BASED ECONOMICS

The implications of knowledge sharing for the new knowledge-based economy are substantial. Knowledge-based competition is generally assumed to require that firms have different knowledge which they then use to create sustained competitive advantage. But knowledge sharing allows firms to access the same basic knowledge to cooperate and compete simultaneously for greater productivity. This, in turn, changes the way that firms must operate, and the mechanisms for governing transactions in the new economy.

Within the firm, it is clear that individuals must share trust for the firm to survive and prosper. With the increasing mobility of human capital, it is no longer guaranteed that the employees of the firm have the same social and cultural background to provide a social basis for trust. By encouraging knowledge sharing at the individual level, the firm gains in two ways. First, it can guarantee that knowledge will flow efficiently to those employees who are in the best position to utilize that knowledge at a given time. Second, however, it bonds individuals together in a collaborative mode to ensure that they work toward common goals, which in turn will drive firm innovation. As Foray (1991) observes, intrafirm cooperation is essential to innovation because the functions and resources of the firm are integrated together into a larger whole. He draws from the work of Aoki and Dore (1986) to show how Japanese firms are better organized through knowledge sharing to achieve higher-order innovation through the development of common, firm-specific knowledge using mechanisms of learning by doing (Carayannis and Alexander, 1998; Carayannis and Roy, 1999; Carayannis and Alexander, 1999; Carayannis, 2001c).

Electronic commerce is tightly linked with the exchange of information and knowledge as these are the key media of exchange that underlie this new form of commerce. As such, the issues that are salient to the area of knowledge economics are also key in understanding the co-opetitive dynamics of electronic commerce (see Figures 3.1 & 3.2). Primary among these are the issues of trust and non-linear change underscored by the concepts of strategic inflection points and strategic capability options. These concepts are becoming increasingly important as business transactions are becoming more digital and the barriers to entry into markets and industries fuzzier promoting more openness in pursuit of win-win business configurations:

> Two major forces—fundamental technological change and a new ethos of openness—are driving through our era, forces that could bring about the long boom, a 25-year global expansion with all its consequences. Five waves of technology—computers, telecommunications, biotechnology, nano-technology, and alternative energy— may bring about big productivity increases that lead to high rates of economic growth, in balance with nature. Meanwhile, we're seeing unprecedented global integration....These two meta-developments lead to increasing integration and prosperity worldwide[24].

Figure 3.1
Dimensions of Business Value from Electronic Commerce

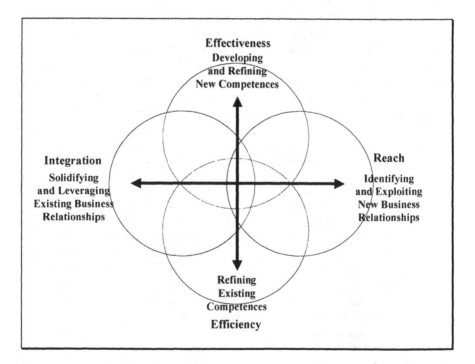

---

[24] *Wired* Magazine, 15 June 1997, pp. 25-30.

Figure 3.2
Nested Integrated Value Nets

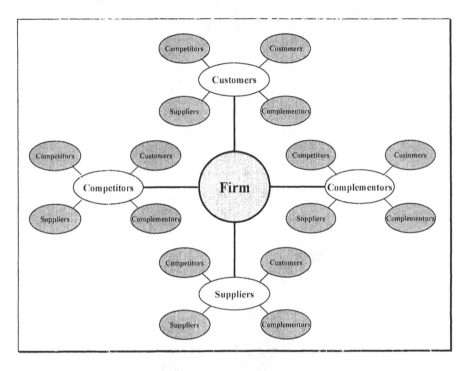

To convert the relationship between outside lawyers and venture entrepreneurs from a generally adversarial relationship to a win-win arrangement requires a change in the expectations of both parties through a change in behaviors and actions. Entrepreneurs must have the expectation that the lawyer truly views the start-up firm as a client, and not simply as a means of generating new fees. In turn, the lawyer needs to expect that the entrepreneur is a promising prospect who will develop into a long-term source of business and a loyal customer. The lawyer does not want a customer who will consume the lawyer's time and attention and then promptly go bankrupt, leaving the lawyer with no revenue to show for that effort.

Any change in expectations can only occur through the demonstration of a credible commitment by each party, backed by behaviors that show good faith. This commitment is intended to show that the entrepreneur and the lawyer each has "skin in the game," meaning that they are willing to make an irreversible investment in the relationship. At the same time, neither party wants to make such a commitment blindly. Instead, trust must be built up over time through a repeated pattern of incremental investments, with each round of investments demonstrating to each party that the other holds a strong belief in the long-term viability of their business relationship. This pattern forms *a spiral of trust*, which generates a shift in expectations (see Figure 3.3).

As the transacting parties have the opportunity to develop a partnership through socialization (S) and interaction (I) that leads to increasingly higher levels of trust (T). In Figure 3.3, the depth in the spiral indicates the level of trust that has been built so as we transition from one stage to the next, more openness and knowledge sharing can take place also per Figure 2.1.

Figure 3.3
The Spiral of Trust

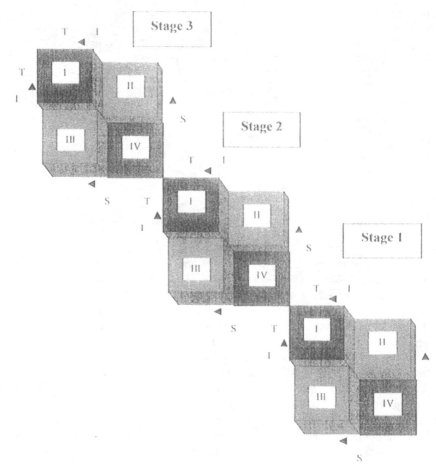

Source: Adapted from Carayannis (1998).

The pattern of commitments which lead to trust will tend to be a series of successive rounds where each party offers a quid pro quo, or a small investment which is reciprocated by the other party. In the case of the lawyer, for example, this means that the lawyer must be willing to give away some amount of advice or expertise without demanding immediate compensation. In classic negotiating terms, this offer provides an opening gambit to provoke the entrepreneur into following through with his or her own commitment. Note that in this stage of the relationship, the entrepreneur tends to hold the most leverage as there is generally a large number of law firms who could provide the same services as the lawyer. There may be instances, however, where there are few law firms willing to take on a risky start-up as a new client, thus increasing the leverage held by the lawyer. The entrepreneur can reciprocate by offering the lawyer some kind of stake in the future expected profits of the start-up, demonstrating that the entrepreneur is willing to sacrifice some long-term reward to secure the services of that lawyer.

The equity-based model of compensation is a vehicle for carrying the entrepreneur and the lawyer through this spiral of trust. By deferring compensation, the lawyer and entrepreneur cement an agreement where the "shadow of the future" (in game theory terms) is cast upon the current relationship. This helps to ensure that neither party will act to undermine the relationship. At the same time, by tying the lawyer's compensation to the overall business success of the venture (based on the eventual stock price post-IPO, or post-acquisition or post-merger), the equity-based compensation scheme helps to align the long-term interests of the law firm and the entrepreneur.

HOW THE EQUITY-BASED MODEL WORKS

As discussed briefly in chapter 2, the equity-based (or equity-for-service) model of compensation works in a fashion very similar to the use of stock options to compensate employees or key company insiders (such as founders)— but obviously with the important caveat that the lawyer receiving the equity is an external service provider. Even the practice of issuing stock options to outside lawyers is not completely new. It is not uncommon for lawyers to serve on the board of directors of corporations, and in such cases the lawyer may receive stock or stock options as compensation for service on the board. What is rather novel about the present application of the equity-based model is that *the company issuing the stock is also the client of the lawyer*, which as we shall discuss presents some potential complications.

A list of some of the more common types of investing arrangements between a law firm and a client include:

1. Performing services for stock.
2. Performing services for deferred fees and stock.
3. Performing services for fees with stock as a premium for engagement/expertise; additionally, as traditional VC dries up, intellectual VC (IVC) will be looked at more closely out of necessity.

4. Performing services for fees with a concomitant direct investment in the client in exchange for stock or founders stock.
5. Performing services for fees with a concomitant investment in a venture capital fund which then invests in a client.
6. Performing services for fees and co-investing during a venture capital financing round.

The Venture Law Group (VLG) Model

One design of an equity-based model of compensation for outside lawyers is commonly credited to Craig Johnson, founder of the Venture Law Group in Menlo Park, California. (Johnson, in turn, claims that the business model for his law firm came to him in a dream one night.)[25] There are a few important caveats to understand before assessing the equity-based model:

1. Most law firms using this model receive only a small portion of their compensation as equity. The bulk of their compensation is still paid in traditional billings.
2. While start-up firms have limited cash reserves to spend on lawyers, they also cannot issue stock options with impunity. Each option issued dilutes the value of the company, so entrepreneurs must be careful about which outside service providers should be rewarded with options.
3. Much of the interest in the equity-based model of compensation was fueled by the growth of the Internet economy and the "dot-com" stock bubble. Now that many Internet firms have seen their market value collapse post-IPO, interest in this model has clearly waned.[26] Still, the equity-based model was used prior to the emergence of the commercial Internet and is likely to survive the current downturn in initial public offerings.

The equity-based model of compensation in law firms is used in conjunction with traditional fee-for-services billing, and is targeted specifically at addressing the opportunities and pitfalls associated with working for entrepreneurial clients. As implemented by the Venture Law Group, the model works something like this:

1. First, the law firm will provide some initial strategic advice to the start-up to help it establish a business plan, obtain financing, and deal with the legal challenges of starting a new business. At the Venture Law Group, the start-up is not charged for this initial level of consultation. In fact, Jerry Yang (the cofounder of the Internet portal site Yahoo!) states that his firm was not billed by VLG at all until after his company had received its first round of venture capital financing.[27]
2. Once a new venture has become an established client, VLG will request the opportunity to purchase an equity stake in the start-up. VLG will take the equity as

---

[25] D. M. Osborne, "When Is a Law Firm Not a Law Firm?" *Inc.*, 1 May 1998, accessed at http://www.inc.com.

[26] Thor Valdmanis, "Fewer Firms Taking Equity Option Instead of Cash Payment," *USA Today*, 25 April 2001, p. 7B.

[27] Osborne, op. cit.

common stock during prefinancing periods or as preferred stock if the company already has financing.

3. Once the start-up has allocated a block of equity available for purchase, approximately 80 to 90 percent of that block will be purchased by VLG Investments, a venture capital fund operated by VLG. VLG Investments in turn is funded by a quarterly investment based on a pro-rated share of the profit-sharing bonus received by each partner in VLG. The partner responsible for the venture client is required to purchase the remainder of the block using his or her personal funds.

4. The equity stake is arranged above and beyond the usual fees that VLG charges its clients. Also, the amount of each investment is very small—typically about $11,000 per client.[28] As many start-up clients offer at least some amount of equity to VLG, the investment fund has a large number of companies in its portfolio (reportedly VLG made over 200 investments between 1993 and 1998).[29]

Variations on the Theme

Many law firms do not allow their individual attorneys to invest personally in clients, reserving that right for the firm. These firms feel that a personal investment by the attorney would represent a dangerous conflict of interest (see Ethical Issues and Compliance section later in this chapter). The VLG approach contradicts this, as Johnson believes that a financial interest in the client provides additional incentive for the attorney to do the best job possible advising and representing the client firm.

There are now numerous variations on how a law firm can establish a system for exchanging services for equity in its start-up clients. Here are a few variables which firms consider when establishing an equity investment program:

- Criteria for deciding to accept equity as payment (under what circumstances will the firm agree to use equity as a form of compensation for services?)
- Amount of the investment (how should the law firm determine how much equity to accept from the start-up client?)
- Timing of the investment (when is it appropriate to take equity-for-services?)
- Format of the investment (how will the legal ownership of equity be established?)
- Fund sourcing (what sources of funds will be used to take the equity?)
- Distribution of returns (how and to whom will the profits of the equity investment be distributed?)

---

[28] Ibid.
[29] Ibid.

Criteria and Process for Accepting Equity

Even when equity is being used as a form of compensation from a client, a law firm should still exercise the same degree of caution as any investor in determining when equity is an acceptable form of payment for services. First, almost all law firms contacted by the authors confirmed that they will take equity as payment only from private firms which have not yet held an initial public offering. In rare cases, some firms have taken equity in public companies—for example, in helping to turn around bankrupt clients. However, the potential returns on such investments tend to be small compared to the situation for start-up clients. The problem is that like any investor, the law firm must be able to evaluate the start-up client's business potential to gain a reasonable assurance that the equity will produce some substantial return. Attorneys, due to their rather risk-averse nature, tend to be particularly concerned that they may end up investing many hours in a start-up client, only to have that client go out of business before its IPO. As noted by Edward Chansky, partner in the intellectual property practice of Levett, Rockwood & Sanders in Westport, Connecticut, attorneys are fearful of the possibility of "if the company doesn't go anywhere, then we just did a bunch of work for which we aren't going to get paid."[30]

Some firms may have corporate transaction lawyers with extensive business experience. These firms may rely on those attorneys to "vet" a prospective start-up client and determine if the company is likely to produce an adequate return on investment to justify accepting equity as payment for services. Other firms without such in-house expertise may choose to wait until one or more venture capital firms has inspected the start-up's business plan and qualified the company for funding. Unfortunately, most start-ups need to have an outside counsel identified *before* obtaining financing, so venture capital typically is a consequence not a precursor to the start-up crunch that motivates the Equity-for-Service approach.

Amount of the Investment

Most law firms put some limit on how much they are willing to take in equity in a client. First, firms will tend to limit the percentage of ownership in a start-up client to a very nominal share—generally following the "two percent rule" as David Schellhase (former in-house counsel at the software firm Vantive) calls it. This amount establishes the commitment of the law firm to its client but does not give the firm control over the management of the client. Some other firms may allow larger shares of ownership; at VLG, Craig Johnson helped to cofound the start-up Garage.com with former Apple executive Guy Kawasaki and ended up owning 8 percent of the firm. Wilson Sonsini generally limits its investments in clients to $50,000 in current firm value.

---

[30] Quoted in *The Connecticut Law Tribune*, 1 May 2000.

Law firms will also hedge the risk involved in equity ownership by limiting the amount of potential revenue deferred by taking equity. Most firms will forego only a small portion of billings (perhaps 5 or 10 percent per year) in exchange for equity in start-up clients. More entrepreneurial law firms may be willing to risk more of their regular income for the chance to win big in taking the start-up public.

Timing of the Investment

The first critical question, after a firm has determined that it will enable the use of equity in lieu of or in conjunction with traditional fee-based compensation, is when the equity investment should take place. This decision is very important, as the timing of the investment establishes the value of the equity interest obtained by the law firm. There are two specific aspects of timing which should be addressed: the timing of the investment relative to the financing of the start-up, and the timing relative to the stage in the business relationship between the start-up and the law firm.

The law firm needs to ensure that its equity in the start-up earns a return sufficient to compensate for the cost of its services and the risk in taking equity instead of fees. However, as noted, the firm may want to take equity only after another investor has assigned an appropriate financial value to the start-up's potential. The law firm may decide to wait at least until the start-up has secured a round of seed financing from outside "angel" investors, joining in that round as an early-stage investor to receive equity.

The law firm should also decide at what point it is appropriate to request equity from a start-up client. At the height of the Internet-driven investment boom in Silicon Valley venture firms, some of the most prestigious law firms required that start-ups offer a share of their corporate equity as a condition for taking the start-up as a client. Demand for outside counsel was so great that start-ups were essentially forced to give up equity for access to the best attorneys. One firm reportedly considered doubling its standard billing rate for any start-up client who refused to offer equity as part of its payment for legal services.[31] Other firms simply use equity as a substitute for some portion of their normal fees, or as a means to secure the deferment of billings or accounts payable by the start-up until after the start-up has acquired cash through an initial public offering.

Format of the Investment

The law firm may not necessarily receive shares of common stock from the start-up in an equity-based compensation deal. In fact, such an arrangement might be the exception rather than the rule, at least where the value of the start-up firm is highly uncertain. A law firm may choose to purchase so-called friends and family shares, which are shares of stock reserved for sale to

---

[31] David Schellhase, "Rethinking the Equity Equation," *The Recorder*, 23 February 2000, p. 5.

outsiders at the discretion of the top management of the start-up. The law firm may also be able to purchase "founders' shares," which are assigned a par value of $1 per share until the start-up's initial public offering is formally priced by an investment bank.

There are a number of other ways for law firms to secure an equity interest in a start-up. One possibility is that the law firm can be issued stock options, similar to a favored employee or executive. These options, once purchased, convert to common shares upon the start-up's initial public offering. Another method is to construct some type of financial derivative which captures the value of the law firm's equity interest. The start-up may issue a warrant, or the right to purchase a specific number of shares at a future time and at a set price. Another popular instrument is a "collar," which establishes a maximum and minimum value of each share to be issued at a later date. These derivatives are useful especially if the value of the start-up has not yet been established by an outside professional.

Sources of Funds for Equity Investments

In cases where the law firm chooses to purchase equity in the start-up, the funds used for the investment need to be procured in advance. Most firms which take this approach reserve some portion of the annual profits shared by the partners to establish an outside investment fund which is used to invest in clients. As an alternative, the fund can solicit contributions directly from the partners—for example, for about $3,000 per partner per year.

Another common variation involves some specific commitment from the "sourcing" attorney (the attorney who is responsible for bringing the start-up on as a client). To cement that attorney's commitment to the client, the sourcing attorney may be required by the law firm to make a personal investment in the client—for example, 10 percent of the law firm's investment. This requirement is usually intended to guarantee that the sourcing attorney will continue to pay close attention to the needs of the start-up. This is similar to the individual investment required by Venture Law Group of its senior attorneys.

Distribution of Returns

One of the most difficult issues in managing equity investments in clients is how to distribute the investment returns earned on that equity. The distribution formula should be based on the strategic goals intended when making equity investments. In many cases, the investment is a substitute for billings that would otherwise be revenue for the law firm. Therefore, the firm may elect to distribute the returns back to the partners who contributed profits to the investment fund. The returns may also be used as a means of generating bonuses for valued attorneys and employees. In some firms, the sourcing attorney receives an additional share of the returns from investments in his or her client. The returns can also be distributed as a post-engagement bonus to the entire team of attorneys who worked on that client's case, similar to the use of contingency fees in civil litigation.

One common use of investment returns by firms during the dot-com boom was as a retention tool. As many firms began to lose attorneys and other professionals to start-ups, those firms tried to use equity investment pools to offer employees the same potential "upside" as stock options in a start-up employer. Some portion of the returns earned by the law firm's investment fund would be reserved for a bonus pool, with the amount of each bonus assigned by the law firm partners. As an added incentive, each employee can be given a share of ownership in the fund which "vests" over a period of years, encouraging attorneys to stay with the firm so that they can gain those future returns. Any attorney who leaves before his or her share vests will lose any claim to those returns; that amount is instead distributed back to the firm or the remaining employees in the pool.

WHY THE EQUITY MODEL WORKS

The equity-based model of compensation is superior to the pure fee-for-services in arranging relations between lawyers and start-ups for reasons far beyond pragmatic considerations such as preserving the entrepreneur's cash. As noted by Professor Ashish Nanda of the Harvard Business School, the start-up could accomplish the same goal by issuing a bond or other debt security to its outside counsel, deferring its financial obligation but without sacrificing equity.[32] By taking an equity stake in the start-up, the law firm is showing that it will accept a share of the risk involved in the venture as a measure of the law firm's contribution to the final performance of the start-up.

Joint Venture and Exchange Contracts

The theoretical basis of the equity-based model can be traced to research on the use of equity joint ventures and equity-exchange contracts between businesses. In a joint-venture situation, each investor contributes some share of the resources of the new organization formed by the agreement, and accepts a commensurate share of the eventual gains or losses from that endeavor. Joint-venture agreements in the high-technology industry commonly include contributions of intellectual assets, such as patents or other forms of legally recognized intellectual property, as one type of investment for which a joint venture participant should receive consideration when allocating the shares of ownership in the new venture. The negotiations process for forming the joint-venture also implicitly includes considerations for less tangible forms of intellectual capital, such as the transfer of management and technical talent from an investor to the new venture.

Viewed in the context of a joint venture, the equity-based model of compensation in the legal profession represents a type of joint venture between

---

[32] Ashish Nanda, *Consulting*, June 2000, pp. 20-25.

law firms and start-ups. Since legal expertise is an essential component of the resources needed to successfully manage the evolution of a new venture from start-up phase to initial public offering and beyond, an equity-based compensation approach can be framed as a recognition of the intellectual contribution of the outside attorney(s) to the eventual performance of the start-up. Note that the use of equity is not only a sacrifice on the part of the entrepreneur—the outside attorney is also accepting a higher level of risk by agreeing to take equity instead of a service fee and therefore should justly receive a premium (in the form of a share of the total returns from stock ownership) if that risk pays off.

The second critical factor beyond risk-sharing in the theoretical analysis of the equity-based model is how the use of equity helps to align the interests and strategies of the law firm and the start-up. In a simple fee-for-services agreement, the performance of the law firm is monitored by the tension between two competing sets of incentives. On one hand, the law firm is motivated to adopt an extractive approach to the relationship with the client, maximizing the number of billable hours charged to the client while investing minimal effort. On the other hand, to ensure predictable and increasing future revenues, the law firm wishes to build a long-term relationship with the client, and therefore will in theory invest the effort necessary to ensure the satisfaction of the client.

Breakdown of the Equity-for-Service Model

Where the fee-for-services model breaks down is in its application to entrepreneurial clients. Such clients often lack very deep legal and business experience. Therefore, they may be unable to recognize whether or not the law firm is in fact investing time and effort commensurate with the billings for that service. Also, in situations such as the business environment in the technology industry in the mid- to late-1990s, law firms had an advantage in their dealings with start-ups. Demand for the services of prestigious law firms greatly exceeded the supply of legal talent. As a result, the pressure on law firms to maintain long-term client relationships was reduced. If one apparently promising start-up ended its relationship with a well-regarded law firm, there were several other start-ups waiting to sign contracts with that same law firm. Therefore, by tying the law firm's compensation to the long-term returns from equity ownership, the equity-based model provided a better mechanism for policing the behavior of the law firm in its dealings with start-up clients.

Finally, the rise of the equity-based model provided greater incentives to assess the actual nature of the services offered by law firms to start-up clients. In many cases, start-ups pursue relationships with well-known law firms not simply for legal expertise. Reputable attorneys in the technology field can also provide the start-up with introductions to existing networks of investors (especially venture capitalists), board members, mentors, and other important contacts. Therefore, simply billing a client for time does not fully capture the value of what a law firm can offer to a start-up client. The equity-based model has the ability to be more comprehensive in ensuring that the total contribution of the outside counsel to the start-up's performance is properly recognized in their contractual agreement

THE EQUITY-BASED MODEL OF COMPENSATION IN PRACTICE

Equity-for-services is not a new idea. In a general sense, anytime a farmer or businessman used his real property or equipment as collateral against a debt generated by a contractor (e.g., a mechanic's lien), an equity-for-service agreement was formed. This is no different in the legal field. Examples abound of the town lawyer who owned a little bit of everything in town because he drafted the druggist's will, or he conducted the real estate transaction for the barber, and so on; and the recipients of these services could not afford to pay up front or even upon completion of the legal work. Accordingly, it was easier to grant a little equity than to saddle start-up or low-margin businesses with bills that would not be paid except in bankruptcy.

In the field of patent law, an interview with Mrs. Muriel Olson, age 97, uncovered that her late husband, Roy Olson, a name partner in a now defunct patent firm in Chicago, knew of many instances during the 1930s and 1940s where patent lawyers who wished to be paid at all had to accept company stock. Although we were not able to uncover any additional first-hand knowledge of equity-for-services agreements prior to these, inventors have been inventing and patent lawyers have been patenting in this country since at least the 1836 Patent Act, if not the original 1790 Patent Act. The 1790 Act authorized the secretary of state, the secretary of war, and the attorney general to grant letters patent for any sufficiently useful and important "art, manufacture, engine, machine, or device, or any improvement therein not before known or used." Thus, since the decision-makers were important and powerful executive officers of the government, it can probably be assumed that attorneys were necessary to obtaining a patent. This is especially so after the 1836 Act when a system of examination was first introduced, thus making the entire process more administrative and complex. It is even conceivable, albeit beyond the scope of this book, that equity-for-patent service can trace its roots to England, where the 1623 Statute of Monopolies allowed 14-year grants of letters patent for new manufactures.

In more recent history, law firms such as Cooley Godward LLP of Palo Alto, California, have been engaging in equity arrangements with their clients since 1963. Although most if not all managing-level attorneys have been confronted with problems relating to working out the payment schedule of particular clients, the practice of investing in clients seems to have been perfected on the West Coast. One observer noted that this wasn't explored by West Coast firms due to any particular entrepreneurial drive, but, rather, was precipitated as a mechanism to maintain viability and compete with the profitable old-line firms from the East Coast for equivalent margins and for new attorneys. In other words, they did it because they had to.

KEY ISSUES IN IMPLEMENTING THE EQUITY-BASED COMPENSATION MODEL

To this end, equity programs have found a place in firms which have suffered at the recent explosion of attorney movement between firms and/or companies. Additional factors which have put a great deal of pressure on law firms to adopt an equity program include the phenomenal growth in entry-level salaries being paid to attorneys, the increased cost of equipment and technology, and the greater spread in profitability between firms which do well and those which do not. Firms which have experienced a loss of attorneys also note the downward spiral which occurs when an attorney leaves, the ability to profit leaves, which leads the firm to a financial situation where otherwise loyal attorneys leave leading to additional lost profits, and so forth. The recent growth and decline of Internet-related industries highlights one area where equity programs played a crucial role.

Real-world Examples

One large 900+ attorney law firm with a focus on high-technology matters, Brobeck, Phleger & Harrison, LLP, experienced a substantial loss of partners and associates a few years ago to their clients, many in the dot-com and B-to-C industries. In one instance, a young partner received stock options from a client which received a takeover offer 30 days later, making the partner's options worth $30 million. In another instance, a fourth-year associate went to a dot-com client to become their in-house counsel and received stock options. Within six months, the options were worth millions of dollars. In a third instance, an associate left the firm, the corporation failed, and the associate returned to a position at the firm. To address some of these situations, Brobeck instituted an Investment Program involving equity investing for the firm's partners, associates, and staff. The benefits of such a plan include (1) supplementing the firm's income, (2) increasing retention by requiring investments to vest over a period of time, (3) providing a program which appeals to entrepreneurial attorneys, and (4) providing a positive aspect to the client-attorney relationship where the client understands that the firm also has an interest in making the company succeed—that is, "skin in the game."

However, the loss of firm attorneys to clients is not limited to firms specializing in high-tech. Milbank, Tweed, Hadley & McCloy LLP is a 135-year-old, 475-attorney, New York "traditional" firm specializing in financing. This firm experienced a loss of attorneys not only to dot-coms, but to the investment banks they served as well. To address some of these issues, they also instituted an equity-based Investment Program that included a Partner Fund and an Associate Fund, the details of which are provided.

Interviews with many of these firms reveal that there are as many ways to structure these equity agreements as there are firms and clients. However, ethical and tax issues have placed some boundaries around these deals. These ethical and tax issues will be explained in detail in the next sections, but suffice it to say that beyond these guideposts, the only other limiting factor appears to be the risk-tolerance of the participants. This is especially true when considering the straight equity-for-service arrangements as opposed to the less risky hybrids which have evolved over time into the dominant form of these agreements.

Ethical Issues and Compliance

The short answer to whether it is ethical for a lawyer to acquire securities issued by a client in connection with performing services for that client is: Yes. The basis for this answer can be found in four main opinions by the ethics committees of the American Bar Association (Formal Opinion 00-418, 7 July, 2000), the New York City Bar Association (Formal Opinion 2000-3), the District of Columbia Bar (Opinion 300, 25 July, 2000), and the Utah Bar (Opinion 98-13, 4 December, 1998). The main issues which apply to equity arrangements arise of out of the canons of ethics relating to conflicts of interest and to the reasonableness of the amount of the fee.

Although most lawyers are familiar with the ethics rules as they relate to certain disciplinary matters such as criminal activities, neglecting a client, and the improper premature use of funds held in a retainer account, they haven't a clue about the proper way to establish an ethically compliant equity program. These issues must be addressed by every firm seeking to develop or maintain an equity investment program and they must be addressed in the correct manner. Failure to do so may actually result in a disciplinary investigation by the local bar association counsel. Although the historical development of the various ethics rules and how to properly comply with them is an interesting topic, it is requires a complex explanation which is already covered in the opinions above. It is also well beyond the scope of this book. Accordingly, only a brief summary of how compliance is achieved is provided here.

Ethics Requirements

Suffice it to say that four main requirements must be fulfilled: (1) the transaction must be fair and reasonable; (2) the terms of the deal are fully disclosed in writing to the client; (3) the client is given a reasonable opportunity to seek the advice of independent counsel; and (4) the client must consent to the conflict of interest/potential conflict of interest in writing [See ABA Model Rule 1.8(a)]. Accordingly, to comply with the ethics rules the firms that have equity programs require their clients to execute a form letter which spells out (in gory detail) (1) the cost basis for the services rendered, (2) the problems with attorney bias, conflict, withdrawal, and privilege; and (3) the encouragement or demand that the client get a review by independent counsel. Firms which ignore this requirement can additionally have the problem, besides bar counsel, that one attorney had in California where he lost his $30 million stake when a client had their agreement voided because it did not comply with Rule 1.8.

The Example of Sailor Mohler

Another situation that can happen to attorneys who invest in their clients is illustrated by the dispute described in an article in *Washington Techway* magazine.[33] The article describes a dispute between an inventor of a heart monitoring device, Sailor Mohler, and his former attorney. Mohler, a 48 year old former Navy veteran who flew missions in Vietnam, who had a degree in physics, and who had a career in the X-ray technology field with the military and then with Pfizer, became a victim in an equity investment situation.

The gist of the story is that an attorney was brought in as president of his company and agreed to perform legal work for a one-third stake in the company until the company was up and running. After the heart device was approved by the Food and Drug Administration (FDA), some of the inventor's friends wanted to invest in the company and the attorney allegedly refused. The inventor then transferred the intellectual property rights to a different company. The attorney and other investors filed suit to get the property back and alleged breach of contract, breach of fiduciary duty, and 13 other counts against the inventor, Mohler. One the investors claimed that the inventor was mismanaging their investment. The inventor's point of view was that his business partners were trying to "steal his invention" and he also filed suit against the attorney's firm, alleging it had neglected his interest as their client. The dispute points out the difficulty of determining who the real client is, when there is a conflict of interest, and achieving a true consent, even where the inventor is a generally worldly and seasoned businessman.

Liability Issues

There are many legal theories which could be used to attempt to attach liability to an attorney's or a firm's conduct as it relates to an equity program. However, the most troubling of these is the breach of fiduciary duty. Since a lawyer-client relationship is a fiduciary relationship, the attorney is held to a higher standard of behavior. One of the problematic areas is the use of a conflict-of-interest claim to convert a simple malpractice claim into a breach of fiduciary duty claim which brings on the possibility of punitive damages where they would otherwise not be allowed under normal circumstances. Another problem area concerns the fact that insurance may not cover liability arsing from entities managed, operated, or controlled by the attorney.

Since every lawyer knows that when "things go south," the first thing clients do is blame the lawyers, it has been suggested that certain limits be placed on the equity relationship. These limits include: (1) utilize an independent person or body to determine the investment decision, (2) seek indemnification, (3) be sure to update the conflicts disclosure as needed, (4) do not acquire too large a stake in the client (e.g., 1-5%), (5) do not exercise control of or be on the board of the corporation, (6) avoid directly benefiting only the

---

[33] Susan Crabtree, "Lawyers in Love," *Washington Techway*, 11 September 2000.

lawyers who work on the client's matters, and (7) stand ready to sell your shares as soon as a conflict arises.

Tax Issues

One of the biggest tax issues relating to equity investments concerns the generation of "phantom income." This type of income tax liability attaches under an accrual accounting methodology whereby stock received for services is booked as income when the fees are waived or when the services are provided. Thus, you could find yourself paying income tax on the fair value of a stock before you have received anything of real value, since it is generally required that you hold the stock until some liquidity event occurs—merger, acquisition, or IPO. This can be particularly problematic when the firm is one of the first investors and there is no third party valuation given to the stock. This problem is frequently solved by timing the investment to occur during a coinvestment in a venture round, letting the VCs set the price per share. However, in a typical investment vehicle like an LLC, payment of the phantom income tax early to avoid large tax liabilities later if it successful by making an IRS Code Section 83 election (if you elect early then any gains in share price would only be taxed as capital gains) can put the tax burden on the partners during the year of the investment and give a windfall to the partners present when the fund vests, say four years later.

A third problem is the valuation of the services. This number can be easily fudged by adjusting the amount of time charged, the dollar amount charged, and/or the hourly rate charged. This makes valuing the services difficult. Finally, one problem not frequently noticed is the time value of fees paid in a fee-for-service versus a stock-for-service arrangement. In the fee-for-service arrangement, part of the fee goes to cover overhead and part goes to profit. In the stock-for-service arrangement, not only must there be an outlay of capital to cover overhead, but profit is not taken in as well. The hurdle which a stock for service arrangement must overcome includes not only the fees deferred and the premium expected for doing so, but also the time value of the overhead lost and the profit not captured.

Chapter 4

Insights from Practice:
Perspectives from Expert Service
Providers

EXAMPLES OF FOR-PROFIT AND NOT-FOR-PROFIT ADOPTING THE EQUITY-BASED MODEL: MOTIVATIONS, EXPERIENCES, AND CRITIQUES

Generally, a common method of setting up an equity investment program is to appoint an investment committee, generally attorneys with a large amount of experience in transactional matters, decide the amount to invest, form a legal entity for investing such as an LLC, which is opened and closed on a yearly basis, develop rules for participation and vesting, and institute selection criteria and standard forms to process the clients which match the firm's interests.

The participation criteria also vary by firm as to whether opportunities to invest in a given client are "firm opportunities," a kind of "one for all and all for one" approach, and whether originating attorneys can also individually participate, a more entrepreneurial approach for the "golden Rolodex" crowd. What are some of the goals to try to achieve in an equity program? The main goals would seem to be as an income supplement with which you can attract and keep the partners, and lawyers who are successful at conducting firm business.

Equity Deals in Industry-University Collaborations

An interesting recent development involving not-for-profit entities, where equity deals are playing a role, is in the area of industry-university collaborations. Historically, universities and their professors generally looked down on industry researchers with contempt and disliked any attempt by industry to "steer" their research by offers of grants, equipment, or advice. As research and development (R&D) evolved, the industry researchers started doing some pretty cool stuff which interested their academic counterparts, and the university didn't think the industry's money was any less green than that from other sources such as the National Institutes of Health (NIH), the National Cancer Institute (NCI), Department of Defense (DoD) and so on. Thus, a few rare collaborations were formed.

Within the last 10 or 20 years, universities have taken to technology transfer, incubators, and in-house start-ups with a vengeance. This activity has been driven by, among other things, increasing competition for research dollars and the realization from some enormously successful institutions that serious money could be recaptured from research that was going to be done anyway as part of the university's mission. It was in this environment that universities started taking equity in the start-up ventures in which their faculty were involved as consideration for transferring the technology out of the university into the new corporation. Similarly, large companies realized that the lines were blurring such that company and university collaboration and contribution were almost inseparable. Companies sometimes provided equipment, sometimes technology, sometimes expertise, sometimes money. Universities, or the research foundations they started, did the same.

Today, industry leaders such as DuPont and GlaxoWellcome are involved in collaborations with universities where technology, money, management, equipment, and lab and office facilities are given to start-ups in exchange for equity. For instance, DuPont may donate some patents and a few experts. The university will provide some grad student interns from the business school and from the microbiology department as labor. The university foundation may provide incubation facilities and a professor or two from the business school as Chief Financial Officer (CFO) or Chief Technical Officer (CTO). The money can come from the state and the foundation and the company and the usual sources, but now it doesn't have to be used to build-out the office and buy furniture. Instead, the money can be put to work advancing the R&D, with emphasis on commercialization.

Interestingly, the pharmaceutical, biotech, and software industries already have a system for this. Usually, small companies will shop around and obtain technology from a local university. The small company will then develop the technology into a patent portfolio and advance the research to a somewhat commercialized stage. Then, the small company hopes and prays for the exit strategy to be fulfilled: the merger, the acquisition, or the IPO. The new equity model, discussed in Chapter 3, short-circuits this middleman approach and allows the large company to reach directly into the university/start-up stage. On the surface, this would seem involve a lot more risk than waiting around to see who survives the first cut in the small-company beauty pageant. However, it would also seem to have the added benefit of allowing the large company to guide a particular technology from the beginning.

Where Does an Equity Program Fit?

Generally, an equity program works best in technology areas, particularly in firms with a high enough deal-flow to provide a decent selection of investment opportunities, and where a firm is experiencing the "downward attrition spiral". This spiral happens when a sudden loss of attorneys results in a loss of profits, which results in a loss of attorneys, and so forth. Another factor to consider is when a firm has a sudden increased cost of equipment and technology and needs to generate some additional revenue.

Case in Point

David Hornik
Associate, Atlas Ventures

Why do VLG and other law firms accept equity from new ventures as payment for services?

The truth is, VLG really didn't adopt an equity-for-service approach. We were quite explicit that we were not exchanging our services for equity. We were really telling them that they needed us on the team and that the price of admission and the continued interest in their companies was some skin in the game so our clients needed to give us some equity—they also gave us the opportunity to invest

I think one of the motivating factors for service providers is that it gave them the first opportunity to make a return on their investment in time that was not directly proportional to their time. The big problem with service providers is that they need to leverage human capital to get any reasonable return (partners in law firms only get rich on the backs of more junior attorneys who are being paid less than they are billing). By taking equity in companies they were representing, a lucky lawyer could make millions on a single client to whom they could have only billed thousands or tens of thousands of dollars.

Smart guys will use it as a part of their revenue strategy because it is really huge when it works. It makes sense to have a little of your intellectual capital invested in a high-risk instrument—particularly when you are a lawyer and most of your equity is very low-risk, plodding dollars for hours of work.

How do you deal with equity as deferred compensation?

You bet on the promising companies by not charging them until they get money. The start-up costs are pretty low so you are willing to bet $10K worth of services against them getting funded. Of course it is a harder bet these days because it is so hard for companies to actually get funded, but in any event, lots of firms would defer billing until a financing (but they always got the money paid once the company had money).

But it makes it really tricky because a law firm has certain up-front expenses (salary, etc.) that it needs to pay in the short term, not the long term....So here is the real problem with timing. The timing of things got all messed up by the crazy market we were experiencing. There were lots of companies having liquidity events after a year or so, which is not normal. We are now going back to a world in which it takes four, five, six years to get a successful outcome from a start-up company, which means that the time horizon is way too long for most service providers. It is hard enough to bet against the uncertainty of a start-up and it is another thing altogether if the payout doesn't come for six years. If that becomes the norm there will be fewer and fewer lawyers willing to defer any compensation for the sake of equity because the time horizon is too long.

Why should entrepreneurs give equity to outside counsel?
Here's my thinking about another reason why equity matters. At the end of the day, as you suggest, professional services are not a commodity. You ultimately get the service level provided by an individual or set of individuals who serve your account. So it really matters who you get, not just what firm. Equity can provide incentive for the right individuals to work on your account (again, it may be the price of admission—a great lawyer may demand some piece of the equity for himself before agreeing to work with a client, which gives him added incentive to be really successful with respect to your company.

Clients liked it because it meant that you put skin in the game—not just intellectual capital but honest to goodness capital. I had one client who said he would not scrutinize my bills until I had billed him more than my firm had invested in his company (a stupid attitude—he always should have scrutinized my bills—but it was the attitude).

I always looked at it this way—the truly successful relationships start-ups have with lawyers are successful because the outside lawyer treats the relationship like he is actually inside counsel—I always viewed myself as outside general counsel to a dozen companies.

The other advantage for an entrepreneur is that it gives the service provider the incentive to pay any attention to the little guys. Without equity, you would always service the big guys first because they pay the most money for the most services. If it were not for the desire to get in on the ground floor of the next Microsoft, no start-up would get top-tier service because it would not be in their interest to take on such clients.

Another big thing is whose call gets answered first—one of the advantages of being really engaged (and often it is the equity that gets you engaged and keeps you engaged) is that you do their work first, you take their phone call first, and so on.

How do you structure the equity deal?

You ALWAYS want to get common stock because it is soooo much cheaper. Common stock doesn't have things like liquidation preference (i.e., you get your money out first if the company is sold) and those sorts of things, but it is usually priced at about one tenth the price at the outset of the company, so if you were to buy 10,000 shares of preferred stock at a buck a piece it would cost you $10,000, whereas the same 10,000 shares of common stock would cost $1,000. Often the firm would get common stock at the inception of the company and then buy preferred stock in the next equity financing. Thus the firms all established stock funds and they invested in their clients.

Law firms may get preferential founders-type stock. There are two kinds of friends and family stock. Often start-ups would raise their initial seed funding from friends and family, in which case it was preferred stock at a price that was higher than the price of common stock but still at a pretty low valuation. Then there is what is called friends and family stock allocation in an initial public offering. That stock is basically stock sold to friends of the firm as part of the IPO. When all stock prices were going up the day the company went public, friends and family shares were like found money. You would be given the right to buy stock in the company at the IPO for $10 per share and the share price would go up to $40 that day, so you would make $30 per share on the first day. So there was real value there. And it too became an issue for law firms. Companies often issued friends and family shares to their lawyers, or the law firms and even to their junior associates. It created a bunch of the same conflicts. If the IPO shares were worth a bunch of money, was that money rightfully the law firm's? Did it give lawyers the incentive to work only on companies going public? These were tough issues when IPOs were hot—probably not such tough issues any longer. Usually the par value is way lower—$0.01 or $0.001 per share, and as I said the common stock price was always lower than the preferred price.

In theory what happens is the value of preferred stock over common stock goes down as the company is more successful because features of preferred stock that give a company down-side protection become less valuable. So as the company does better, the board of directors often increases the assumed value of the common stock to reflect the closing of that gap. The reason you want to keep your common stock price low is that for certain tax reasons you have to price stock options at approximately the common stock price or the stock option will not qualify for preferred tax treatment (deferred tax, etc.), so if the common stock price gets too high then the employees see less value in the options. But if you underprice the options then you may have to take an accounting charge when the company goes public. So it can be an issue....

This is not always a good deal for the entrepreneur. It isn't that they want to protect their valuations—what they want to protect is their fully diluted percentage ownership in the company—they want to make sure that they are not diluted to the point of owning a disinteresting piece of the pie—and equity is a zero sum game.

Worse yet, the standard terms of a venture financing have the company that is getting financed paying for the attorney for the investor—that number is usually capped and the cap is negotiated but that number has gone up over time (it used to be $10K, then $15K and now I think it is not unusual to see $20K). So I think you can count on the typical venture financing costing at least $25K from the company to get done between the attorneys' fees for the company and the attorneys' fees of the investor.

Are attorneys allowed to invest personal funds into clients?
Some places it was required (to keep a check on the money going out of the firm investment fund) and in some instances it was allowed. Again, the point was to allow people to get a stake in the outcome. Since it was the individual attorneys who would be doing all the work and adding most of the value it was considered appropriate to give them a slice of the equity themselves.

Is this kind of compensation scheme important for retention of associates?
This may or may not be the actual structure but kind of doesn't matter.... VLG and other Silicon Valley firms were all the same—VLG, Gunderson, Wilson Sonsini, Perkins Coie, and Fenwick—we were all doing the same thing. You established a fund that was a partner fund and then you invested out of it. For associate retention during the heyday they would create an associate pool and invest some portion on behalf of the associates. The theory was that if the associate pool was viewed as having enough value, the associates wouldn't leave the firm to join one of their clients (which was happening all over the place).
The flip side of this occurred when the market was red hot. Lawyers would blow off companies that weren't doing well because there were real opportunity costs associated with time—you had to make the most of your time and spending it on companies that would not have big return on equity was not a good use of your time. This absolutely happened. The hot companies got their calls returned first.

What are the drawbacks of equity-for-services?
So this is why the equity-for-service approach is a bad one in anything but an over exuberant market—service professionals are entirely unqualified to make investment decisions. They know how to be lawyers or accountants but they (1) don't know how to evaluate the value and likely success of a potential client, and (2) even if they knew how, they don't have the time to reasonably do so....Often they will use reasonable criteria like they will agree to it if a top-tier venture capital fund is investing, but other times they will just be random. At my old firm the basic process was to ask my partner Buddy and me if we thought it was a good investment and if we said yes (based upon nothing more than a little market knowledge and a guess) then we would do the deal.
However, service providers have the advantage of portfolio theory. If you get equity across a range of companies and a range of areas (high-tech, biotech, etc.) you are more likely to make money in the long run.

Again, the big issue here is the cost of the stock. If you buy the stock when the company is formed, it is the equivalent of being given the stock for free (at a tenth of a penny, it is a good deal in virtually any outcome other than bankruptcy). As the value of the stock increases with financings and business success, the firm has to pay more for the stock and therefore it is harder to justify—it becomes a bigger bet.

Other firms solicit interest from partners in the investment. So if there is a company where there is an investment available a memo will be circulated and interested will be stated. Then the investment will be divided up among those who want to participate.   This becomes an issue when the deal is oversubscribed. Then how do you choose who gets to invest and how much? People would compete for hot deals.

Craig Johnson is one of the few characters out there who can actually do a bit of bridging between lawyer and VC. He does have the connections. He can make the introduction. The interesting thing is that he isn't really doing the law stuff any more. A good friend of mine is doing all his legal work while Craig does all the schmoozing. One problem with the equity model is that when it works it makes you rich and you have no incentive to be a lawyer any longer. When VCs get rich they try to find the next company because it is a game and they are addicted. When lawyers get rich they retire. Period.

There was a lawyer at VLG who represented a red-hot networking company. When the company went public the partners' individual equity was worth something like $7M. It was some consolation to the partnership that the whole partner piece was worth something like $50M, but partnerships don't really dig one partner getting rich while the others do not. It creates jealousy.

Oh yeah, here's the other big problem. It was hard to give people an incentive to work on something that didn't appear to have a good equity outcome. Partners and associates to work on public companies seemed like a waste of time—they would not be worth any more in equity. So places like VLG tried to dump clients after they went public. This ended up biting them in the ass because when there was a downturn, the private companies all went belly up and the public companies had been pushed to other firms, so places like VLG had major cash issues because they didn't have enough work.

It is a total double-edged sword. I definitely worked harder because I thought I could make a difference and make some more money. By the way, to give you a sense of the magnitude of it, I represented two clients in 1998. I had been given the opportunity to invest $10,000 in each at their inception but VLG had a policy at the time that did not allow it, so I could not. I sold both companies one year after I incorporated them for something like $500M in combination and my $20K would have been worth $800,000, so we are talking about BIG payouts in relatively short times (there were six founders of the two companies—four made in excess of $20M and two made in excess of $15M— for one year's work; man was that good while it lasted).

What are some ethical problems in equity-for-services?

Here's the problem—and I'm sure I'll get into it later as well—lawyers were completely mercenary. During the heyday, not only did lawyers charge the maximum rate, but they ALSO insisted on equity. VLG was NOT taking equity in lieu of cash, it was taking it on top of cash. The supply of experienced lawyers was so constrained that lawyers could demand not only to be paid at the market rate but to also get 1 percent of the common stock in a company. In many instances in the late 1980s that turned out to be worth hundreds of thousands of dollars if not millions. I agree that equity aligns interests. but I am not sure that equity is a substitute for paying too much money for lawyers (the good news is that now the demand is constrained so lawyers are needing to charge less and demand less equity).

Potential cases?

The interesting thing that was happening during the heyday was firms were differentiating themselves based upon contacts to the venture community, familiarity with start-ups and so on. I even got a company to hire me to do the sale of the company because I had contacts in all the major portals (Yahoo!, Excite, Lycos, etc.) and would be able to shop the deal around for them. The company (Sonique) ended up giving my firm just under 1 percent of the total deal size to act as their attorneys. I got the price of the deal up from $35M to $65M and the firm made about $600,000 for about $100,000 worth of my time. Better yet, the guys who owned the company bought me my Porsche! But the deal structure was very much like equity. We got a piece of the deal and the reason we did was because I had the contacts and the ability to move their deal forward, not just do the legal documents. The same was true with new company representation—I would often pitch companies that they had to give me equity because I could get them in front of VCs, had done a bunch of mergers and acquisitions in the space, and could introduce them to companies they were interested in speaking with. To my mind that is really the role of VCs, which is why it is what I now do at August, but all the good lawyers were (and I'm sure still are) pitching themselves as the guys to get your company rolling.

PROBLEMS WITH BUSINESS BASED ON BILLINGS INSTEAD OF PARTNERSHIPS

Last year, taking stock for payment from dot-com start-ups seemed like the path to Internet riches. Maybe it wasn't so brilliant after all. Not long ago, Web designers, lawyers, executive recruiters, landlords, celebrities, professional athletes and others with goods or services to offer technology start-ups were accepting—in some cases demanding—stock in lieu of, or on top of, cash for their services to up-and-coming companies. Many of those taking the stock figured it was almost riskless because they were selling picks and shovels to the gold miners. It turns out that many ended up with fool's gold.[34]

The equity-for-service approach we are discussing here is not immune to cyclical trends and even fads. The Internet bubble and the "new economy" business models have recently given way to a less exuberant mentality, often leading to the other extreme:

> "Taking stock in your clients is generally a thing of the past," says Jonathan Nelson, chairman of Organic, whose own stock has plunged to less than $1 a share from an offering price of $20 in February, 2000. Taking stock in young companies hasn't sent most to the poorhouse, because the majority who did also took at least enough cash to cover their expenses, using stock to sweeten the deal. "What we're not getting this year is gravy," says Margit Wennmachers, a founder of public-relations firm OutCast Communications, which took stock in a number of clients.[35]

The equity-for-service approach has been widely adopted as we see here. In this case, it is an exchange of virtual estate for real estate, literally:

> Soroush Kaboli, a real-estate owner and broker based in the Silicon Valley, says companies offered him stock or warrants on top of rent as an incentive to let them into his buildings. He concedes he might have been able to charge slightly more to a potential tenant with no stock to offer. Among the companies that gave him stock or warrants were Webvan, community site Homestead.com and Niku Corp., which supplies online software to professional service firms. While Mr. Kaboli has made some money from Niku, there hasn't been any payoff from Webvan or Homestead (which earlier this year pulled its planned IPO). But Mr. Kaboli says he went into the business of taking stock with the understanding that only a fraction of venture-backed companies succeed. Almost exactly a year ago, he predicted: "In a year or two years, I'll either be talking in a very happy way or I'll be crying on your shoulder."[36]

Overall, the equity-for-service approach enables service providers to convert their labor-intensive and hard to scale practice to a scalable business.

INTERVIEWS WITH EXPERT SERVICE PROVIDERS, INVESTORS, AND ENTREPRENEURS

Along with finding third-party information on this issue, during the period of October 2000 to June 2001, we also interviewed a number of law firms,

---

[34] "Fool's Gold? Stocks Taken As Payments Were a Bust," *Wall Street Journal*, 18 December 2000, Lisa Bransten, staff reporter.

[35] Ibid.

[36] Ibid.

consultants, venture capitalists, and entrepreneurs to solicit their opinions on the pros and cons of this approach. It is interesting that we received a wide array of opinions and perspectives. We list the results of our interviews by firm category, firm name, and position of person interviewed. We believe that this indicates that the IVC approach is still in its early stages and has not been fully established or proven yet. These were open-ended interviews that were partly based on the following set of questions:

1. Please discuss your experience and practice in terms of choosing between cash upfront versus equity compensation by your clients.
2. When do you choose which venue and why?
3. What has the trend been over the last ten years in the IP law practice with respect to equity-based compensation and in what niches has it been more pronounced—start-up firms or large firms as well?
4. Does accepting equity as compensation for legal services present conflicts of interest; when, how, and why could they be mitigated?
5. Does accepting equity as compensation for legal services help entrepreneurs better leverage expert services or does it help more the law firms that participate in the stock issue? When, how, and why?
6. What is the spectrum of legal and business models involving equity for services—which are the two extremes and who is an outlier and who is closer to the center among some IP law firms you could mention?
7. Is the industry in which the client operates relevant and influential on the equity for a fee model?
8. Does industry turbulence and firm rivalry increase the likelihood of equity-for-service or not and why?
9. What are some best practices in the context of the questions so far and who has adopted them?
10. What are some lessons learned from the experience and practice to date with respect to the equity-for-service model?

Interviews with Law Firms

Venture Law Group

The Venture Law Group is often identified as the quintessential law firm for start-ups, and is widely credited with pioneering the practice of taking equity in clients as a component of a professional engagement. As noted earlier, VLG did not originate this practice, but it might be said that VLG founder Craig Johnson raised the practice to a new level by using it to transform the role of outside counsel in assisting start-up clients.

VLG was formed in 1993, when Craig Johnson left his position as a partner at the powerful firm of Wilson Sonsini Goodrich and Rosati due to his dissatisfaction with the way the firm dealt with start-up clients. In an interview, Mr. Johnson claims that the concept of VLG came to him in a dream.[37] Some of his supporters cite this as simply Mr. Johnson's flair for the dramatic. In any case, he did institute some practices which were quite different from traditional

---

[37] D. M. Osborne, "When Is a Law Firm Not a Law Firm?" *Inc.*, 1 May 1998.

law firm management. First, he established the firm without the use of "name" partners—VLG has retained the same corporate name no matter who has been named as a partner. Second, he extended profit-sharing beyond the pool of partners to all employees, including associates, paralegals, and secretaries. Third, he decided to limit the size of VLG to a rather modest number of attorneys, with each attorney serving only 15 to 20 clients at one time (whereas other large law firms may have 30 to 50 clients per attorney).

Most important, Johnson established a system under which VLG takes equity in selected clients where it has a strategic interest in the future of that client. VLG directors (the equivalent of partners in conventional law firms) emphasize that this equity stake is not taken as payment for services. In a few cases, VLG may take equity as part of an agreement to defer billing until after the client receives its first infusion of venture capital. But more commonly, VLG will simply purchase a small equity stake in the client—rarely more than 1 percent of the total ownership.

Generally, the equity stake is structured as preferred stock to avoid diluting the founders' interest in their own company (although after the start of the Internet boom in 1997, VLG did adopt the practice of other law firms in taking common stock). The preferred shares would be convertible upon the client's "liquidity event"—an IPO, acquisition, or other means of making the stock fungible. The actual equity investment is not made directly by VLG, but instead by an external fund called VLG Investments. This fund is run by an investment professional and also makes investments in start-ups which are not clients.

Another area where VLG diverges from the practice of some (but not all) law firms is in encouraging, or in some cases requiring, that individual attorneys make a personal investment in the clients of VLG. This is generally the lead attorney for that client, or the one responsible for bringing the client to VLG. According to one director at VLG, this practice is intended more as a "reality check" on the viability of the client as a long-term customer and an investment by the firm (in both funds and attention). In simple terms, if the responsible attorney is not willing to put any money into that client, there is reason to doubt why the firm should invest its own money.

VLG attorneys do not see any particular ethical problems created by the practice of taking equity stakes in their clients. In fact, VLG asserts that the primary motivation for the practice is to ensure that the interests of the firm and its attorneys are aligned with those of the entrepreneur, not to make more money for the firm. To guard against any potential claims of deception from clients, VLG does issue each client an engagement letter which spells out in great detail the terms of VLG's investment and the issues that the entrepreneur must consider in accepting that investment. (VLG also advises new clients to consult an outside attorney on the terms of the investment agreement.) But while Craig Johnson and others play down the significance of the monetary gains involved, those investment returns are a critical component of VLG's compensation strategy. The truth is that by limiting the number of clients that VLG will accept, and by focusing mostly on privately held start-up firms, VLG cannot support the expenses of running a law firm on billable hours alone. The firm needs the returns from its investment fund to supplement its other revenue sources and to provide its professionals with compensation comparable to or exceeding that available at other law firms.

Still, entrepreneurs do not object to sacrificing some portion of their ownership to VLG. According to VLG attorneys, most are pleased that VLG is willing to show its long-term commitment to their venture using actual dollars rather than empty promises. One client, Amyl Ahola of the Web-hosting firm TeraStor, told a reporter from *Inc.* magazine that VLG is "geared to providing the kind of support that you need as a start-up....The service we've gotten has been surprisingly, consistently positive."[38] Clearly, VLG has not had difficulty in convincing its clients to accept its investment funds. In 1999, VLG held stakes in all 17 clients which went public that year.[39]

VLG is sometimes criticized by other attorneys for not being a law firm, but instead acting more as a consulting firm. Craig Johnson not only accepts this characterization, but he reinforces the image with his own statements. He tells potential clients to "Think of us as a McKinsey or a Boston Consulting Group for start-ups, with the added value that we can actually do the deals."[40] In another article he claims that VLG is "a combination of a very good corporate/securities law firm, a consulting firm, a venture capital fund and an investment bank."[41] Although much of this approach is an issue of strategy, observers also note that Johnson's unique position as a long-time dealmaker in Silicon Valley helps VLG to sustain its business model. One Silicon Valley executive notes that "Craig is one of the few characters out there who can actually do a bit of bridging between lawyer and VC. He does have the connections. He can make the introduction. The interesting thing is that he isn't really doing the law stuff any more." While VLG still focuses on legal work, many of the top partners are working more as close advisers to clients rather than simply as outside counsel. As a result, they are able to claim larger equity stakes than if they were simply providing legal services.

During the technology boom of the late 1990s, VLG invested in a number of clients who succeeded in achieving either prolific IPOs or were acquired for large sums of money. These clients include not only the Web portal Yahoo! but also eToys, Foundry Networks (a networking company whose share price increased 525 percent on its first day of trading), Cerent (acquired by Cisco Systems for $6.7 billion), and Hotmail and WebTV (both acquired by Microsoft).[42] The interest held by VLG and partner Josh Green in Foundry Networks was worth over $16 million after the client's IPO. In another deal, for client SnapTrack (which developed a location technology for mobile phones), Johnson received stock in acquirer Qualcomm that was valued at $22 million as

---

[38] Ibid.

[39] Debra Baker, "Who Wants to Be a Millionaire?" *ABA Law Journal*, 86 ABAJ 36.

[40] Osborne, op. cit.

[41] Baker, op. cit.

[42] Bethany McLean, "The Big-Idea Guy," *Fortune*, 3 April 2000, p. 265[c].

of 21 March, 2000. Johnson claims that VLG's portfolio in the year 2000 reached a value of over $100 million.

For obvious reasons, the collapse in the share value of technology stocks which began in May 2000 has hurt VLG's business model. In April 2001, VLG announced that it expected to miss its revenue targets for the year by 10 percent. The firm's results worsened over time—although VLG originally stated that it would not lay off any attorneys, in May 2001 the company let go nine associates, citing worsening economic conditions as the reason.[43] Partner compensation and profit-sharing is also expected to shrink. VLG has also cut back on its recruiting, and has taken cost-cutting measures such as subleasing some office space and reducing office recreational outings.[44] These steps were not unusual among Silicon Valley law firms (and technology-oriented law firms nationwide). Still, since VLG is more dependent than other firms on its investment returns and profit-sharing for both compensation and operating funds, it may be feeling the effects of the technology downturn more than its competitors.

VLG presents one potential future model for the intellectual venture capitalist, where a firm goes beyond simply providing professional services to acting as a mentor to start-up clients. This makes VLG a more attractive work environment to entrepreneurial attorneys than some other firms. Associates report that the firm has an organizational culture which is "innovative, interesting and exciting."[45] Craig Johnson also claims to have changed the internal dynamics of his firm, so that attorneys are not focused only on logging billable hours.[46] Associates also mention that "Partners don't 'dole out work' so much as 'work with' associates," building more of a team-centric atmosphere.[47] The key point is that not all professional service providers may have the expertise, connections, and reputation needed to play this role.

Cooley Godward

Cooley Godward is one of the leading firms in the Silicon Valley region, with origins dating back to the firm's founding in San Francisco in 1920. Based in Palo Alto, the firm had 688 attorneys worldwide as of 2001, with 157 partners. The firm has two primary departments, business and litigation. Practice areas cover a wide range of expertise, including antitrust, intellectual property, real estate, and tax. The firm has a long history in the area of emerging companies. In 1959, Cooley Godward formed Draper, Gaither and Anderson, the first institutional investment partnership organized on the West Coast. It was also the counsel to some of the first high-technology firms in California, such as National Semiconductor and Genentech. The firm has

---

[43]Vault.com, "Venture Law Group P.C.," company snapshot, accessed at http://www.vault.com on 6 September 2001.

[44] Renee Deger, "Down But Not Out," *The Recorder*, 19 April 2001, p. 1.

[45] Ibid.

[46] Susan Orenstein, "Lawyers Need Equity, Too," *The Industry Standard*, 3 April 2000.

[47] Vault.com, op. cit.

expanded into markets in other states, including Colorado, Washington, and Virginia. In a survey by *American Lawyer* magazine on "Lawyers for the New Economy," Cooley was mentioned most often by high-technology executives as intellectual property counsel, and third for overall legal representation.

Cooley Godward has been at the center of growth in Silicon Valley. Profits per partner have more than tripled over the past decade, from about $220,000 in 1990 to $665,000 in 1999. Profits at the firm in 1999 topped the firm's then-record 1998 performance, growing by a full 39 percent to hit $78 million.[48] The firm managed the initial public offerings for such firms as eBay and Qualcomm. These benefits extend down to associates; along with its competitor, Gunderson Dettmer Stough Villeneuve Franklin & Hachigian, Cooley Godward was one of the first Bay Area law firms to increase starting salaries for first-year associates in January 2000. As of 2001, starting salaries reached $125,000 per year (exclusive of bonuses).

Cooley Godward has been one of the most aggressive firms in taking equity in clients. As early as 1986, the firm held 108,000 shares in client Amgen when that firm held its public offering.[49] In 1999, the firm held equity in 20 of the 23 IPOs that the firm assisted on.[50] To a large extent, one factor in the firm's investment strategy is to use the funds to support attorney retention, especially during the Internet boom of the late 1990s. Alan Mendelson, partner in the firm's Palo Alto office, noted in an interview, "Retention is a very big issue....We have lost significant numbers to [start-up firms]."[51] Part of the compensation structure for the firm includes the Investment Bonus Program. Through this program, each associate receives a portion of the profits the firm realizes from its investments in privately held companies and from the sale of "directed shares" purchased by the firm in conjunction with public offerings. Distributions of these profits are made to associates four times per year. The fund is structured as an outside partnership, called the Cooley Investment Fund.

Cooley Godward differs from some of its Palo Alto competitors by barring individual attorneys from owning stock in their clients. This reflects, in part, the egalitarian and team-oriented culture of the firm. Alan Mendelson also commented, "We think the notion that individual partners could become individually wealthy is not conducive to the type of firm we want to build."[52] Another partner, Jim Linfield of the firm's Boulder, Colorado, office, states, "We treat these investment opportunities as firm opportunities....This becomes part of the glue within the firm because everybody benefits from the firm's success. It aligns our interests with our clients and no one attorney gets rich on any particular deal."[53] The company did increase its equity demands as the IPO market became hotter in 1999 and 2000. Mark Tanoury, business chair at the

---

[48] Cited by Vault.com at http://www.vault.com.
[49] "Legal affairs," *The Red Herring*, 1 May 2000, p. 70.
[50] Baker, op. cit
[51] Ibid.
[52] Ibid.
[53] Marsha Austin, "Lawyers Trading Services for Stock," *Denver Business Journal*, 14 April 2000, p. 1A.

firm, noted that the firm's equity stakes in clients taken during early 2000 were typically twice the size of previous transactions.[54]

Even with the advantages for recruiting and compensation, Cooley attorneys emphasize that the major purpose of investing in clients is to establish and solidify the firm's relationship with those firms. Partner Mark Tanoury states that "Clients like for us to invest in their companies....For the most part, they take it as a vote of confidence."[55]

Wilson Sonsini Goodrich & Rosati

The law firm of Wilson Sonsini Goodrich & Rosati (WSGR) was originally founded in 1961 as McCloskey, Wilson and Mosher. It has since grown to be perhaps the most important law firm in the high-technology sector, representing clients including Hewlett-Packard, Novell, and Seagate. The firm has more than 800 attorneys, 147 of whom are partners, and over 1,700 support staff. WSGR is headquartered in Palo Alto, and has regional offices in Austin, TX, Kirkland, WA, McLean, VA, Salt Lake City, UT and New York, NY.

Wilson Sonsini also has a long track record of representing start-up clients up to and beyond their initial public offering. The company was the first law firm for Apple Computer in 1979. Since then the company has assisted clients with literally thousands of public offerings, including 100 in the year 2000 alone. In 2000, the firm represented start-ups in 43 IPOs.

Investing in start-ups is a long-standing tradition at Wilson Sonsini, in contrast to most other firms. The firm was making equity investments in clients starting in the 1990s and even earlier. During the Internet boom of the late 1990s, the high profile of Wilson Sonsini enabled the firm to choose its clients carefully. For example, name partner Mario Rosati (who also manages the firm's investment fund, WS Investments), commented that he only accepted about 25 percent of the companies who requested his representation.[56] As a result, the firm owned equity in start-ups which executed some of the most successful IPOs of all time. Wilson Sonsini represented the software company VA Linux, which on December 9, 1999, saw its shares rise from an offering price of $30 to $239.25, the largest opening-day rise of any IPO. At the close of the trading day, the shares owned by Wilson Sonsini and its partners were valued at $24.5 million. That amount was dwarfed by the market value of Wilson Sonsini's investment in another client, the Internet grocery delivery service Webvan. At the end of Webvan's first day of trading, Wilson Sonsini held over 2 million shares valued at over $51 million.[57] Moreover, partner Judith O'Brien and Wilson Sonsini owned shares in Avanex Corporation, with an investment value which peaked in March 2000 at over $114 million.

---

[54] Orenstein, op. cit.

[55] David Howard, "Dot-com Scams," *Smart Business*, 14 August 2000.

[56] Shaun Neidorf, "Silicon Valley Lawyers Embrace VC-like Role," *Venture Capital Journal*, 1 October 1999.

[57] Baker, op. cit.

However, the company's investment value decreased dramatically in the following months.[58]

Despite the slide in technology share values in the year 2000, Wilson Sonsini has managed to convert a fair amount of that paper wealth into actual returns to partners and associates. According to Mr. Rosati, the firm generated about $12 million in profit from its investment fund in 1999. On a per-partner basis, the value of the fund exceeded the profitability of the company ($700,000 per partner).[59] Even in 2000, when most technology stocks lost considerable value, Wilson Sonsini was able to make money on its equity investments. During the last eight months of 2000, the value of the firm's fund increased by 130 percent, where the value of most of its competitors' equity stakes decreased. Even when the "lock-up period" on the firm's shares in Avanex Corporation expired, that stock was worth $47 million[60] However, it is not clear whether Wilson Sonsini sold its shares at that time, or later after the value of those shared continued to slide.

Wilson Sonsini uses its investment fund for several purposes. One is clearly for partner compensation—partners are generally allowed to invest in their clients, after Wilson Sonsini has been offered the opportunity to invest. Generally, any engagement with a client made during the Internet boom also included the requirement that Wilson Sonsini be allowed to expand its ownership stake in subsequent venture capital funding rounds. Wilson Sonsini also used its fund to boost compensation for associates as well. First-year associates are paid approximately $125,000 per year, which is below the average prevalent in Silicon Valley. That compensation is adjusted by substantial bonuses funded by WS Investments.

Wilson Sonsini is not immune to the problems involved in the equity-for-services model, however. The firm's involvement with Webvan came into question when the Securities and Exchange Commission (SEC) forced a delay in the start-up's IPO due to a violation of the "quiet period" ruling, when companies registered for an IPO are not allowed to talk up their stocks. At that time, Wilson Sonsini partner Jeffrey Saper was a member of Webvan's board of directors, which some observers found a questionable practice. Also, the firm has been struck by the downturn in venture capital activity in 2001. In that year, the firm cancelled its annual company retreat to Pebble Beach, California. Still, Wilson Sonsini is better equipped than most firms to weather the fluctuations in the stock market, as its broad range of practice areas (including antitrust, litigation, and intellectual property) make it less dependent on start-up clients for revenue.

Brobeck, Phleger & Harrison LLP

Brobeck Phleger was one of the largest and most prestigious law firms operating in the technology field. Based in San Francisco, the firm had over 900

---

[58] Susan Beck, "The Razor's Edge," *The American Lawyer*, May 2000.

[59] Orenstein, op. cit.

[60] Renee Deger, "Stock Market Survivors," *The Recorder*, 7 December 2000, p. 1.

attorneys and 3,200 clients in the technology sector.[61] The firm was also among the first law firms to raise the salaries of first-year associates in 1999 to combat the growing competition for legal talent presented by Internet start-ups—with starting salaries reaching $125,000 per year in 2000. The equity-based model provided the means for Brobeck to maintain sufficient profits for partners while increasing compensation for non-partner attorneys.

Brobeck, Phleger & Harrison billed clients by the hour for legal services, but four years ago also began making independent investments in select clients. At the time, about half of the firm's then 375 attorneys were in corporate law and half were litigators. Overall, 150 attorneys worked in the firm's high-tech practice areas. Apparently, the retention tool did succeed, at least during the height of the Internet stock boom. Brobeck first rewarded associates by raising the salaries of first-year associates in its San Francisco offices from $100,000 to $125,000 per year. The bonuses (including compensation from the associates' fund) were added on top of that amount. In 1999, Brobeck grew by 45 percent, making it the top large law firm in nonmerger growth for the year, according to the *National Law Journal*. While other leading firms lost large numbers of associates, Brobeck was able to retain its lawyers and also saw its recruiting totals increase substantially in 1999 and 2000.[62] Brobeck also instituted a more liberal policy towards associates who left to join clients. One such associate left the firm to become in-house counsel at a start-up. When the venture failed, he was allowed to return to Brobeck without adverse consequences. In 2001, about 60 percent of the firm's 900 attorneys did corporate work, mostly for high-technology clients.

Although Brobeck's venture investing was not done through a separate legal entity, they did funnel investments through a "stand-alone" fund. "We don't want to confuse our engagement to invest in legal services—that's the business we're in—versus choosing where we really want to invest, which is going to be a much smaller percentage of our clients," said Carmelo Gordian, chairman of the firm's business and technology group based in Austin, Texas.[63] An investment professional ran the firm's investment fund and maintained a formal process for determining which clients got seed capital. For Brobeck's "partner fund," the company set aside a small percentage of its operating budget to make investments in suitable start-up companies. The major objective of this fund was to make money for the partners, rather than to improve the relationship with a particular client. From this fund, the firm would generally invest a small amount (between $50,000 and $300,000) per opportunity. The fund would liquidate its stock upon the start-up's IPO, or it might simply hold the stock for a later sale or distribute the shares back to the partners. Investments in target firms were made only when the Internet company was raising money from other

---

[61] Davan Maharaj, "More Firms Are Willing to Work for Stock Options," *Los Angeles Times*, 24 January 2000, Monday, Part C; 1.

[62] Cameron Stracher, "Beyond Billable Hours," *The Wall Street Journal*, 12 February 2001.

[63] Rebecca Mowbray, "Professional-services Firms Accept Shares of Start-ups Rather Than Cash Payments," *The Houston Chronicle*, 23 April 2000, p. 1.

sources at the same time. The fund made 75 to 100 investments a year, turning it into the firm's own high-tech mutual fund. Some partners added more than $1 million to their annual compensation during 1999 and 2000.[64]

As a retention tool, Brobeck also maintained an "associates' fund." Each year, the firm invested $2,500 on behalf of each associate into the fund. To qualify, an associate needed to have been employed for at least one year at the firm. The associate's interest in that investment would vest after the associate had logged a certain number of billable hours (thus preventing an associate from leaving prematurely and taking the money). The entire investment would be forfeited if the associate left to join a competing law firm. However, if the associate left for a position which was not at a law firm (for example, to serve as a general counsel to a client), that person could recoup a share of the original investment if he or she returned to Brobeck at a later date. Note that the partners of the firm actually made the investments into the fund, not the associates. Also, Brobeck instituted a number of other programs to promote associate retention, including a mortgage assistance plan, free laptops for employees, flexible telecommuting arrangements, business casual dress, morale-raising events, and profit-sharing.

According to an analysis in the *American Bar Association Journal*, Brobeck held equity in 13 companies which held initial public offerings in 1999.[65] The firm earned significant returns on several start-ups where it has held investments. The firm was an investor in such ventures as Broadcom, NetZero, and Rhythm Connections, and by early 2000 had built a stock portfolio worth tens of millions of dollars, according to Chairman Tower Snow.[66]

Brobeck attorneys made the strong distinction between their "investments" through these funds and taking equity in exchange for services. Mr. Snow noted, "Equity is fine, but you may not be able to liquidate the equity two or three years down the road…you need money to pay the bills."[67] The firm avoided any potential conflict of interest by only rarely taking what Washington, DC partner Kevin Lavin called "a very small percentage" of a client's equity in exchange for agreeing to *defer* (not replace) Brobeck's normal legal fees. In such cases, according to Mr. Lavin, the equity offer was accompanied by an engagement letter with "extensive disclosures", and Brobeck recommended that the client retain another outside law firm to help in negotiating the final agreement with Brobeck.[68] Also, by spreading its investments across a large number of clients throughout the firm's 11 offices, Brobeck ensured that the future of the firm was not dependent upon a single client (thus avoiding the need to treat equity-based clients differently from fee-for-service clients).[69]

Brobeck lawyers claimed that their clients were pleased by the decision of the firm to invest in their stock. "The clients have really reacted positively.

---

[64] Ibid.
[65] Baker, op. cit.
[66] Maharaj, op. cit.
[67] Ibid.
[68] Loomis, op. cit.
[69] Mowbray, op. cit.

They get a kick out of the idea that we want to become a long-term partner," according to John Hayes, corporate securities attorney in the firm's Denver, Colorado office.[70]

As a historical footnote, in early 2003, the Brobeck firm was dissolved. Although there have been published articles about the reasons behind this (and which we will not address here), many interesting questions concerning equity for services deals arise out of such an eventuality. The first is whether and the extent to which such practices contributed to the firm's demise or rather provided it with much needed opportunities and revenues during a difficult economic downturn. The second, concerns the disposition of the stock held by the firm after its demise and its impact on client-entrepreneurs. To the best of our knowledge, equity-for-services deals did not induce the firm's demise. As the disposition of the firm's assets is still pending as of this writing (Spring 2003), we felt it would be inappropriate to address this issue further.

Perkins Coie
Buddy Arnheim started his career at Brobeck, Phleger & Harrison, one of the top technology law firms based in San Francisco. He and a group of other lawyers at Brobeck left the firm in 1996 to form Gunderson Dettmer Stough Villeneuve Franklin & Hachigian in Menlo Park. In 1998, Arnheim was recruited away from Gunderson to help form the Menlo Park office of Perkins Coie, a San Francisco firm, and specifically to establish that firm's equity-for-services activity.

Please discuss your experience and practice in terms of choosing between cash upfront versus equity compensation by your clients.

At Brobeck, taking equity in association with other compensation for services has been the model for some time, even before I arrived there. For example, members of the firm invested in Cisco when it was first formed. However, even when I was there, Brobeck had no formal policy behind the process for taking equity. It only happened if you were smart enough to ask the client at the opportune time. In 1995, Brobeck began formulating a policy on equity ownership in clients. There was a lot of activity, but no formal policy ever emerged.

We formed Gunderson with the intent of taking equity from the beginning. Also, at the start of the firm, the associates wanted the opportunity to participate in equity investments by the firm. We set up a policy where all investments went through a central, external fund; 90 percent of returns were given to partners, while 10 percent went to associates. After about the first 3 ½ years, minor liquidity in the fund was achieved, but I had left by then so I'm not sure how well they did.

In 1998 I joined Perkins Coie to start their Menlo Park office and to institutionalize a fund to run the equity-for-services deals. We ask for common stock upon engagement with the client and the right to invest alongside VCs in

---

[70] Austin, op.cit.

future rounds of financing. The investment fund is funded by contributions from most, but not all, partners at the firm. We take no more than 10 percent of the total value of the financing round. Any stock purchased sits in the investment fund entity and the returns are shared among the partners.

We've been fairly successful....Perkins Coie started taking equity in the first quarter of 1999. We've invested at a moderate pace, and were able to leverage some quick liquidity events—maybe 12 to 18 months after the investment. To be honest, we lost our shirts on many of those investments, but a lot also achieved reasonable liquidity on many others, where we at least broke even. Of course, one nice return can make up for a lot of losses—our best outcome was from a client that was sold to Microsoft, because we received Microsoft stock and could liquidate immediately.

A typical case is our investment in Avantgo [a software developer for data access and content delivery to handheld computers]. The company IPO-ed at $12, but after our "lock-up" period expired the value was only $4 per share. Also, it's very thinly traded, so there's not enough volume to support our selling our stock all at once.

What has the trend been over the last ten years in law practice with respect to equity-based compensation and in what niches has it been more pronounced—start-up firms or large firms as well?

When equity-for-services was pioneered by Wilson, Sonsini and Brobeck, it mostly attracted interest due to the mystique of investing. It was a cutting-edge practice. Over the past ten years, taking equity has become institutionalized. It used to be a thing that just happened. You could take equity in a client if it was presented to you. Usually, this involved a private company that was already doing a financing round. The attorney had to meet SEC requirements [as a "qualified investor"] and get permission from his firm.

In 1996, you saw the concept of not just investing, but taking founders' shares in newly formed companies at very low cost, with a fantastic potential for returns. At Gunderson, we shunned this practice—our attitude was, why would we deserve those shares when we weren't founders of the firm? Conflict of interest was also a deterrent. With founders' shares, you can accumulate significant ownership of the client—maybe 1 to 3 percent, making potential conflicts more significant. The same conflict is present when making an outside investment in a client, but to a much smaller degree.

Does accepting equity as compensation for legal services present conflicts of interest; when, how, and why and how could they be mitigated?

As a lawyer, you're in a better position to empathize with a client if you have a stake. Since it's the firm's stake, you're not handicapped by equity. If you have a share of the equity, you're able to directly see the benefit of your contribution. If the stock is preferred shares, you may have less incentive—but with common stock, you're aligned with founders. Second, we've never had enough of an interest to make a difference either way. As an outsider, you can feel the same emotions as insiders.

We have policies that could amplify or mitigate conflicts of interest. We use a vesting schedule (have to engage for 12 months to "earn" equity)—that keeps you attuned to the client. But after vesting, do you have same incentives? Yes (if stock has positive value). We have a clause that can accelerate vesting if start-up is sold—that could give an incentive to the law firm to recommend sale over IPO for personal gain. But other shareholders can always veto the sale. At the same time, if investors back the sale, the law firm wants the best terms on the deal, just like anyone else.

It's interesting that no business polices these investments in the way that lawyers do (among professional service firms). In litigation, the application is very different—your job is to try to color the truth. In transactions, you're mostly conveying facts to the client—no incentive to color the truth, so there's less opportunity to lie for personal gain.

Does accepting equity as compensation for legal services help entrepreneurs better leverage expert services or does it help more the law firms that participate in the stock issue? When, how, and why?

Emerging growth companies need to make decisions quickly rather than worry about every detail of financing. The value of having a law firm as an investor is in getting access to complementary resources rather than getting best deal on each term.

What is the spectrum of legal and business models involving equity-for-services—which are the two extremes and who is an outlier and who is closer to the center among some IP law firms you could mention?

Venture Law Group is clearly at the vanguard of the practice. VLG got over the conflict-of-interest issue early on, for example, about taking founders' shares. They used founders' stock to justify their work in nonlegal services—executive recruiting, introductions to investors, things like that. They also used founders' stock as a screening factor, only taking those clients who agreed to offer founders' shares. After VLG broke the ground, other firms started taking founders' shares. Wilson Sonsini is also very aggressive about getting equity as part of any deal with an emerging company. Cooley Godward and other firms in the area are less so—they make requests for equity rather than demands.

What are some best practices in the context of the questions so far and who has adopted them?

One key practice is to invest in clients rather than taking equity in lieu of anything—billings, whatever. Smaller firms can take equity-for-services, but there are clear drawbacks. Perkins Coie won't do it, because it's complex from an accounting and tax point of view. If your law firm takes equity-for-services, the equity is taxable income if any profit is earned. Say, for example, you take $100,000 in stock for services—you can't sell the stock, but you still owe the taxes on that $100,000. Also, we have 160 to 170 partners, and each partner would have to report his or her own share of that equity as income. The start-up would in effect now have 170 new shareholders. Under SEC regulation, that start-up becomes a de facto public company in terms of disclosure requirements, but doesn't get the benefit of an IPO.

The best way is for the investment partnership to hold onto any money earned, otherwise the law firm has to distribute all returns at the end of each year. If you really want to take equity for non-legal services, you can figure out other venues.

What are some lessons learned from the experience and practice to date with respect to the equity-for-service model?

Timing clearly means a lot, especially when talking about the Internet boom. Perkins Coie has done OK based on timing. The early movers did much better—if you invested in 1995 to 1997, you made out well. *Some* people made a lot of money. With the current environment, most firms are still investing, though much more carefully.

Overall, the practice has slowed down just because there are fewer fundings happening. However, we still continue to request the opportunity to invest in emerging company clients, and have made investments in many cases. At the same time, down round (e.g., financing round where the dollar value per share is reduced), generates a lot of emotion on shareholders whose shares are compressed dramatically. In this case, we will talk more honestly and compassionately with founders—this increases credibility and gives us better perception. My general belief is that there is a point when firm's equity ownership will get high enough to compromise objectivity—it has to be well over 5 percent. Usually the amount we're talking about, is not really not enough to sway an individual lawyer.

Most companies are seeking institutional investment—not family businesses. So irrespective of the industry, if that's the pursued path, it won't matter. Some industries have faster growth rates and quicker liquidity—so the provider will tend to get less share as liquidity increases. Growth trajectory matters more, as does the time horizon of expected liquidity. It also depends on whether the start-up intends to be bought or wants to IPO.

The practice is here to stay—even in the 1990s, partners had received equities in a company called Vigaro (garden fertilizers)—it IPO-edand was bought, and guys did well. But this still won't be the primary source of compensation—just an augmentation. Equity may be 10 to 20 percent of partner income. It does make sense to institutionalize policies—this can lead to strange animosities among attorneys, based on compensation versus effort.

The legal industry in general is consolidating like accounting firms. Small partnerships are not surviving. Mid-sized firms don't have deep enough expertise to really serve their clients. As consulting firms have bought tax lawyers, law firms are facing nontraditional competitors. Law firms are going outside law—managing trusts, based on estate planning. So the legal industry will change and morph.

As the competition increases, the likely scenario is that fees will get compressed and prices will go down, so alternative billing structures will need to make up for that contraction. Equity is clearly one possibility. But this is not the primary driver—primary is still competition among law firms.

Firms need to conform to securities law for accredited investors—junior associates just can't play.

Milbank, Tweed, Hadley & McCloy LLP, Partner

Milbank Tweed is a 475-lawyer firm that has been in existence on Wall Street for over 135 years. Due to the dot-com work, they had technology issues and equity plans thrust upon them by clients. Although the core of the firm is banking, the firm has been moving toward tech the last five or six years. Although they did not experience a loss of associate attorneys to dot-com's, they did experience a loss of attorneys to become general counsels of investment banks. The original plan was only to provide some work and to add interesting work opportunities.

In this firm, although the investment plan is run by the executive committee, the selection process is performed by a three-person investment committee which consists of three senior transactional attorneys. One of these guys spends roughly 40 percent of his time looking over opportunities and they are roughly about as selective as Pillsbury Madison Sutro is rumored to be which is that they turn down two for every one taken.

Milbank offers both a partner fund and an associate fund. The partner fund is administered by a three-person, democratically elected executive committee. The associate fund is a mirror image of the partner fund, but it is not funded by the associates. Rather, it is funded by the partners. The partner fund is organized as a separate LLC each year which can invest in clients and all opportunities are firm opportunities. Milbank's program provides for stock-in-lieu-of-fees opportunities, but the firm is not in the start-up stream as much as other high-tech firms are since they have a more traditional, financing focus. They generally invest pre-IPO and utilize the extensive experience of the transactional attorneys on the Investment Committee to screen candidates. The screening and selection is primarily based upon the business plan and interviews with the client. For a partner to be eligible to participate in the investment fund, they must be present at the firm at the end of the year.

Brown & Wood LLP, Partner

Since its founding in 1914, Brown & Wood has established a preeminent position on Wall Street. Its practice has focused on the capital markets and its client base on investment banks and major financial institutions. The firm was ranked as the top counsel for both managers and issuers of U.S. debt, equity, and equity-related offerings completed during 2000, according to Thomson Financial Securities data. In addition to a large New York office, Brown & Wood has maintained offices in San Francisco, Los Angeles, Washington, D.C.,

London, Beijing, Hong Kong, and also has a strong Korean practice. As of September 2000 Brown & Wood had an investment fund in operation for about one year.

In May 2001, the law firms of Sidley & Austin and Brown & Wood merged to become Sidley Austin Brown & Wood, a significant legal power in the international arena. The combination of these two legal authorities creates a new kind of law firm. The two firms meld a 235-year combined legacy of service and legal innovation. The merger creates a firm of more than 1,325 attorneys and combines the highly-rated and inventive capital markets practice of Brown & Wood with Sidley & Austin's full array of corporate, banking, regulatory, intellectual property, and litigation capabilities. It is not known if the investment fund survived the merger.

Kirkpatrick & Lockhart LLP, Partner

This is law firm that advises other law firms on how to practice the equity-for-service approach.

Interest in law firm investment funds has been around for many years and this interest has increased in the past 10 years. It recently has attracted more interest in the DC area (because of the Netplex, the dense agglomeration of Internet and telecommunication start-up firms in the area).

The Wilson Sonsini model is to never take stock for fees. Instead, firms tend to take options/warrants in return for fee deferral. Most law firms are not set up to deal in illiquid compensation, and this is one of the challenges of working with the equity-for-fee approach along with potential conflicts of interest. Law firms need high cash flow (especially for salaries, information technology, etc.), and can ill-afford to have illiquid equity investments, at least in large amounts. Moreover, there are pressures on partner compensation rates as a result of raises in associates' pay, and this exacerbates the challenges against the equity-for-fee approach. A motivation to adopt this approach is the promise of a long-term relationship with a client, as many of the current start-ups will eventually grow to become large firms and potential big clients for the law firms. The equity-for-fee model is needed to attract a stream of new clients in new industries driving the U.S. economy. Also, pressure from competition with other law firms may make the equity-for-fee approach a competitive differentiator.

Moreover, adopting this approach keeps us more competitive, allows us to attract younger lawyers, and is particularly needed to get California clients— where we recently opened an office. In connection with this, Kirkpatrick has a large investment management practice complementing our legal services. Law firm funds resemble hedge funds and the risk is that we may create an investment fund that then has to be regulated by the Securities and Exchange Commission (SEC) in taking the equity for fee approach. No one has been prosecuted yet by the SEC but in each case we may get a "no-action" letter from the SEC to protect from liability.

Regarding the reaction we see from the venture capitalists, there are two perspectives: on the one hand, VCs are happy to see lower legal expense as IP work is costly and litigation fees can sink company. However, they do not like to share the pie—especially since equity could be offered to public otherwise. So, often investment banks and venture capitalists may resist offering equity for fee to law firms and the lawyer is often given stock as a friend and adviser of the entrepreneur, not due to VC initiatives. There is always a tension that is mostly constructive between VCs, founders, and lawyers.

In terms of how significant this trend is, we're newcomers—my impression is the personal relationship between founder and lawyer benefits from added trust and a higher degree of engagement from both parties. The equity-as-fee model can cement the lawyer—client relationship. Clients still pick a lawyer based on the quality of the law firm, not the use of stock-for-fees approach.

However, to make this work, the law firm must have a rigorous vetting process and judge investment opportunities in clients for their appropriateness based on: quality of management and the client firm, honesty, Internet as vehicle for fraud, reasons that the law firm may not want to work on a business deal, actions that may invite SEC enforcement, the knowledge of /relationship with client, etc.

It is critical to make the process institutional to protect the partner from pressure from the client. In this sense, Kirkpatrick will not make co-investments with any client. We are also ready to lose a client if the circumstances warrant it. I believe that the "deal lawyer" will also likely not face conflict of interest under this approach.

Piper, Marbury, Rudnick & Wolfe

Piper, Marbury is a full-service law firm formed by the merger of the Baltimore-based Piper & Marbury with the Chicago-based firm Rudnick & Wolfe. Both are firms with lengthy lineage—Rudnick & Wolfe was founded in 1936, while Piper & Marbury traces its roots back to 1854. The combined firm has 822 employees worldwide, making it one of the nation's 15 largest law firms. The firm's largest offices are in Washington, DC and Chicago. Piper & Marbury had the reputation for focusing more on venture capital, high-technology, and intellectual property law, while Rudnick & Wolfe brought expertise in real estate law.

Starting in 1998, the company adopted a policy for taking equity in clients. Unlike West Coast firms, which emphasize the strategic aspects of equity-for-services and also demand equity from clients in return for their attention, Piper, Marbury adopted the practice primarily to accommodate the limited funds available to their start-up clients. In fact, the website of the company as of 2001 features a section on the company's flexible billing policy to fit the needs of its clients. As a result, rather than taking equity on top of normal fees (as practiced by the premier West Coast firms such as Wilson Sonsini or Gunderson), Piper, Marbury tends to take equity in lieu of at least some portion of their regular billings, or as a warrant against deferred fees.[71] The company has tended to take equity reluctantly, at the request of clients, rather than requiring it as a condition of service.

In early 2000, Piper, Marbury established a venture capital investment fund, primarily to benefit the firm's attorneys. This move followed similar initiatives in venture investing at other firms operating in the Washington, DC area, including Akin, Gump, Strauss, Hauer & Feld; Hogan & Hartson; Patton Boggs; and Shaw Pittman Trowbridge. Piper, Marbury also resolved to become more aggressive about taking equity interests in exchange for legal services.[72] The company in 1998 established a policy of when, where, and how it would take equity. These investments are managed through an investment fund which is legally separate from the firm itself.

Under the Piper, Marbury policy, the firm takes equity only in pre-IPO clients. The general rule is that the firm will take no more than 1 percent ownership of any client, for a total investment value of between $20,000 and $50,000. The equity stake is obtained in conjunction with a regular round of funding by a venture capital group, and the firm invests only once in each client. In this way, Piper, Marbury does not have to determine the valuation of the client's business, but instead relies upon the valuation set by a third party. In general, Piper, Marbury will take no more than 50 percent of its estimated fees in the form of an equity investment. Another potential use is to accept equity in exchange for deferring normal billing for services until the client can conduct an IPO. Overall, one partner at Piper, Marbury estimates that less than 1 percent of the firm's revenue is tied to equity stakes in its clients.

Piper, Marbury screens any start-up clients before agreeing to take equity as partial compensation for its services. The firm uses criteria similar to those used by a typical venture capitalist, evaluating the client based on its business idea, technology, people, management skills, and presentation. To help in the screening process, the firm's emerging firm practice works closely with several venture capital firms and "angel" investors, receiving referrals from those investors as well as putting its clients in contact with potential sources of capital. One partner estimates that 10 to 20 percent of the firm's start-up clients are sourced through referrals. One advantage cited for working with venture capitalists is that these investors are intimately familiar with the client's prospects for business success, including the number of competitors or potential competitors and similar factors. By taking equity in conjunction with an investment by an outside VC or angel, Piper, Marbury can base its own investing decision in part on the judgment of professional investors. This can create some conflicts, however, as one partner pointed out that "quality money asks for as much ownership as possible." As a result, the venture capitalists may attempt to "squeeze" the law firm out of participating in an investment round in order to maximize the value of their own investment.

---

[71] Conversation with Piper, Marbury partner by the authors.
[72] Susan Crabtree, "Lawyers in Love," *Washington Techway*, 11 September 2000.

As of late 2000, the Piper, Marbury investment fund had a value of approximately $2.8 million, of which about $500,000 consisted of investments made for an "associates' fund." While the rest of the fund benefits the partners of the firm, the associates' fund is a recruiting and compensation tool for non-equity lawyers. The profits from that fund are vested to each associate based on their years of service at the firm.

While compensation and retention are important factors in developing the Piper, Marbury fund, the most important reason is to support the firm's business model for servicing emerging company clients. The firm is structured to take on a client in its earliest stages, with the hope that the client will stay with Piper, Marbury through the IPO and beyond. Due to the uncertainty of business survival for start-ups, Piper, Marbury needs to take on a large volume of new clients. On average, according to one source, the firm signs on one new client every day, and can expect that in any given month a few clients will be acquired and at least one will fail (that ratio may have increased since the passing of the investment boom in technology companies). As a result, Piper, Marbury has a high turnover in its emerging company client base, with each client staying with the firm only for 24 to 36 months on average. By taking on a large number of start-up clients, Piper, Marbury can maintain a steady flow of investment returns, and also reduce the overall risk of its equity fund by spreading its investments across a large number of clients in its portfolio.

Interviews with Venture Capital Firms

Draper Atlantic
An interview with a partner at Draper Atlantic indicated that the company has not had that much experience in these matters. He indicated that many of the aggressive law firms will defer fees for pre-funded early-stage companies and may take some equity warrants as part of compensation. Of course, as the companies mature, a lot more fees become more cash-based. Also as the market worsens, it is expected that fewer law firms want to take the equity risks depending on the attitude of the individual firms: some think it's a major conflict; others are not very concerned. This partner did not know of any firms that take all fees in equity; it is usually a mix of fees and equity. Lately, many firms with which this partner was familiar were re-examining that policy and wanted to take all cash to avoid market risk. In general, factors that influence such decisions are: (1) the financial condition of the law firm, (2) the stage of the company, and (3) market conditions.

NextGen Capital, Washington, DC Venture Capital Firm
One partner commented that equity-for-service does not seem to be applicable to venture firms, except as it might relate to the board of directors— "We generally do not take either cash or equity from our companies. If cash, only for expense reimbursement. If equity, NextGen partners sign it over to the fund. We would take cash only if the expenses of attending the board meetings

are extraordinarily high. We would take equity only if all of the other board members are taking something; it would not be a practice initiated by NextGen. In fact, unless the directors were outsiders (neither management or investors), we would frown upon a board that was enriching themselves in this manner. I have seen it [the service-for-equity approach] become more common over the past 10 years, but I have no real data for you. "

Generally speaking, it seems that the partner is not in favor of corporate counsel taking equity instead of cash compensation, as it causes a conflict of interest: "There are plenty of good lawyers out there that do not require equity for expert advice. I think this helps the lawyers more than it helps the companies".

An Interview with an Angel Investor—and the CEO of a Biotech Start-Up

The angel investor and the biotech start-up worked very well together, and the arrangement was very advantageous for both parties. Eventually, the biotech start-up hired the angel investor as their Chief Financial Officer, paying him partially in salary and again in part with actual shares. The angel investor has been so pleased with his experience in equity-for-services that he has signed off on a similar arrangement with an outside patent law firm. Under this arrangement, the IP law firm bills the biotech start-up directly for all expenses (patent filing fees, photocopies, etc.), but the billable hours logged by the partner on the engagement are paid in stock rather than cash. In an interesting development, the angel investor has also received two presentations by outside clinical research organizations, which have offered to run the trials of the biotech start-up's therapeutics with partial compensation in equity.

The angel investor sees several clear benefits from his equity-for-services arrangement with the biotech start-up. First, by allowing him the option to take compensation as stock or cash on a quarterly basis, the angel investor can adjust his risk exposure based on his assessment of the company's financial status (which he knows well as their CFO) by changing the balance of cash versus equity in his compensation. Second, cash conservation is clearly a priority for the start-up, so deferring or replacing fees paid by issuing stock is almost always an advantage. Third, based on past experience, the angel investor believes that as long as the technology of the start-up is solid, he can expect to earn much higher returns by accepting equity-for-services than in simply billing by the hour. Finally, the equity stake helps to motivate the angel investor and maintain his interest in the firm. The angel investor is in fact semiretired—he admits that he is working for the biotech start-up not to earn a high salary, but more due to his interest in entrepreneurship and medical technology. By taking an equity stake in the firm, the angel investor gets to play the part of both venture capitalist and service provider, making a key contribution to the success of the start-up. In this sense, he sees equity-for-services as a direct analog to employee stock ownership plans (ESOP), which can help to maintain employee loyalty and commitment to an employer.

The angel investor acknowledges some criticisms of the stock-for-services model, but discounts most of them. He calls the potential for conflict of interest problems "a stretch"—he is hard-pressed to think of a situation where an equity interest in the firm would make him work against the long-term interests of the start-up rather than for them. He does admit that the outside auditor of the firm should not be paid in equity. Since the auditor has a fiduciary responsibility to the shareholders, that viewpoint would clearly be tainted if the auditor also held stock in the client. Even in a case where the consultant may push for a decision that has greater personal short-term benefit than long-term benefit for the firm, the angel investor emphasizes that "we're all big boys." The most that the consultant should do is try to persuade the firm to follow his recommendations, but the firm's top executives are the ones who make the final decision. In almost any situation, the outside service provider, be it a law firm or consultant, should be "an advocate for the firm." If that service provider has a vested interest in the client due to an equity position, then it simply reinforces the provider's responsibility to that client.

Entrepreneurs should not be overly concerned that issuing equity-for-services will dilute their ownership stake, according to the angel investor. If the start-up has a lot of cash on hand and is concerned about dilution, then this *is* an issue. But for most early-stage start-ups, "cash is king". Stock value, in the angel investor's view, is an "all-or-nothing" proposition—the stock is worth $0 if there's no market for it, or it's worth $50 if it can be traded. If the company is already raising capital at $1 per share, then there is no disadvantage in paying a service provider at that same rate.

For the service provider, the angel investor admits that accepting stock is a gamble. He has personally worked with five start-ups, and in one case taking stock did not pay off. Still, he believes that by working for a firm, he is acting as a part-venture capitalist, investing his time and knowledge in that company. The angel investor calls himself "an old-fashioned financial type," who believes that stock value is a function of earnings per share rather than inflated expectations. If the service provider has a realistic evaluation of the prospects of a start-up client, then taking equity clearly has more benefits than risks. And even in a market downturn, venture capitalists scale back their investing but they don't stop funding companies. Service providers should view their own business in the same way—they may need to be more selective, but the equity-for-services model still works.

Interviews with Entrepreneurs—Founders of New Ventures

Founder of Early-Stage, High-Tech Venture
So far our company has not had any experience in choosing between the two options as it relates to compensation for service providers. We are, however, discussing with our consultants the possibility of paying them in

equity versus in cash. We are also contemplating using bartering as another way to save cash. What we have done, though, in the past is give stock options to some key service providers as an incentive tool.

Conserving cash is usually the main reason why we will use equity compensation. Another reason is the hope of establishing a tighter relationship between our company and our service providers by giving them a stake in the success of our company.

Law firms in general have been taking equity-based compensation during the Internet boom but that trend seems to be going down with the burst of the Internet "bubble". Our law firm did not seem to think that accepting equity as compensation for legal services presented conflicts of interest. During the Internet boom, accepting equity as compensation for legal services was more to the benefit of the law firms. Now I would think that such a practice will be more to the benefit of the entrepreneurs.

Technology companies seem to be adopting the equity-for-service approach more than others as their industries are more competitive and they have more intense needs for cash conservation and customer acquisition. Overall, the IVC approach made some service providers some real good money in the midst of the Internet boom. I am not sure now but I am assuming that it is not working well.

C.E.O. of Major Biotech Testing & Development Firm

I don't feel that our involvement in IP has been a "driver" for our firm, neither have we any significant involvement in using equity with direct clients (for reasons discussed below). For at least two reasons, we have declined all offers of accepting equity rather than cash payments for our testing and development services. These reasons are (1) the perceptions by other clients that (a) we might give preferential treatment (such as pricing, access to testing slots or scientific personnel) to those with equity interests, and (b) we might disclose information beneficial to those with the equity arrangement (and, conversely, detrimental to another client); (2) the fact that we would be acting as "investors" when we do not have the time or expertise to make the judgments required to substitute our cash for an equity payback. Relating to this last point, there is no evidence that we are losing business by not financing prospective client business by declining equity, and, in fact, we believe we are stronger in the service market since we are known to have this "no equity entanglements" approach.

Our firm operates in a highly regulated environment (with the Food and Drug Administration, Occupational Safety and Health Administration, Environmental Protection Agency (OSHA) , etc.). Technical and process changes therefore must be widely accepted and practiced to be generally acceptable for regulatory submissions. In this environment, IP has not been a significant factor for developing or protecting our expertise, so our interactions with IP attorneys have been limited to hazard a guess, though we have seen less discussion in equity for legal services over the past nine years (since I have been here, "on watch")....I believe that if the equity is held separately from the engagement partners—that is, in a "blind" fashion—it should not be too much of an obstacle.

I would think that over time equity-for-service should help both about equally, should it not? Perhaps that is too academic a view, though. In the short run, my feeling is an equity-for-service deal would help the entrepreneurs, simply because the transaction takes place first, and, I just don't think the attorneys have the full expertise (and time) to properly evaluate the deals.... Unfortunately we don't have enough experience to have "data points," see a "spectrum," or "name names"....regarding the spectrum of legal and business models you allude to.

I think in our experience, yes, it does matter what industry the firm belongs to. If direct clients are in a position of power—to hold deals hostage, so to speak—then that could enforce the rule (whether equity is needed to penetrate the market, or, as in ours, it's basically a no-no)....

As mentioned—rivalry can cause firms to indicate to clients that conflicts of interest (COI) exist for a competitor (because they hold an equity interest). It doesn't take long in a highly competitive marketplace for people to begin pointing out even perceived problems.... In our particular niche market, equity is not used—nor does its use appear to confer any competitive advantages. We think the converse is true actually.

President and CEO of Biotechnology Firm
Please discuss your experience and practice in terms of choosing between cash upfront versus equity compensation by your clients.

I'm currently using this arrangement with a public relations firm called Policy Advocates (Jerry Parrott). Their normal fee is $5,000. Under our agreement, they are charging $3,000 and will purchase common shares at the last-round price of preferred shares used by the VC—they will end up with about 1 percent of ownership. They don't do this with all clients—instead they do it with firms they think will be acquired or will IPO. I have a relationship with a marketing research firm which has purchased options (priced at 25 percent of last preferred price). Company SP (a pseudonym), purchases shares valued at $3 for $0.90. We get a discount equal to value of the investment (not amount paid for options). They feel that VCs know how to value. I worked for a venture capital firm for 2 years—they paid me about 1/3 of normal market rate, and 2/3 made up in equity from the VC's portfolio firm. The compensation was performance-based—my assignment was to identify alliance partners to buy the company or its products. I got equity if I closed the deal. I was successful in one case and not in another. I now have equity in another private firm, which acquired my original client, but this firm has not IPO-ed so I can't liquidate my holdings.

When do you choose which venue and why?
The answer depends on your risk tolerance—I'm a high-risk-taker or I wouldn't be in the biotech industry. A lot has to do with my comfort with the company and the comfort of the client—some clients said no, we don't want to

dilute our base. I tried to educate them that equity is internal cash, and external cash is more expensive. In many cases, I succeeded in convincing them to use equity to pay service providers.

To manage the speculative risk, I evaluate the company (a due diligence investigation). I look at the business plan to see if it's reasonable. I always take some cash component to pay my own bills—I try to get some positive cash flow. But if I feel confident, I always try to take equity.

Does accepting equity as compensation for legal services present conflicts of interest: when, how, and why, could they be mitigated?

I'm a director for a public firm. They hired a public relations (PR) firm. The PR firm informed the company that they would purchase 500,000 shares, at a time when the stock was at a market low. Later, the company did not like the service of the PR firm and fired them. The PR firm then then dumped the stock which drove down the stock price. They also shorted on additional shares to punish the client. This is a very big concern in public companies.

When I was at Univax I had a couple of law firms (IP and an outside counsel). The problem was whether there was a conflict-of-interest about the advice I was getting. Patent lawyers might push certain applications which, if they didn't have an interest, they might not. In biotech, your market value is often tied to size of your patent portfolio, so over-patenting will tend to inflate your stock price artificially. My internal counsel also had a lot of concern about using equity to pay for legal services.

As you know, external auditors can't own stock in audit clients. For me, this is a big concern. In general, I have a great concern about law firms, less about others. A lot of conflict-of-interest issues involve how much equity the service provider owns. If you're under 1 percent ownership, I'd say it's no problem. If it's 5 percent I would be very concerned. I would allow up to 5 percent but never over.

Does accepting equity as compensation for legal services help entrepreneurs better leverage expert services or does it help more the law firms that participate in the stock issue? When, how, and why?

As founder, I've always tried to push equity to conserve cash. With law firms I see all kinds of COI problems. I see it as I want an independent person who does not feel that their response would benefit them in any way...so again I feel that if they have a big equity position, they might want to alter their advice.

The potential conflict in this case is, what if the service provider is not making its numbers. If you have a successful IPO, the service provider will see that you have issued them stock at a low price and now you're doing well. If they decide to sell it may force down the value of your outstanding shares and reduce your liquidity.

What is the spectrum of legal and business models involving equity-for-services—which are the two extremes and who is an outlier and who is closer to the center among some IP law firms you could mention?

Morgan Lewis & Bockius—I approached them with equity, and they said that they never take equity in clients.

What are some best practices in the context of the questions so far and who has adopted them?

You don't want to give preferred shares to an outside service provider. The service provider should not have voting rights. If you have stock, you have voting rights—if you have options, you don't have that until they are exercised, unless you're already a public company. The service provider, in that case, could take the options, convert them immediately, and sell them. That might put pressure on your stock price, especially if you're a small company and very thinly traded. However, if the stock is already moving up in the market, the sale might generate interest and benefit the start-up.

You do have to pay tax if you take common stock in exchange for services. You have to pay the tax on the market value of the shares. If you take options, you don't have to pay tax until you exercise those options. For example, in one case, I got penny options and have 10 years to exercise—I would pay tax on the strike price when I convert them to shares.

What are some lessons learned from the experience and practice to date with respect to the equity-for-service model?

As a consultant, you always want public stock if it's available. I want options from private firms because you can get them at a low price, and the tax is deferred.

Interviews with Management Consultancies

KPMG Senior Partner

Remember that I am a public services guy and the equity positions offered by our clients are normally restricted to application service providers (ASP) and other outsourcing ventures. Arguably, sometimes there are incentive-fee contracts, but these have more to do with contractor performance than with equity in the sense you mean it.

Generally, our decisions are based on the standard risk/reward analysis. The kind of equity compensation offered is normally in the form of transaction fee-based arrangements for ASPs. Really, it comes down to evaluating risk and reward; as well as some subjective assessment of the client's capacity to absorb it's own risk. A lot of government entities are under severe pressure from their vendors and citizens to go "e." Cost pressures also drive this. Interestingly, in the hot economy of the late 1990's, government spending would have been expected to expand. However, in today's cost/value world, the pressure continued to deliver more for less. This can create desperation strategies. We avoid these because no equity deal is without risk to the client.

Just like they say in Las Vegas—make sure you can afford to lose because you may not win. Also, there can be circumstances where taking an equity position could obviate other opportunities. For example, if you set up a digital marketplace for a city, and the city wants to buy services which you offer on a competitive basis, can you bid? Is that worth the equity? Per my last answer, the Internet has created service and cost reduction opportunities which did not exist before. This has resulted in an increase in service requests for e-procurement and some internal service outsourcing.

Two years ago, it became the rage for governments to issue a request for proposal (RFP) to set up digital markets at no cost to them. Unfortunately, this concept is too often based on a myopic view that transaction volume rules the value equation. Actually, it began to introduce risk management concepts to the government that they were really not ready to absorb.

In government, owning a digital market could limit your ability to participate in that market. We are also a new IPO. Prior to the IPO, our potential for conflict-of-interest with SEC clients was significant. (This was even true in government, where our assurance services could impact public debt offerings.) Most of this has passed with the IPO but remains for the other Big 5 (now 4).

The answer is captured in five words: *What is the value equation?* The fact is that many entrepreneurs lack the cash to obtain the first-rate consulting support they need. The consultants would like to develop lasting relationships with the next Microsoft. There is no single solution to this equation. Arguably, the professional service firm may have more ability to absorb near-term cash losses than the "dot.coms".

In the government, most of the emphasis is on e-procurement. This is pretty vanilla—You operate the marketplace and you keep $X or Y% of the transaction stream. That and the basic ASP for enterprise resource planning (ERP) and bill collections, etc are the norm and near the center. The outliers are the ones that think of the value equation beyond the immediate and obvious. In Texas, for example, they figured out that the real cost of e-procurement could well be in the incremental costs of 53 state agencies, dozens of counties, hundreds of cities, and thousands of schools, institutions, and the like who would be spending Texan tax and charity dollars to accomplish the same thing over and over again. Texas commissioned a single RFP to set up a digital market with terms and conditions which would encourage the agencies, counties, cities, and others to use a master contract rather than contracting on their own. Not mandatory, but compelling!

Governments mostly try to finance their systems enhancements using contractor cash. There is not a strong incentive to have equity in the City of X.

Yes—mostly this has to do with the nonprofitable incentive: Get the client!! It seems like every significant procurement brings out the government in nonmarket firms. This confuses the market, particularly with new players who don't have the stomach for more than a couple of quarters' investment in this "government stuff," where you definitely go in for the long haul.

Overall, the challenge and the opportunity lies in being able to figure out the value equation. If your experience is based on "get the client" then you'll lose (and some major players have lost dearly by not understanding this).

The e-world can be insidious for the unprepared. The e-buzz creates an atmosphere like a Friday happy hour at college—mate, mate mate! But, what are you really looking for? When equity is involved, you better be looking for a relationship, and not just a quick score.

Part II:

Using the Equity-based Model: Primer and Cases from Practice

Chapter 5

IPR Primer:
A Brief Overview of U.S. and
International IP Laws

This chapter explains intellectual property, a critical issue which any entrepreneur must address to receive funding from venture capital sources. It then discusses the value provided by IP lawyers as service providers.

BASICS OF INTELLECTUAL PROPERTY RIGHTS

What Is a Patent?

A patent for an invention is a grant of a property right by the United States government to the inventor (or his heirs or assignees), which acts through the Patent and Trademark Office (PTO) (see examples of patent abstracts in the Appendix). The PTO is responsible for examining the patent application and granting the patent. An applicant may also submit a granted patent to an additional examination if the validity of the patent is in question. The PTO also makes determination regarding who is the first to invent the invention in question.

The PTO does not otherwise determine whether a granted patent is valid, that is the responsibility of the courts. Patent infringement actions are brought through the U.S. court system and validity and infringement are the two main questions to be answered in most patent lawsuits.

There are a few types of patents: utility patents, design patents, and plant patents. Utility patents are what is commonly thought of when people refer to a "patent." Utility patents are granted to the inventor(s) for 1) new and 2) unobvious "process, machine, manufacture, or composition of matter." Design patents cover the new and ornamental design for an article of manufacture. Plant patents cover new and distinct varieties of plants which a person has invented, discovered, or asexually reproduced. More on these topics is covered in the below.

The term of a utility or plant patent is 20 years from the date the patent application is filed at the Patent and Trademark Office, subject to the payment of maintenance fees. The term of a design patent is 14 years and does not require maintenance fees.

The right conferred by the patent grant extends throughout the United States and its territories and possessions. The right applies to the actions of individuals or corporations (see making, using, selling, or importing) and also applies to importation of patented goods. International protection is obtained on a country-by-country basis. Two major treaties govern international cooperation in patent law: the Paris Convention and the Patent Cooperation Treaty (PCT).

The right conferred by the patent grant is, in the language of the statute and of the grant itself, "the right to exclude others from making, using, selling, importing" the invention. What is granted is not the right to make, use, sell, or import, but the right to *exclude* others from making, using, selling, or import the invention. Thus, a patent is said to grant exclusionary rights or exclusive rights. Patent rights can be thought of as a bundle which are separable. The right to make, alone, may be infringed and remedy sought through the courts. The rights to use and sell also are distinct, and any activity which falls under one of them may be stopped by a patent holder and damages recovered. Not all patents cover all three rights, however. Where a person has developed a new process for making an old compound, they would have the exclusive right only to make the compound using their process. Another example might be where a person has invented a new cancer treatment by administering aspirin. If patented, the inventor would have exclusive rights only to the use—that is, "method of treating cancer by administering aspirin,"—and not to aspirin itself (since aspirin is not "new"). See also http://www.uspto.gov for further information.

Since start-up companies have limited amounts of cash with which to spend on very many competing needs, it is important to be very judicious in the use of both the amount of expenditure and the timing. Although not popular with their vendors, start-ups must realize that to survive they may have to resort to paying only those vendors who demand payment, and to pay those at the very latest date, and in the least amount possible. However, keeping current with one's bills has its own benefits, especially when listing outstanding balances on applications for a line of credit or an equipment lease. In those situations, it may make more sense to pay down those amounts.

This pendulum swing must be balanced, however. As noted previously, some service providers will not work for a start-up if there is a risk of nonpayment. This is especially true for attorneys. Start-up companies typically use only a few lawyers. They need a corporate lawyer to provide financing and securities-related services. They need employment lawyers to manage their growing workforce. They need a tax lawyer or accountant or both to provide expertise on everything from their salary and benefit plan to ensuring that the company does not financially overshoot or undershoot its goals as stated in the business plan. Lastly, they need an intellectual property lawyer and, preferably, a patent lawyer if the company is a technology company.

Sometimes start-ups prefer to obtain these services all under one roof. Some law firms provide this type of cradle-to-grave attention and try to provide staff attorneys who can handle each specialty. Some firms do very well in this regard. Others do not. And although there are as many reasons that a client-attorney relationship does not work as there are clients and attorneys, the main problem area is trust. A start-up must trust its advisors. Sometimes these relationships can develop under one roof, sometimes it requires more than one firm. Sometimes it may be advantageous to have more than one firm at your disposal.

Since patent law can be one of the more expensive areas but can also be one of the most predictable from a cost standpoint for technology companies, we have chosen to profile some relationships between patent lawyers and start-ups. To understand the cost and variables which add to the predictability, we have provided a brief summary of the basics of IP law. After the summary, case studies are provided which illustrate the various real-life concerns, facts, and outcomes in the equity-for-service area.

What Is a Copyright?

A copyright protects the creations of an author, artist, musician, and so on, against copying, such as literary works, dramatic works, musical works, artistic works, architectural works, sculptural works, or computer software works. In some instances, copyright law also confers performing and recording rights. The copyright goes to the form of expression rather than to the subject matter of the creation. The term of copyright is equal to the life of the creator plus 70 years or for anonymous or pseudonymous works, it is 95 years from publication or 120 years from creation.

A description of a machine could be copyrighted as a writing, but this would only prevent others from copying the description; it would not prevent others from writing a description of their own or from making and using the machine. Certain packaging brochures can be copyrighted as well as any sculptural aspects of consumer products. Copyrights, although not now commonly pursued by manufacturers, provide for powerful remedies including injunctions against further use of a copyrighted work as well as money damages. These injunctions, which are comparatively easier to obtain in a copyright case, can be applied to a component vital to a business and can shut a business down until the dispute is resolved or settled. This can be an important weapon for U.S. manufacturers. Copyrights can also be used as additional weapon in the arsenal of U.S. companies who manufacture patented items for export to other countries. Copyrights are registered in the Copyright Office in the Library of Congress. Information concerning copyrights may be obtained from the Register of Copyrights, Library of Congress, Washington, D.C. 20559, (telephone 202-479-0700). International protection is obtained on a country-by-country basis. The Berne Convention governs international cooperation between countries concerning copyright issues.

What Is a Trademark?

A trademark indicates the source of a product. This relationship between mark and source in the mind of the consumer is called goodwill. Goodwill is where the value resides in a trademark. One mark, Coca-Cola, has been reported as having a goodwill worth over $40 billion. Trademark rights may be assigned, provided the owner maintains a system for oversight of the quality, and provided the "goodwill" is also explicitly recited in the assignment. A trademark relates to any word, name, symbol, or device which is used in trade with goods to indicate the source or origin of the goods and to distinguish them from the goods of others. Trademark rights may be used to prevent others from using a confusingly similar mark but not to prevent others from making the same goods or from selling them under a nonconfusing mark. Similar rights may be acquired in marks used in the sale or advertising of services (service marks). Trademarks and service marks which are used in interstate or foreign commerce may be registered in the U.S. Patent and Trademark Office. Manufacturers have used trademark law to also cover the color of a product (pink insulation) as well as the shape or configuration of a product (wine bottle). Trademarks may also be obtained at the state level, but prevent use only in that state. Federal registration is all that is necessary in most circumstances and provides the benefit of access to federal courts.

Trade dress is similar to a trademark in that it is an indicator of product source, but relates to the packaging configuration, color, font, size, and so on of a product. Trade dress has also been extended to restaurant configuration (e.g., a colorful Mexican-themed restaurant).

Other Rights

A trade secret is any information which provides a competitive business advantage. Trade secrets may be privately enforced in state court or enforced by the Justice Department under the new federal trade secret law. Trade secrets are enforceable only if reasonable steps had been taken to keep the information secret—that is, confidentiality agreements, separation of recipe into component parts, locks and other physical plant security efforts, employee agreements, and so on.

A shop right arises during the course of employment from employee activities which provide valuable products or services. These rights automatically accrue to the employer in most states unless specifically waived under contract.

A mask work is the three-dimensional image or mask used to produce semiconductor chips. The mask shields the substrate on the chip from the etching process. It is similar to a copyright for a sculptural work, but specifically provided for under its own statute.

International Patent Filing Costs and the Stock-for-Services Paradigm

The decision and costs surrounding the international filing of a patent application can be one of the single most expensive aspects of patent procurement. Just to file and not including the legal fees to obtain, a European and Japanese equivalent to a U.S. patent can cost an additional $10,000 to $25,000 for an average patent application. Almost all of this cost is for translation fees and governmental filing fees. The lawyers haven't even started working yet!

However, this is a problem. The fact that these fees are for translations and governmental fees means that the stock-for-services paradigm will generally not work to allay these costs. At a minimum, translators are not known to accept these types of deals since human translators employed by the companies want cash on the barrelhead for their efforts. Additionally, most entrepreneurs would not want to trade their stock to a governmental body under any circumstances.

Nonetheless, there is an opportunity to defer some of the costs after the initial filing when the law firms who do international patent work engage their counterparts in foreign countries and begin examination and negotiation with the particular host country's patent office. A brief overview of how international patents are obtained is first required.

Patents are national in origin; meaning that if you want a patent, you must apply for it in each country. Think of it as a license to use that country's courts to enforce your patent rights against theft. To obtain a patent in a foreign country after filing a U.S. patent, the inventor's attorney will generally have the patent application translated into the host country's language and filed at the requested patent office. In a few countries, patents are granted upon filing and passing a minor formality check. Switzerland, Luxembourg, South Africa, and Australia are some of the major countries who currently use this mechanism. Most major market countries will send the application to a specially trained patent examiner who will review the application to see if it is new, is properly described in the application, and is an advance over what came before. The expertise of good patent lawyers in each country comes in handy for any strategy requiring deviation from the norm. Unfortunately, each country takes it's own stand on genetic organisms, business method patents, software inventions, bioinformatics, medical treatment, and the like, and this requires knowledgeable U.S. counsel to identify the problems and good overseas counsel to work it through the system. Eventually, after some negotiation with the patent examiners, agreement is reached and patents are generally granted in most circumstances.

The idea of paying these overseas patent lawyers in stock is particularly interesting to U.S. corporations, the foreign lawyers themselves, and their U.S.

counterparts. The costs of developing and maintaining a large portfolio around a single product with a few backup products, all filed in the countries where the product will be sold or where competitors need too be excluded, can be $500,000 per month. During personal discussions with many European patent attorneys, they are generally very interested in this phenomenon, but do not believe that they would be allowed to engage in such practices because of the severe ethical restrictions, actual or perceived, on professional conduct. In particular, German patent firms have restrictions not only on accepting stock, but also on the size of the firms (they must be generally small by U.S. standards). Similar to the United States, they must also be specifically registered to practice patent law and must be fluent in multiple language requirements to practice before the European Patent Office (EPO). Thus, significant regulatory restrictions would have to be changed to export such a system to Europe. Nonetheless, the extremely high costs of obtaining international patent coverage has already initiated discussions among corporate and governmental bodies for years, but none of the suggestions to date have involved the sort of risk-distribution by requiring non-U.S. attorneys to have some "skin in the game."

NATURE OF IP LAW AND ITS ROLE IN ENTREPRENEURSHIP

IP law is one of the most expensive fields of legal expertise. As evidence, consider that the top ten patent winners in 1998 spent an average of $10,000 to $30,000 per patent over a two-year period for developing the application, prosecuting the patent, and seeing it through to approval and received around 2,000-3,000 patents per company per year. This amount of $30,000 to 90,000 per year, does not include R&D costs or postpatenting costs. These numbers serve to illustrate the level of expense and commitment involved in obtaining patents. Entrepreneurs must understand the value of carefully protected intellectual property as the foundation for a new business. IP has a "locked" value which is not unlocked until you invest in it (using licensing, alliances, etc.). IPR also includes a potential opportunity cost for insufficient protection—that is, if a firm does not secure protection for its intellectual property, it could lose potential sales or licensing fees, and may even lose an advantage over its competitors. Here is where an outside patent counsel often provides value. By framing the patented innovation properly in the application, the lawyer can expand the range of the invention and its potential influence on the market. Discussions with the inventor should elicit the uniqueness of the invention and understand implications for market creation and capture.

The fundamental dilemma for the entrepreneur is understanding the market failure in IP. The cost of protecting a valuable idea may form a barrier to securing the necessary protections. Also, the value of patents is diminished if patenting is pursued as a fad, not a business decision. In biotechnology, for example, firms are patenting SNPs (gene fragments) without understanding their true utility—these patents are filed primarily to pre-empt similar filings by competitors. The problem with this approach is that it ends up lowering the perception of the value of an IP lawyer, since the lawyer becomes a "paper mill" for applications. It also detracts from the desirability of the lawyer role. The client and lawyer should focus not only on managing property, but the knowledge behind the property.

OBTAINING IP COUNSEL—SOME CONSIDERATIONS

Business executives also need to understand why it may be preferable to use outside counsel for IP work to supplement, or in some cases replace, in-house counsel. One problem is that inside counsel (especially in large firms) tend to leverage their financial power. Corporations may prefer to control costs and be able to fire their lawyers at will. They may want the lawyers inside the firm, but they do not want to be "married" to them.

In addition, the role of the in-house counsel is primarily to protect the firm against sources of risk. This risk-averse attitude is sensible in most cases, but not in cases of technological venturing. Instead, outside counsel tends to be more proactive. As one technology manager at a major university puts it, "in-house lawyers tell you why you can't do what you want; outside lawyers tell you how you can pull it off."

Lastly, outside counsel and inside counsel each have expertise that can not be captured by a single internal employee. Outside counsel are exposed to a broad variety of corporate problems and their solutions. Inside counsel are privy to a deeper understanding of their companies' requirements. Interestingly, inside counsel sometimes hire outside counsel in order to provide an "outside" report to top management. In reality, both outside and inside attorneys are fully aware that inside counsel frequently have the best understanding of both a problem and its solution. However, a "credibility dance" is necessary to get management to endorse the advice of their in-house lawyers.

USING PATENT PORTFOLIOS FOR MERGERS, ACQUISITIONS, VALUATION AND PARTNERING

Some companies don't have to be told why they should bother with patents.[73] IBM has let it be known that they collect on the order of $1 billion per year in licensing patented technology that they developed through their R&D programs, but which they can't or won't pursue themselves. Clearly, patenting inventions they don't even plan to commercialize for themselves is working for them.

The patent system has experienced tremendous growth in recent years, primarily because the system is working. It cannot be denied that if your company is not getting patents you should ask yourself why not. Although many factors are responsible, in ten years Microsoft has gone from having one patent to having over 800. Oracle, Sun Microsystems, Novell, Dell, and Intel have all had similar growth. Patent licensing revenues have increased from $15 billion in 1990 to over $100 billion in 1998. Even universities have gotten into

---

[73] By Todd Juneau, Esq, Unpublished Draft.

the act, generating over \$611 million in licensing royalties and starting over 300 new companies from academic research in 1997 alone.

Blocking Patents

Patenting products you plan to sell makes sense on its face. The granted patent or patents which cover your product give you some insurance against nefarious infringers (i.e., thieves). But what about patenting your competitor's product which he or she plans to sell? Yes, this is not only possible but it is done all the time. You may ask yourselves how can I patent my competitor's product? It's called a defensive patent. Let's say for instance that a competitor develops soy oil as a nutritional supplement. They also get a patent which covers (1) purified soy oil and (2) methods of using soy oil as a nutritional supplement. Your business is automobile tire reclamation and you have discovered that purified soy oil is very good for softening tires in order to recover carbon black, steel belts, and so forth for reselling to manufacturers. You decide to get a patent on the new and unobvious use of soy oil in tire reclamation. The new use of an old composition is a very patentable invention. Better yet, although your competitor has the patent on purified soy oil and has indicated that they might supply you with some if you're willing to pay a premium for a patented product, they are not capable of using their own patented product, purified soy oil, to reclaim tire components because you have filed for and received a "blocking patent". This situation can result in a stand-off or in cross-licensing and frequently actually results in cross-licensing where both parties can come to an agreement on reasonable terms and the perceived gain is greater than the perceived threat.

THE "NEW ECONOMY" REALITIES

But how does this work if my business is in the new economy? Patenting software, network architecture, and methods of processing data have been patentable for a long time. Recently, the State Street Bank case upheld the validity of a patent to Signature Financial Group on a method covering a hub-and-spoke system for pooling money between various mutual funds in order to reduce costs and maximize return. Most people have heard of the Amazon.com "one-click shopping" patent where little Amazon stopped Goliath Barnes and Noble from moving into their turf in a testament to the power of patents. The stories go on and on. For example, Stac Electronics defeated Microsoft in 1996 and Fonar defeated General Electric in 1997 in patent trials. Software patents are filed every day and granted every Tuesday at the Patent Office. Everything from software which controls processes for production of your product to software for distance-learning from universities to software which removes cookies from your computer are patentable and patented. Why do these companies spend their precious company resources in this manner? Because by and large, the system works.

An Example: Software/Electronic/Network/Systems

How exactly does this apply to software, electronics, networking, or other systems? Simple, the same tools used in the soy oil example above apply to these industries and you don't have to rely solely on a business-method patent. For example, your insurance company (or hospital or bank or telecommunication company) wants to improve efficiencies in the way it does its business. Like any good business, you first collect data on its current practices, analyze the data to see if there is a better way, and install a set of revised procedures and a feedback mechanism in order to solve the problem. If this new system is novel (i.e., hasn't been done before), and provides a commercial advantage, there is good chance your system is patentable. So then what do you do with such a patent? It depends on how expansive you were able to claim the invention. If you are the first company to provide such a system to an entirely new market, you may be able to get a patent which excludes everyone else from entering that market. Further explanation of the value of this is not required. If you get a patent which is not so broad, you can at least protect your system from being used by competitors or from walking out the door with your former employees. By making tangible your intangible assets, immediate value is obtained for the company.

Nontechnology Industries

But what if my business is a small, non-technology business? What relevance do patents have for me? First of all, patents can and should have many uses even for non-technology companies. Patents can be obtained for the shape of your packaging (design patents last 14 years). Patents can be obtained for "anything under the sun made by man" according to the Supreme Court of the United States. This definition is limiting to you only if your business plan encompasses products intended for sale outside our solar system, or of course, anything not made by mankind. Accordingly, whether your business involves mechanical, electrical, or chemical products or processes, you can probably get a patent on it if it is new and not an obvious variation on what came before. Examples include methods of food processing, making detergent, making cancer drugs, making wood-grain laminates, making electricity, or outputting data from a software program. Compositions include any purified naturally occurring compound, purified genes, purified proteins, new forms of silicon for computer chips, carbon recipes for steel, and the list goes on and on. Devices include heart pumps, gas pumps, tire pumps, carburetors, assembly line machines, and so forth. All these and more can be found on the Web at the U.S. Patent and Trademark Office Website, www.uspto.gov, where anyone can check out whether that idea they just had has been thought of by someone else. It is important to get with the program and realize that a patent audit can identify processes, compositions, and devices which may be patentable for just about every industry.

Keeping Out the Riff-raff

Patents, as discussed, can be used as insurance against theft. This is pretty straightforward. If somebody makes, uses, sells, or imports your patented invention, you can enjoin them from further activities and demand that they disgorge any profits they made since they started. However, look closer and notice that the four rights available under patent law stop manufacturers (make), end-users or resellers (use), distributors (sell), and importers (import). This effectively excludes competitors from the U.S. market if you have a U.S. patent and any other market where you have a national patent for that country.

Patents and the required litigation costs associated with them can be used to deter theft and thus maintain market share from those unwilling to pay the price to challenge a patent. This is so mainly because patents are by law presumed valid by the courts and must be proven invalid by any challenger by clear and convincing evidence, a high judicial hurdle to overcome. It keeps out the riff-raff since if they cannot pay $10,000 to $100,000 per *month* in litigation costs, they should not attempt to challenge the patent.

Keeping Honest Companies Honest

Patents can also be used to keep the large companies honest. Look at Barnes and Noble, they have stayed away from one-click shopping while the lawsuit is pending since they are fully aware that if they don't prevail against Amazon they may be subjected to triple damages for being a "willful infringer". Excluding your competitors from the market should be evidence enough to convince most people that the system works.

But what else can a patent be used for? As discussed above, defensive patents can force cross-licensing and give you an advantage over those without defensive patents when talking price with a supplier. If you have a defensive patent and negotiate an exclusive cross-license, then no other companies can access the market. This kind of bootstrap monopoly is frequently found in the patent strategy of many start-ups with experienced patent counsel, since it is a quick way to get into a previously closed game. Obviously, it can also get a start-up noticed (the "spill my drink on you to get you to notice me" approach) which can be an advantage for companies seeking a buy-out, corporate partnering, corporate joint venture, or other type of corporate relationship, especially where the patents can be used to add value to the deal.

For example, Guilford Pharmaceuticals licensed some nerve-growth technology in the form of U.S. and foreign patent applications to Amgen for $466 million. It should be noted there was no product on the market at the time, just R&D wrapped in patent protection. This kind of patent-portfolio/R&D packaging happens all the time. It makes you wonder what the definition of a product really is; is the product the FDA-approved drug that results from the clinical trials or is it the patent portfolio itself? A patent program can also be used simply to quantify, evaluate, and recognize important R&D within an organization.

OTHER CONSIDERATIONS IN A COORDINATED PATENT PROGRAM

But what if none or only some of my competitors are active in the patent arena? Clearly, this can indicate an opportunity or a deadend and should be viewed with an open mind. Some industries are well suited to understanding and incorporating patent strategies into their larger goals. Some are not. Cosmetic formulations can be patentable, but patenting the changing styles of lipstick color doesn't make sense given that it takes about two years to get a patent. However, many industries are so well developed in their patent strategy that they take into account that it takes roughly two years to get a patent and do not introduce a product until the marketing, sales, advertising, and patent strategies are completed. Of course, this requires an investment in coordination and training (do not try this in the absence of professional guidance). Accordingly, this type of integrated strategy ensures market share and dominance for the long term.

The Downside of Not Participating in the Patent World

A few examples illustrate this best. Xerox in 1979 had developed most everything in the later windows operating systems including pull-down menus, pop-up windows, and scalable windows. They even drafted patent applications but, importantly, did not file them. It has been estimated that even at 1 percent royalty rate (which is low), the royalties would have topped $500 million for the sample period between 1984 and 1988. In another example, VisiCalc was developed by Dan Bricklin in 1979. He decided not to patent it and it became the basis for Lotus 1-2-3 and Microsoft Excel. In a last example, Kodak had entered the instamatic film market in 1976 when Polaroid owned a great many patents in this area. At the end of the day, Kodak was ordered to pay $925 million, forced to shut down a $1.5 billion plant, lay off 700 workers, and spend an additional $500 million to buy back the cameras it had sold. Legal fees over 14 years topped $100 million.

The proper use of patents can provide enormous power over markets and competitors. Companies which use patent strategies are successful while those that do not must rely on other tools. Some of these tools may include ensuring that you have the best personnel, having non-patented trade secrets, maintaining the best product, and ensuring that your sales and advertising force consistently drives your customers toward your product and not your competition. However, isn't it usually necessary for survival of a business to use all of the above? The questions then becomes whether an equity-for-service program can supplement these best practices.

Chapter 6

Intangibles Valuation Primer:
A Brief Overview

This chapter discusses the state of current views, approaches and methods in the United States regarding the valuation of IP. It focuses on the three specific forms of IP recognized by U.S. federal law:[74]

- patents, dealing with functional and design inventions;
- trademarks, dealing with commercial origin and identity; and
- copyrights, dealing with literary and artistic expressions.

The next section provides a background on the increased recognition of IP value in the U.S. business world, and how that has led to the development of a highly sophisticated discipline of IP valuation.

---

[74] A fourth form of IP, trade secrets, is protected in the United States under various state laws but not by federal law.

INTANGIBLES VALUATION FROM THE ATTORNEY'S PERSPECTIVE

To expand a bit further upon the dynamics and motivations for attorneys which are a natural result of a stock for services deal, we need to analyze it as between "worker drone" attorneys and those who are partners or members of the law firms which engage in the transaction.

In many corporations, just as in many other industries, there will usually be a single attorney designated as the client-contact attorney. This person is similar to a job-site foreman and manages the project or projects. Sometimes this is the originating partner, (i.e., the partner who originated the client's choice to come to the firm), sometimes it is a junior partner or senior associate who works for an originating partner. Of course, there may be teams of project managers and other variations from firm to firm, but the point is that there will generally be attorneys who are sharing in the risk and those who are not.

In a first scenario, an originating partner may agree with the client to substitute receipt of stock for receipt of fees, either outright or as consideration for a fee deferral. This principal partner is then acting like a bank. In the same sense that a bank makes a market and absorbs part of the risk by freeing up capital, the partner is acting like a knowledge banker. This knowledge banker role is the result of taking part of the risk of non-payment in exchange for a premium (e.g., accepting equity), and lending the legal services to the client in need.

The viewpoint from the working attorney's perspective is the same as that of a "paying" client. The problem is identified, attorneys give the client some options for going solutions: the work is authorized, performed, billed, and the worker attorney gets paid. The upside is the vicarious exposure and attendant training which results from being directly involved in these types of transactions and with these types of clients. The only downside is any fallout from a lower cash flow and/or higher risk to the employee's organization.

The upside for the originating partner is that he or she "buys" the legal services at "cost" and trades them at full value. Thus, an originating attorney can claim an exposure of 100 percent of the worth of the services, but in fact, is putting out 20 percent-40 percent depending on the generosity of the firms' compensation structure.

In another scenario, the client may be a more savvy client who has been through this all before and decides to take a "divide and conquer" strategy toward the law firm billing practices by offering the shares directly to the working attorney and bypassing the more rigid hierarchical structure of many firms. Of course, the first problem is that the originating partner has not been compensated or reimbursed for any client development costs such as travel, entertainment, outreach, and so on. This resentment can easily be overcome by sharing any stock received in a fair manner in order to make direct compensation to those responsible for its existence. The next problem, however, is more dramatic. What if the associates or working attorneys start in-fighting over the opportunity to work on clients which have marketed themselves as the next big thing? Of course, this will have, and has had for some firms who have been victims of this, an erosive effect on law firms and replaces cohesiveness of the team with self-seeking behavior. Left unchecked, this attitude will break established firms apart, this "tear the pages out of the only book in the school library so nobody else can get a good grade on the project" attitude loses the only reason for doing the deal this way in the first place, which is to help clients by reducing their need to expend precious capital. Thus, even within a certain amount of deal-flow in a stock-for-services environment, a governed balance would appear to prevail as well as a stronger option than a capitalistic free for all.

VALUATION OF INTELLECTUAL PROPERTY: TOOLS, METHODS, AND PRACTICES

In the United States, awareness of the value and significance of intellectual property to business success grew substantially in the 1990s. A study of the U.S. economy found that in 1982, "tangible" assets accounted for 62 percent of the average company's market value, while in 1992, that share declined to 38 percent.[75]

Several corporations are leaders in recognizing that intellectual property has the potential to generate long-term revenues. One consultant, with extensive experience in IP valuation with industrial companies, estimates that only the 100 largest companies in the United States are in a position to invest in IP and to realize substantial returns from that investment. Smaller companies lack the resources, particularly in time, necessary for changing their corporate cultures to value IP.

Industries where intangible assets are a greater share of firm value and where licensing is more common tend to be much more aware of the value of IP. Leading industries cited by these experts include clothing, computer software, pharmaceuticals and chemicals, telecommunications, and consumer goods. Within these industries, there are great differences in the sophistication of approaches to IP valuation.

In the United States, awareness of the value and significance of intellectual property to business success grew substantially in the 1990s. Some companies, particularly those in so-called knowledge-based industries (generally referring to high-technology sectors such as electronics, software, and biotechnology), consider their main business to be the creation, accumulation, and protection of IP. For example, Texas Instruments reports that the largest contributor to the firm's annual profits is its IP department, through both licensing and damages received from successful patent litigation. In the ten years between 1986 and 1995, Texas Instruments received a reported $1.5 billion in licensing royalties (more updated figures are not available), and estimates state that its income from

---

[75] Cited in Karyl Misrack, "Valuing Intellectual Property: The Science and the Art," *The Colorado Lawyer*, August 1997, pp. 85-91.

patent litigation is even higher.[76]   Some firms now produce only IP. For example, many firms in the ASIC (application-specific integrated circuit) industry produce semiconductor designs, and then license all those designs to other firms which fabricate and sell those circuits. A study of the U.S. economy found that in 1982, "tangible" assets accounted for 62 percent of the average company's market value, while in 1992, that share declined to 38 percent.[77]

As the recognition of the value of IP increases in the United States, businesses are also increasing their awareness and sophistication of methods for estimating the actual financial value of IP. In the 1950s, when IP was viewed mostly as a natural but unexploited result of company operations, firms rarely bothered to place a specific value on a particular item of IP. Today, there are several different approaches to IP valuation, with a wide variety of exact methods corresponding to each approach. There are a number of consulting firms which specialize in the valuation of intellectual property for clients, and some firms which do substantial amounts of licensing or other transactions involving IP have in-house staff with IP valuation expertise.

In the 1990s, the experts from the IP and finance fields began to cooperate on developing more sophisticated valuation methodologies. These apply quantitative financial techniques to the analysis of the qualitative factors identified by the IP experts. Today, there are four basic approaches to IP valuation, with a variety of methods corresponding to each one: heuristic method, cost method, market method, and economic method. These four approaches will be addressed later in the chapter. According to interviews with experts, the most comprehensive valuations use a combination of methods and approaches to derive the IP value.

The most important feature of IP valuation activities in the United States is that any given item of IP always has several different values. The exact method chosen for an IP valuation depends first on the business context of the valuation, and second on objective of the party conducting the valuation. A third factor in valuation is the regulatory or contractual requirements of the transaction context. There is no single methodology which is best for every case of IP valuation, as these factors vary among transactions. There are general industry practices where some methods are more commonly used with particular transactions—see Table 6.1, later in this chapter, for a review of those practices.

The preferred methodologies in different fields also vary. For example, IP licensing professionals and IP appraisal consultants use the most sophisticated methods, which are hybrids of the various approaches. Tax accountants tend to favor the market approach, as the Internal Revenue Service has identified this as its preferred method of IP valuation in transfer pricing. Venture capitalists rely more on their own industry knowledge and assessment of start-ups in valuing the IP for an equity investment. Investment bankers involved in mergers and acquisitions are more likely to favor the economic approach, since they are

---

[76] Twila Gamble and Jennifer Tanner, "The Strategy of a Licensing Campaign," *Intellectual Property Today*, September 1996, p. 50.

[77] Cited in Misrack, op. cit.

interested in valuing the entire business and not simply isolated intellectual properties.

THE VALUE OF INTELLECTUAL PROPERTY IN THE UNITED STATES

During the economic boom in American business after World War II, intellectual property rights were viewed as a means of maintaining an archive of a firm's creative output, with no value beyond simple record-keeping.

There are several reasons why patenting was not considered an important activity. Most U.S. corporations in the postwar period were concerned primarily with expanding their products and markets, but not necessarily with exploiting all of the intellectual resources created by that expansion.

In the case of patents, since licensing was relatively rare, there was not a developed market which assigned values to patents. Also, patent litigation was relatively rare, because patents were difficult to protect in court. Therefore, even when firms filed for intellectual property protection, they lacked the ability and the incentive to enforce those rights against infringement. This attitude began to change in 1980, when the U.S. Congress established the Court of Appeals for the Federal Circuit (CAFC) in Washington, DC. This became the ultimate forum for resolving all U.S. patent disputes. The CAFC made the protection of patents easier, and its rulings also helped to establish clear definitions of patent infringement. This made patents by themselves more valuable to firms.

Until recently, firms viewed the management of their intellectual property as a cost center. New inventions and other assets were protected only if they added a key product or service to the firm's lines of business. The firm's intellectual property office, usually a department of the general counsel's office, recorded any patents or other intellectual property rights granted, paid the necessary fees, and did not attempt to do anything with that property. A number of pioneering companies, such as Texas Instruments (mentioned above), Dow Chemical, IBM, and DuPont, take a completely different view of intellectual property. These companies view their intellectual property as true assets, resources which should be exploited fully if the firm is to operate at peak efficiency. This new view shifts the patent and IP tracking function from a cost center to a profit center. It explicitly recognizes that all of a firm's intellectual property has some value, and that the job of the IP office is to maximize the leveraging of that value by the firm.[78]

DIFFERENCES IN PERCEPTIONS OF IP VALUE ACROSS FIRMS AND INDUSTRIES

Several firms are leaders in recognizing that intellectual property has the potential to generate long-term revenues and even promotes the creation of

---

[78] Rick Mullin, "Intellectual Assets," *Chemical Week*, December 11, 1996, p. 26.

additional intellectual property. Thus, "intellectual capital" such as IP displays the same properties as financial capital, in that an investment in IP buys a productive asset which can be used to acquire or create other assets.

While the terms "intellectual capital" and "knowledge management" are now very popular, there are still relatively few companies which have taken a comprehensive approach to estimating and exploiting the true value of their IP portfolios. While various IP valuation experts note that awareness of the importance of IP is substantial and growing among U.S. firms, they add that few have acted on that awareness.

Dow Chemical Corporation is among the most aggressive U.S. firms in valuing and exploiting its intellectual property. In 1995, the company's executive committee resolved to increase Dow's licensing revenues from $20 million per year to $125 million per year by the year 2000, and over the same period to reduce its tax liability by $40 million over ten years by selling or giving up unused patents. The company appointed a vice president for licensing, and began construction of a database which would store information on all 30,000 patents held by the company.[79] Dow also began to value those patents systematically, in part to identify those which should be shed from the firm's patent portfolio. This system was extended to include the valuation and licensing of non-IP intellectual assets, such as process know-how and corporate operating procedures (for example, environmental safety methods). Dow conducted a comprehensive benchmarking study which found that only two corporations in the world were comparable to Dow in their IP valuation and tracking programs. Dow also has its own IP valuation procedure, called the Technology Factors Method, which was developed for the firm by Arthur D. Little & Co.

IBM is another firm often cited for its forward-looking policy on managing its IP portfolio, particularly in software. IBM received more U.S. patents than any other company in 1997, with a total of 1,724. The current chairman of IBM, Lou Gerstner, initiated the move to make IBM an IP powerhouse, and to exploit that IP to its fullest potential. In 1995, IBM earned $646 million from licensing of IP to other companies. Recently, it has been reported that IBM's revenues exceed $1 billion annually.

Starting in 1996, the company began contacting other software companies to demand royalties on products that IBM perceived were infringing on its software patents. Companies targeted by this campaign include Adobe Software (desktop publishing), Computer Associates (enterprise software), Intuit (personal finance), and Oracle (relational database management). IBM has demanded that these companies pay 1 to 5 percent of gross sales on all products using IBM-patented technology, with the exact ratio based on the number of patents infringed.[80]

---

[79] Ibid.
[80] Ira Sager, "Big Blue Is Out to Collar Software Scofflaws," *Business Week*, 17 March 1997, p. 34.

IBM now conducts a preliminary valuation on all patent disclosures submitted by its researchers. Those deemed to have economic potential are classified into three categories based on the expected revenues from those patents. The researchers involved receive a bonus based on the number of their patents placed in each category. Exact details of the valuation methodology used by IBM are not available.[81]

IP appraisal experts are unanimous in the opinion that most U.S. firms do not have in-house valuation capabilities, and that their valuation activities are almost completely transaction-driven (that is, companies value only an item of IP if it is involved in a potential license or similar deal). Industries where intangible assets are a greater share of firm value and where licensing is more common tend to be much more aware of the value of IP, and invest more time and resources in managing and valuing their IP portfolio. Leading industries cited by these experts include:

- the clothing industry, particularly fashion houses with strong brands;
- the computer software industry (both copyrights and patents);
- pharmaceuticals and chemicals (due to prevalence of licensing);
- telecommunications;
- consumer goods.

Even within these industries, there are great differences in the sophistication of approaches to IP valuation. For example, Lucent Technologies is extremely active in enforcing its patents and pursuing potential infringers, but it is very poor at estimating patent value. The president of a leading IP appraisal firm notes that IP consultants retained by Lucent almost always estimate the value of Lucent's IP at levels far higher than Lucent's internal valuation. Experts also agreed in general that firms with substantial tangible assets, such as steel and aerospace companies, are slow to appreciate the particular value that IP contributes to their operations.

EVOLUTION OF VALUATION APPROACHES AND METHODS

The practice of IP valuation evolved from two different streams of practice. The first stream comes from the financial analysis field. During the 1950s, corporate financial managers would value patents when necessary for licensing or other situations. These managers estimated the revenues from products based on those patents over the life of the patent, and then discounted those cash flows by an estimated risk factor to calculate its net present value. In the 1960s, Bruce Henderson of the Boston Consulting Group and others pointed out that IP could have value after legal protections had expired, because firms could use the term of protection to advance along a learning curve and to establish barriers to entry

---

[81] Chris O'Brien, "IBM's Patent Penchant," *The Raleigh News and Observer*, 13 January 1998, p. D1.

by competitors. This led financial analysts to model several values of each item of IP based on different assumptions.

Awareness of the sensitivity of IP value to changes in key assumptions about its revenue potential led the investment banking industry to develop more sophisticated modeling techniques in the 1980s. By 1990, investment banks were running Monte Carlo simulations, where computer algorithms would compute huge numbers of possible values based on changes in assumptions, and then estimate the most reasonable value based on the risk factors for that item of IP. Also, the 1980s were a period when many high-profile mergers and acquisitions included extremely high valuations based on the IP of the target firm. For example, in the RJR-Nabisco merger, an estimated 80 percent of the $25 billion value placed on the deal was attributed to intangible assets such as intellectual property (mostly the consumer brands owned by the two firms).

Despite the application of advanced financial methodologies to IP valuation, the outcomes of these efforts were not reliable. A 1994 study by Bank of America of its past involvement in mergers found that in 75 percent of the cases, the original value estimated for the IP in the deals was totally inaccurate. In such cases, the buyer often divested key elements of the acquired firm because it could not make enough money of the IP that it had bought.[82]

The second stream of practice came from intellectual property managers in U.S. corporations and professional appraisal firms. Through the 1960s, most IP was valued with what a long-time valuation consultant calls the "gray-beard" approach—a respected manager with years of experience in the field of application for the item of IP would be consulted, and that manager would "stroke his gray beard" and give his subjective estimate of the item's value. In the 1970s and 1980s, corporate IP managers would conduct a simple income analysis, but then apply a long list of qualitative factors to modify that value up or down.

In the 1990s, the experts from the IP and finance fields began to cooperate on developing more sophisticated valuation methodologies. These apply quantitative financial techniques to the analysis of the qualitative factors identified by the IP experts. The increased attention to IP valuation by tax authorities in the late 1980s, starting with a 1988 White Paper on IP in transfer pricing by the Department of the Treasury (the parent agency of the Internal Revenue Service), also increased awareness of the importance of calculating IP value through sound economic methods.[83]

---

[82] This history is taken primarily from Robert Boyden Lamb, "Economic and Financial Issues in Intellectual Property," in Melvin Simensky et al., *The New Role of Intellectual Property in Commercial Transactions: 1998 Cumulative Supplement* (New York: John Wiley & Sons, Inc., 1998), pp. 11-34.

[83] Cited in Gordon V. Smith and Russell L. Parr, *Valuation of Intellectual Property and Intangible Assets* (New York: John Wiley & Sons, Inc., 1994), p. 14.

PRINCIPLES OF INTELLECTUAL PROPERTY VALUATION IN THE UNITED STATES

The most important feature of IP valuation activities in the United States is that any given item of IP always has several different values, even using the most precise and sophisticated methodology.

Value is assumed to be a subjective concept. The two most important variables affecting the outcome of a valuation process are the identity of the organization that will use that valuation, and the business context in which that valuation is used. These two variables are inextricably linked in determining the final value of the IP.

This is illustrated by the fact that two different organizations using the same methodologies to estimate the value of an item of IP will almost always produce two different values. For example, a valuation done by the company which owns the IP may differ from one done by a potential licensee, since the licenser will (in most cases) want to maximize the compensation received, while the licensee will want to minimize that compensation. Even this rule has its exceptions. In one notable case, the National Institutes of Health intentionally refused to accept an offer for a very lucrative licensing agreement for a pharmaceutical technology because the licensee demanded exclusive rights to the technology. The NIH instead accepted a lower valuation of the IP for a non-exclusive license, because it felt that as a government agency it should encourage broad diffusion of that technology to multiple licensees instead of an exclusive deal.[84]

In the United States, it is assumed that the most "objective" measure of the value of an item of IP is its "fair market value." This is defined as follows:

> Fair market value is the amount at which a property would exchange between a willing buyer and a willing seller, neither being under compulsion, each having full knowledge of all relevant facts, and with equity to both.[85]

In this idealized scenario, the competing interests of the buyer and seller balance out to provide an unbiased valuation. Since a buyer will not purchase an asset for an amount greater than the benefit that he or she would receive from that asset, and a seller will not willingly give up an asset for less than the expected benefit, a second definition is:

> Fair market value is equal to the present value of the future economic benefits of ownership.[86]

---

[84] Cited in a presentation to the Washington, DC chapter of the Technology Transfer Society by Dr. Maria Freire, Director, Technology Transfer Office, National Institutes of Health, 13 March 1997.

[85] Smith and Parr, *Valuation of Intellectual Property and Intangible Assets*, op. cit., p. 144.

[86] Ibid., p. 146.

These two definitions give rise to two of the primary valuation approaches: the market approach and the economic approach.

APPROACHES AND METHODS FOR INTELLECTUAL PROPERTY VALUATION

Since the value of an item as assessed by an individual is largely dependent on the subjective bias of that individual, calculating a value for use in a business transaction requires the use of a formal and logical methodology which can convince others of the validity of that value.   However, there is no single methodology which is best for every case of IP valuation, due to considerations such as access to necessary data, the nature of the IP, and the context of the transaction.   Therefore, IP appraisal experts in the United States have developed several different methods for IP valuation.   New methods are developed to increase the quantitative and objective component of the valuation, and hence eliminate as much as possible subjective, qualitative, and nonrational valuation factors.

Overview of the Four Basic Approaches

Based on a survey of the literature on IP valuation, experts have broken down the various valuation methodologies into four basic groups, or approaches:

- The Heuristic Approach. This approach relies on the "5 and 25 percent rules" and "rules of thumb" or other simple formulas, often with little logical basis, to estimate the value of an item of IP.
- The Cost Approach. This approach is based on the "book value" of an item of IP as it would be recorded on the balance sheet of a company. It equates value with the cost to replace that item of IP with another functionally comparable item.
- The Market Approach. Based on the first definition of "fair market value" given above, this approach posits that if value is determined by the price determined in an open-market transaction, an item of IP can be valued by finding the price assigned to other comparable items of IP in uncontrolled transactions.
- The Economic Approach. Based on the second definition of "fair market value," this approach uses all available data—including discounted cash flow/net present value method and the profit split method—to estimate the actual future cash flows generated by the item of IP over a period of time, as well as a terminal value at the end of that period and convert those figures into a net present value for the item.

Table 6.1 shows the contrasts between the different approaches on four factors: the basis of the value assigned, the source of data analyzed in calculating the valuation, the value captured by the method, and the advantages and disadvantages of the methodology which affect its ability to capture the value of the IP completely and accurately.   As discussed in this section, all four are used in current practice to calculate IP value under different circumstances.

TABLE 6.1
Overview of Four Approaches to IP Valuation

	Heuristic Approach	*Cost Approach*	*Market Approach*	*Economic Approach*
Basis of valuation	Best judgment or industry practice	Cost to reproduce or cost to replace	Price determined in an open market transaction	Value received over time under uncertainty
Data Source	Intuition/ industry experience	Internal accounting statements	Public data on prior transactions	Internal financial data
Value Captured	Best guess or industry average	Past investment minus depreciation and obsolescence	Value as perceived by a rational third party	Expected value received over useful life
Advantages of method	Simple, direct and fast	Data readily available	Accepted view of "fair market value"	Theoretically superior
Limitations of method	Very inaccurate/ unrelated to real value	Excludes premium or discount from market forces	Data difficult to obtain/ comparables not available	Assumptions and expectations may be inaccurate

The exact method chosen for an IP valuation, just as the final value calculated, depends first on the business context of the valuation, and second on the objective of the party conducting the valuation. For example, a valuation done to price a patent for licensing will use a different methodology than one for a tax assessment, since the objective of a license (from the IP holder's perspective) is to maximize the royalty paid by the licensee, while the objective of a tax assessment may be to minimize the royalty paid by the licensee (which will reduce the taxable income of the IP holder).

A third factor in valuation is the regulatory or contractual requirements of the transaction context. For example, valuations for tax assessment require an appraisal by a third-party expert, such as an accountant or an IP valuation consultant.[87] During negotiations for such transactions as interfirm licensing, joint venture formation, or corporate acquisitions, the licensee or purchaser of the IP will usually require that the IP in the deal be priced by an independent appraiser. While the appraiser may have an incentive to manipulate the valuation to favor his or her client, that party also will want to maintain the appearance of impartiality to protect his or her reputation.

---

[87] Weston Anson and Mark Edwards, "A Summary of Current Tax Trends and Issues Affecting Intellectual Property," *Intellectual Property Today*, August 1996.

Finally, the sophistication of the parties in the transaction, and their opinion on the significance of the IP in the transaction, play a major role in the methodology chosen. For example, unsophisticated firms tend to use heuristics such as the "5 percent rule" because they lack the resources or inclination to conduct a sophisticated valuation, or simply because little information is available to establish an exact value.[88]

This section discusses both the theoretical and practical aspects of using various methods grouped under each approach.

The Heuristic Approach and Methods

Heuristics are those methods where a general formula is used to determine the value of the IP without any investigation of the specific details of the IP item itself or its business context. The value is tied only to a very broad algorithm, to observations about the general market environment, or even to little more than the intuition of an expert in the industry or technology field of the IP.

Heuristic Methods of IP Valuation
Primary examples of heuristics include:

- The 5 Percent Rule. This rule sets the royalty for a licensed item of IP (generally a patent) at 5 percent of net sales for the product or business based on that IP. This rate appears in licenses across industries and types of technology and is a historical and traditional rate chosen for its ability to fairly distribute risk and share success between the party who is taking the lead in commercializing a product.[89] Although it should be noted that there is no known explanation why 5 percent is the level chosen.[90]

- The 25 Percent Rule. This rule is a derivative of the 5 percent rule and has been thought to be a reasonable rule for companies making a profit in the 10 percent to 20 percent range. The 25 percent rule relates to profits and the 5 percent rule relates to net sales. For example, assume that $1,000 of product is sold and generates a 20 percent profit, or $200. Twenty-five percent of $200 is $50, which also happens to be 5 percent of net sales (.05x $1,000 = $50). Again, this rule was developed in an attempt to make a fair determination to share risk and success between the developer and the party responsible for commercializing the product. Although fairly simple in explanation, one source has reported that this rule is only for setting royalties in interfirm licensing based upon gross profits of the business unit using the licensed IP. It is thought that this level is meant to recognize the costs of business borne by the licensee, and should not be used in calculating a royalty rate.[91]

- Industry Norm. This method bases the royalty rate on what is believed to be the standard range of royalties for the industry of the business involved (generally expressed as a percentage of net sales).

---

[88] Gordon V. Smith and Russell L. Parr, *Intellectual Property: Licensing and Joint Venture Profit Strategies*, Second Edition (New York: John Wiley & Sons, Inc., 1998), p. 177.

[89] Albert E. Muir, *The Technology Transfer System: Inventions - Marketing – Licensing – Patenting – Setting – Practice - Management – Policy* (New York: Latham Book, 1997).

[90] Ibid., p. 177.

[91] Ibid., p. 173.

Applications of the Heuristic Approach

Heuristics are almost completely discredited as a method for valuing IP, especially by investors. According to one practioner, these methods continue to be used only due to the ignorance of the firms that use them. In many IP-based transactions, the value of the IP is simply not calculated with any great accuracy or detail, according to a consultant. Another IP valuation consultant reports that a significant share of valuations used in transactions are based on "gut feeling."

Although heuristics are inaccurate, unsophisticated, and often misleading, they have the advantage of enabling a firm to conduct its valuation much more quickly than a formal method. Therefore, the heuristic approach can still be used in two general situations. The first is when the appraiser lacks the motivation or information needed to conduct a more sophisticated valuation. In such cases, the parties to a transaction simply use heuristics as a substitute for a full-blown valuation, mostly to save on time and costs.

Second, even a sophisticated firm may use heuristics when it believes that the value of the IP does not justify the investment necessary to do a complete valuation. For example, during his tenure at a major manufacturing firm, one consultant found that asking an experienced business manager the value of the IP under his management yielded an amount that was generally within 20 to 30 percent of the value calculated using a more formal method. Therefore, for less significant businesses (defined by the firm as those with the potential for $2 million or less in annual revenues), the business manager's estimate of IP value was used in place of a comprehensive valuation. An industry technology transfer executive notes that in that firm, the company will generally not do a formal valuation for very standard technologies (such as biological research materials), especially if they have a revenue potential of $50,000 or less.

The Cost Approach and Methods

The cost approach values IP based on how much investment is required to develop that item of IP, or one which is functionally the same. The question of the actual economic benefit of owning the IP is not addressed. Instead, "it is an inherent assumption with this approach that economic benefits indeed exist and are of sufficient amount and duration to justify the developmental expenditures."[92] This assumption itself is not always valid, revealing a major limitation of the cost approach. While an item of IP may cost a considerable amount to develop, the actual economic benefits of that IP can be eliminated by external events. For example, a particular technology can be superseded by a more advanced technology, which reduces the value of the IP for the older technology. This concept of "economic obsolescence" is omitted from the cost approach, as shown below.

---

[92] Russell L. Parr and Gordon V. Smith, "Quantitative Methods of Valuing Intellectual Property," op cit., *The New Role of Intellectual Property in Commercial Transactions*, pp. 39-68.

Cost-based Methods for Valuing IP

There are two basic methods for valuing the cost of an item of IP. Both methods can be used to achieve an estimate of the fair market value of the IP.

- Cost of Reproduction New (CRN). This method calculates the actual amount invested as if the company is creating the same item of IP again. The total expenditures for all developmental activities and investments (such as labor, R&D costs, overhead, and administrative costs) make up the "book value" of the IP.
- Cost of Reproduction (COR). This method uses the cost required to develop an item of IP which is u in function and potential to the item being valued. For example, if a technology is protected by a patent, then the value of that patent is the cost that a competitor would have to spend to develop that technology without violating the patent (called "inventing around" the patent), plus a premium to represent the opportunity cost given that the competitor will be late to market.

It is readily apparent that these two methods will produce different values, since the first (CRN) measures the cost of creating exactly the same IP being valued, while the other (COR) measures the cost of creating a different item of IP with equal utility. For example, the COR amount for a patent will be much less than the CRN if it is relatively easy for a firm to "invent around" that patent. If the cost of "inventing around" the patent is much less than the cost of reproducing that patent, a firm will instead create the substitute.

In both of these cases, the estimated cost is only the first step in obtaining a useful financial value for the IP. As with any other asset recorded at "book value", the effects of time must be applied to the asset value using accepted methods for depreciation of intangible assets (such as the straight-line method, etc.). Different classes of intangible assets are depreciated at different rates; for example, in 1997 the Financial Accounting Standards Board officially declared that software can be depreciated over 36 months.

To obtain the fair market value of an item of IP using the cost-based methods, an appraiser first takes the COR or CRN, then subtracts the appropriate amount for the physical depreciation of that item. Then, an estimated amount for "functional obsolescence" is subtracted; this amount represents the fact that newer technology or IP may supersede the item being valued. Finally, an amount for "economic obsolescence", representing the extent to which the general economic environment may devalue the IP.

For example, a patent which is used in a particular industry will decline in value if the profitability of that industry falls significantly. Therefore:

$$\text{Fair Market Value (FMV)} = \text{COST} - \text{PD} - \text{FO} - \text{EO}$$

Where COST is calculated with either the CRN or COR method, PD is physical depreciation, FO is functional obsolescence, and EO is economic obsolescence. [93]

---

[93] Smith and Parr, *Valuation of Intellectual Property and Intangible Assets*, op. cit., p. 199.

Applications of the Cost Approach

In using this FMV, an additional factor could be applied to represent the time value of money. For example, if a firm is licensing a technology from another firm, the licensee will add some amount on top of the FMV to compensate the licensor for the time as well as funds that it invested in the technology.

The cost approach has several limitations, as outlined by Smith and Parr:

- The cost approach does not account for the effect of demand, commercialization effort, and other external variables on IP value.
- The cost approach does not address the timing of the benefits received from the IP, which may have its own value to the IP holder.
- The duration of economic benefit is not calculated, so the cost approach does not help to predict when the IP's usefulness has ended.
- The risk involved in commercializing the IP is not generally included in the analysis.
- The actual factors to be used to estimate the effects of obsolescence are difficult to identify and calculate.[94]

Despite these drawbacks, the cost approach is still used in some cases. In particular, for emerging technologies where the actual market potential is unknown, the cost approach may be the only valid method for valuing the IP in those technologies. One notable case cited by a senior consultant is the purchase of the original DOS (disk operating system) software by Bill Gates in the early days of Microsoft. Gates paid the inventor of DOS only $10,000, but that investment went on to generate hundreds of billions of dollars of value for Microsoft. Since no one at the time of the transaction could have predicted the impact and success of DOS and its descendants, Gates was perfectly justified in simply estimating the cost of developing DOS and paying its inventor that amount plus a small profit. Another consulting firm executive notes that COR is useful for pricing a tightly focused technology or in consumer goods, where reasonable substitutes exist for the item being valued.

The Market Approach and Methods

Market approach methodologies base the value of the IP on the value assessed by the open market for that type of IP, following the first definition of "fair market value." This approach assumes that the market operates efficiently and with near-perfect information flows, and therefore will judge the value of a class of IP better than any individual. In reality, of course, there are various factors which lead a particular open-market transaction to distort the true value of the IP being exchanged. This is the major weakness of the market approach.

---

[94] Ibid., pp. 203-204.

Market-based Methods of IP Valuation

There are three generally accepted varieties of methodologies which conform to the principles of the market approach:

- Comparable Transaction. This method compares the IP being valued to other IP that have been exchanged in prior licensing deals where the terms of that exchange are known. It then calculates value based on the royalty rates from licenses for IP deemed most *comparable* to the IP being valued. While some comparable transactions can be found from within the firm which owns the IP being valued, the most objective data source is a market transaction between two unrelated firms (also called the Comparable Uncontrolled Transaction or CUT method).
- Comparable Profits. The Comparable Profits Method (CPM) looks at businesses which are deemed comparable to the business based on the IP being valued, using such factors as market coverage and competitive strength. The average profit margin for businesses in that industry is calculated, and subtracted from the profit margin for the "comparable" business. The value of the IP is set at some fraction of that difference. An alternate approach is to find two companies, one with IP comparable to the IP being valued and one without, and to use the difference in their profit margins as the *excess earnings* that the IP produces.
- Residual Value. This approach takes the *market value* of the business being valued (the market stock price of the firm multiplied by the number of shares outstanding) and subtracts the net working capital (monetary assets) of the firm and the *book value* of is tangible assets to derive the value of the intangible assets of the firm. This value is then allocated among different types of intangible assets possessed by the firm, including software, human assets, business practices, and customer goodwill. The allocation process involves analyzing the variation in performance with other comparable firms to isolate the economic contribution of each type of intangible asset. Thus, the value of the IP portfolio of the firm is the *residual value* remaining after all other assets have been accounted for.

Applications of the Market Approach

The market approach is probably the most widely used mechanism for valuation, as most business representatives agree that the market is the most efficient mechanism for determining the *true* value of IP. There are two major problems in using this method. First, firms generally keep the terms of their licensing agreements confidential, so the actual price of IP in the market may be unknown. Ernst & Young has analyzed Securities and Exchange Commission filings to compile a database of 8,500 licensing agreements which can be searched to find the market price of *comparable* IP.

Second, it is often difficult to find a truly "comparable" item of IP for the one being valued. IP licensed in past agreements may differ in several aspects. Ernst & Young looks at several variables in each licensing agreement to determine the extent to which the IP licensed is comparable to the one being valued, including:

- Industry or field of use
- Term of the licensing agreement
- Exclusivity

- Termination clauses
- Technical assistance
- Relationship among parties
- Technology or type of product/IP
- Geographic coverage
- Sublicensing
- Use of trademarks or trade names
- Payment terms and structure

Any differences between a licensing agreement analyzed and the proposed transaction for the IP being valued affects the degree to which the prior agreement can be used as a market comparable for determining price.[95] An executive with an economics consulting firm points out that licenses are often discounted for the possibility that the IP contained in them are not completely valid or may be easily infringed, so they may not capture the full economic value of the IP.

While the comparable transactions method looks at licensing agreements for discrete items or bundles of IP, the comparable profits method looks at IP value as part of the integrated operating capabilities of the firm. It essentially values the effect of IP on the overall performance of a business, which captures more than the value of the specific IP itself. For example, comparable profits indicate to some extent the level of effort and success in commercializing the IP, not simply the strength of the IP. The difficulties in implementing this method are first, finding a publicly traded firm whose IP is truly comparable to the IP being valued (as in the comparable transactions method); and second, calculating a valid "normal" industry profit level for comparison, or finding a comparable firm with no IP which is used as the benchmark.

Residual value is used primarily in business valuations, since it uses econometric formulae which are familiar to financial advisors hired by institutional investors, takeover artists, and acquiring firms. In more general IP valuations, residual value is not commonly used because the methods for valuing non-IP intangible assets are not well-established and require more refinement before they will be accepted by IP valuation experts.

The Economic Approach and Methods

One weakness of the market approach is that it assumes that the market judges the true value of the IP. In many cases, the value assigned by the market to an IP business is due to factors other than the value of the actual IP.

For example, CUT can skew the calculated value of the IP because the transactions surveyed may have special licensing clauses which affect the royalty rate established in those agreements. The economic approach is based

---

[95] J. Merwin and R. Warner, "Techniques for Obtaining and Analyzing External License Agreements," in Russell L. Parr and Patrick A. Sullivan (eds.), *Technology Licensing: Corporate Strategies for Maximizing Value* (New York: John Wiley & Sons, Inc., 1996), pp. 187-206.

on calculating the true benefit enjoyed by the firm which owns the IP, not on the value perceived by an external market. This is most often accomplished through a detailed financial analysis of the business utilizing the IP, integrating known data with forecasts of expected revenues and/or profits.

The weakness of the economic approach is that it tends to treat the value of the business and the value of the technology as conceptually equal by using equal discount rates. In fact, since discount rates are based largely on risk, and since the business risk and the technology risk of a firm may not be the same, the business value can differ substantially from the IP value.

Economic-based Methods of Valuing IP

- Discounted Cash Flow (DCF). This set of methods refers to any which calculates the basic Net Present Value (NPV) of the IP by projecting the future cash flows from that IP over a series of years and discounting those flows by a specific discount rate, such as the Weighted Average Cost of Capital for the business. Following traditional financial analysis methods, the NPV of a capital investment is calculated as:

$$NPV = \sum_{t=0}^{n} [CF_t /(1+k)^t]$$

In this equation, *t* refers to a specific time period (generally one year), *k* is the cost of capital during that period expressed as a percentage, and *CF*$_t$ is the expected cash flow (in or out) in period *t*. A net outflow of cash in a period is expressed as a negative number, while a net inflow is a positive number. In the context of valuing a patented technology, outflows of cash would include the royalties paid as part of the license, as well as the capital investment needed to integrated that technology into a product or process. Inflows of cash would include revenues generated or costs saved using the technology in a product or process. Note that while the cost of capital for a project may vary over time, for simplicity most companies assume that the cost of capital is a constant.
- Profit Split Method (PSM). This method simply splits the profits earned by the business using a piece of IP between the licensor and the licensee, based on the relative contribution of each to the technical and commercial success of the IP. These contributions are based on the amount that each invests towards the full development of a commercial product from the IP, including research and development, marketing costs, distribution networks, and advertising.

These methods can also integrate other factors to change the calculated value of the IP based on characteristics of the underlying technology (in the case of patents). According to Udell and Potter some factors to consider are:[96]

- The importance of the invention. This refers to the significance of the technology in the context of its surrounding product or process. A technology which makes a

---

[96] Gerald G. Udell and Thomas A. Potter, "Pricing New Technology," *Research-Technology Management*, July-August 1991, pp. 14-18.

small modification to a product or process is likely to have a lower value than one which results in a substantial improvement.

- The strength of IP protection. The type of intellectual property right used to protect the technology may vary in its strength, as in the choice to protect software IP using copyright or patents.
- Competitive structure of market (and licensee). If the new technology is used in a market which already has a dominant competitor with high barrier to entry, it is less likely that the technology will result in commercial success. Of course, if the dominant competitor is the licensee, it may be willing to pay a higher royalty rate because it could then block potential competitors from using that technology.
- Investment required to commercialize the technology. The scale of investment can affect the uncertainty of the overall NPV, since the larger the investment required, the greater the uncertainty that exploiting the technology will pay off for the licensee.
- Stage of development. Related to the above factor, technologies which are in early development stages face greater uncertainty that they can be successfully developed for commercial use. Therefore, less-developed technologies will be valued lower than those which are ready for commercialization.
- The competitive advantage offered by the technology. Similar to the first factor, which deals with the technical benefits of the technology, this factor address the market advantage realized by using the technology, such as reduced product price, improved ease of use, and other features.
- The profit margin resulting from use of the technology. Since royalty rates are generally set as a percentage of net sales, the increase in the gross profit margin of the licensee will raise the potential royalty rate.
- The extent of the innovation. Some new technologies, such as the semiconductor, can revolutionize entire industries. More radical innovations promise greater benefits, but are also more uncertain, because the success of those innovations depends on a huge range of factors.

For mainstream IP appraisers, especially in the accounting profession, the Discounted Cash Flow method is viewed as the first-best approach for deriving IP value. Therefore, it is used most heavily in transactions where the parties depend on the advice of accountants, such as business loan calculation, venture capital financing, and mergers and acquisitions (including leveraged buyouts). The key to this method is the calculation of the proper discount rate.

The Profit Split Method is useful in any business where two or more firms share ownership of an IP item, through assignment or licensing. Since it depends on the actual income from that IP, it is easy to audit the appropriate amounts that each firm should receive from the joint venture or licensing agreement. This method is also described in the regulations of the Internal Revenue Service as an acceptable method for valuing IP in transfer pricing situations. However, according to an accounting firm executive experienced in such cases, the actual implementation of the Profit Split Method requires reporting extremely detailed financial information which makes it a difficult method to use in practice.

COMPARISON OF THE FOUR BASIC APPROACHES

In general, these four approaches have continued to evolve toward an ideal level of technical sophistication which captures the comprehensive value of IP to a business.   However, the more advanced methods in the market and economic approaches are also more difficult to use, because they involve gathering information which is not readily available or forecasting cash flows which are difficult to predict. Figure 6.1 illustrates the relationship among the four approaches in terms of their difficulty of use and technical sophistication.

Figure 6.1
Comparison of Four Basic Approaches

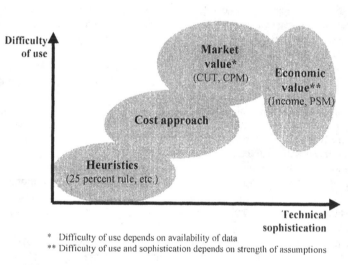

*   Difficulty of use depends on availability of data
** Difficulty of use and sophistication depends on strength of assumptions

©1998 Washington| CORE

One way to increase the accuracy of IP valuation is to combine the various approaches and identify the area where the resulting values overlap. One such hybrid, the relief from royalty method, combines market approach methods to balance the economic approach methods for a more exact judgment of IP value.

The "relief from royalty" method represents the state-of-the-art in IP valuation, in terms of technical sophistication and conceptual clarity. The IP value is calculated using the DCF method of the economic approach. Then, methods from the market approach, including CUT and CPM, are used to calculate a range of fair market values for the IP. The final IP value is set as a point where the appraised economic value and market value match. According to IP valuation experts, relief from royalty is the most widely recognized method in their profession for obtaining a valid estimate of IP value. However, most of their clients do not fully understand the significance of this method compared to those of other approaches. Therefore, while it is used for all types of business transactions, it is still used in a relatively small share of transactions, because only the most sophisticated firms will pay the cost of conducting such a valuation.

Figure 6.2
Sample Valuation Investigation Process

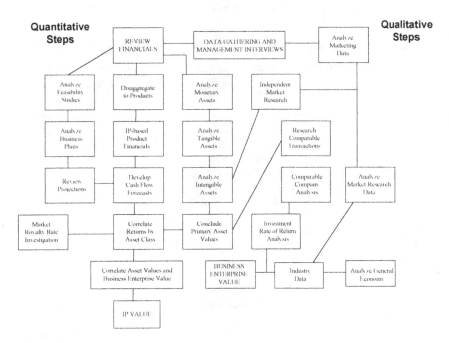

Source: Smith and Parr (1999).

Figure 6.2 shows how a number of approaches and methods can be combined in a typical IP valuation process. This approach integrates the use of comparable transactions, comparable profits, discounted cash flow, and residual value methods. According to various experts, the process outlined in this figure is much more comprehensive than most IP valuations conducted in the field, and also in the opinion of Wes Anson, is a somewhat outdated procedure because of its reliance on older financial analysis methods and data. Still, it is a good illustration of how a variety of approaches help to inform the development of a comprehensive IP valuation.

APPLICATION OF IP VALUATION IN BUSINESS TRANSACTIONS

As stated above, IP valuation is generally not performed, and also not very meaningful, unless motivated by some business transaction. The valuation is designed to serve the ends of the appraising party in the negotiations surrounding that transaction. Therefore, whether intended or not, the final value obtained for IP will vary depending on the underlying business context. This section describes some common situations where IP valuation is necessary, and how those situations affect the conduct of the valuation and its result.

Business Situations Requiring IP Valuation

There are a number of business situations where a firm might need to provide a quantitative and valid financial value for its intellectual property, including:

- Intrafirm transfers of IP. Exchanges among subsidiaries of a firm or between a holding company and its related firms (commonly referred to as transfer pricing).
- Interfirm transfers of IP. Exchanges between two unrelated firms, such as in a license, or the transfer of IP by two firms within a cooperative context, such as the formation of a joint venture or strategic alliance.
- IP valuations within the context of an overall business valuation. Situations where an enterprise with significant IP holdings is being valued. Such situations include valuation for a loan (using IP in as collateral in a security agreement), valuation for liquidation (as in a bankruptcy or foreclosure), valuation for a merger or acquisition, and valuation for the assessment of estate taxes.[97]

This section deals with common transactions in all three categories. Again, as has been noted, the choice of IP valuation method depends in large part on the type of business transaction which motivates the valuation. Very few, if any, businesses value their IP just to have that knowledge—there is almost always in mind some final transaction for exploiting that IP. The exact method used in a transaction is selected based on several factors, such as any regulatory requirements (for example, the Internal Revenue Service specifies which methods are acceptable for transfer pricing analysis), the preference of the other parties in a transaction (such as an investment bank for a merger and acquisition, or a potential licensee), and common industry practices which have evolved over the years.

Table 6.2 shows which methods are most commonly used in different transactions, based on conversations with IP appraisal consultants and a review of the literature. Discussions about why each particular transaction tends to use a specific set of methods are presented in the following sections.

---

[97] Misrack, op. cit.

Table 6.2
Commonly Used Methods by Business Context

Method	Interfirm Transactions		Tax Assessment	Business Valuation	
	Inter-firm License	Joint Venture	Transfer Pricing	Investment/ Financing	Mergers & Acquisitions
Heuristics					
25 Percent Rule	✓				
5 Percent Rule	✓				
Industry Norm	✓				
Cost Approach					
Cost of Reprod. New		✓		✓	
Cost of Replacement	✓			✓	✓
Market Approach					
Comparable Transaction	✓	✓	✓	✓	✓
Comparable Profits	✓	✓	✓	✓	✓
Residual Value					✓
Economic Approach					
Discounted Cash Flow		✓		✓	✓
Profit Split Method	✓	✓			
Hybrid Approaches					
Relief from Royalty	✓			✓	✓

Intrafirm Transfers: Transfer Pricing and Holding Companies

When two affiliated firms (through a parent-subsidiary relationship or holding company-affiliate relationship) exchange goods or services, they have the opportunity to structure the transaction in a way which creates substantial tax benefits to the corporation as a whole. By overpricing the transaction, income is transferred away from the unit facing the highest corporate tax rate and to the unit with the lowest corporate tax rate. As an example, take the case where a U.S. corporation has a foreign subsidiary in Ireland, a nation with a very low corporate tax rate. If the Irish subsidiary creates some item of IP, it can then license that IP to its U.S. parent. If the license is structured so that the parent is paying a very high royalty, then that royalty is recorded as an expense on the U.S. parent's income statement and as revenue on the Irish subsidiary's statement.

This reduces the taxable income of the U.S. parent, and increases the taxable income of the subsidiary. Since the Irish unit faces a lower corporate income tax rate, the overall tax paid by the corporation is reduced. Figure 6.3 illustrates this use of transfer pricing to avoid taxation.

U.S. federal tax regulations over transfer pricing started early in the 20th century, but assumed their present form with the Tax Reform Act of 1968.[98] This law amended Section 482 of the Internal Revenue Code to require that the value of a transfer of intangible assets is "commensurate with the income attributable" to those assets. The IRS issued a white paper on inter-company pricing in October 1988, and based on the responses to that report, proposed three methods for setting transfer prices: the Comparable Uncontrolled Transactions method (the same as the Comparable Transactions method described earlier), the Comparable Profits Method, and the Profit Split Method. The final regulations implementing Section 482 were issued on July 1, 1994.

Transfer pricing happens in domestic as well as international IP transactions. Due to favorable Delaware state tax laws regarding intangible assets, a company can choose to form a Delaware Investment Holding Company (DIHC), an entity which is incorporated in the state of Delaware but whose operations are centered elsewhere. The company transfers ownership all of its intangible assets to the DIHC, which then licenses out those assets out to its affiliated operating companies for a royalty.

---

[98] Information in this paragraph is taken from Gordon V. Smith and Russell L. Parr, *Valuation of Intellectual Property and Intangible Assets, Second Edition, 1998 Cumulative Supplement* (New York: John Wiley & Sons, 1998), pp. 31-40.

Figure 6.3
Transfer Pricing as a Form of Tax Avoidance

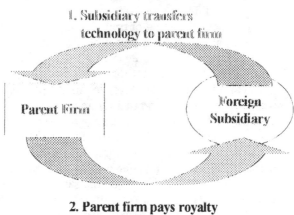

1. Subsidiary transfers
technology to parent firm

Parent Firm

Foreign
Subsidiary

**2. Parent firm pays royalty
to subsidiary firm**

**3. Parent firm taxable income reduced:
Taxable income=original income-royalty**

The royalties on those licenses are recorded as an expense for the operating companies, reducing their tax liability in their state of operation. Various state tax authorities now have their own rules on transfer pricing across state and national borders.

The IRS regulations focus on establishing prices based on (1) fair market value, as determined by (2) an "arm's-length" transaction between two unrelated parties of (3) a "comparable" intangible asset. The concept of "comparability" focuses on the following aspects of the transaction or its participants:

- Function (the role of the parties in developing and using the IP asset)
- Contractual terms (compensation, warranties, technical support, exclusivity, etc.)
- Risks (all considerations of business and financial risk factored into the transaction)
- Economic conditions (similarity of industry, product market, and geographic market for the transaction)
- Property or service (direct comparison of the asset in the transaction to the asset being valued)

These principles show that the U.S. Internal Revenue Service favors the market approach over others in transfer pricing cases. This is apparently because the IRS prefers a method which relies primarily on external data, not on internal corporate data. Using external data allows the IRS to confirm the value of the intellectual property independent of data supplied by the firm.

While the regulations state that the IRS will accept "other" methods of valuation, an accounting firm executive notes that in an IRS investigation, the taxpayer must first show why it cannot use one of the three prescribed methods before it can apply a different method. For convenience, most companies simply use the CUT method instead of trying to apply a different method. One executive notes that it is often not possible to find an exact comparable transaction, but it is a better use of time to find a reasonably-similar transaction and modify the price according to the differences, rather than to use a completely different method. The Profit Split Method is viewed as more accurate, but accountants have found that the regulatory requirements for using this method are too burdensome. The objective of a transfer pricing analysis is not necessarily to get the correct value for the IP, but to get a value which is the most defensible in an IRS investigation or tax litigation.

The valuation of IP using a transfer pricing method will generate a value different from other methods used to value the same IP in a different business context. The IRS requires that the value from a transfer pricing analysis be comparable or related to the value generated by a previous valuation process. For example, if a firm had received an offer from a third party to license a patent, the transfer price assigned to that patent should be roughly similar to the offer, but not necessarily the same. An accounting firm executive mentions that in almost every transfer pricing case she has worked on, the client firm does not have any existing estimate of the IP value. Now, however, the IRS does require firms to maintain a record of their transfer pricing valuations every year so that in case of an investigation, the IRS has an existing set of data that they can examine.

Interfirm Transfers: Licensing and Joint Venture Formation

In licensing transactions between unrelated parties, actual valuation practices vary widely. IP appraisal experts state that heuristics, especially the 25 percent rule or the 5 percent rule, are still used frequently. One problem that arises is that because these heuristics are so common, many industries have royalty rates which average 5 percent of gross sales. Thus, when an appraiser tries to find comparable transactions in that industry for a market-based valuation, the result is likely to come out to 5 percent for completely non-logical reasons. As a result, one consultant states that his firm does not even consider transactions more than three years old when doing a market-based valuation, because those transactions almost invariably are based on the 5 percent rule.

Among companies which are involved in significant licensing activity, most turn to a consulting firm such as Consor in San Diego, the IPC Group in Chicago, and AUS Consultants in New Jersey. These firms have their own proprietary valuation techniques and guidelines, generally focusing on the market approach, the economic approach, or a hybrid. (As stated earlier, the cost approach is used only with emerging technologies.) The consultants stress, however, that they will first meet with the client and develop a unique valuation procedure based on the particular situation, affected by such factors as the business objective, availability of data, and nature of the transaction. There is, however, a fairly logical flow of questions that are answered during a valuation. For example, in any analysis of an external licensing agreement, the most important factors determining comparability are the industry of use, the nature of the technology transferred (including any ancillary assets or services, such as training), and whether or not the agreement is exclusive. After that, there are minor considerations which determine the risk borne by the parties to the transaction, such as how much more investment is needed to commercialize the IP.

Another key consideration in the valuation of IP for licensing is the structure of the royalty or other compensation. For example, an agreement could require that the licensee also sign a supply contract with the licensor. A valuation consultant mentioned a recent case where the transaction involved an advance fee, the receipt of equity in a joint venture, stock warrants for when the joint venture holds an initial public offering, and other mechanisms. The firm needed to calculate the present value of each element of the compensation and compare the total to the overall value of the IP, to see if the two values were roughly equal.

Firms that principally license out IP are also fairly experienced in IP valuation. Two representatives of public-sector tech transfer organizations mentioned that their staff is trained in IP valuation. Still, they also rely on consultants to conduct valuations in particularly significant or complex negotiations.

IP is playing a more significant role in joint-venture formation. U.S. firms are now commonly contributing only IP to joint ventures established in foreign countries, rather than contributing monetary or tangible assets. According to industry experts, firms almost always choose to receive equity as compensation for IP contributed to a joint venture, as this has tax advantages over transferring IP through a license or a financing arrangement. The basic method of valuation is to analyze the net present value of the joint venture with the IP contribution and without, and estimate the excess earnings enabled by the IP. Since many joint ventures involve research and development on emerging technologies, the cost approach is also used.

IP in Business Valuation: Collateral, Venture Capital, and Mergers and Acquisitions

IP transactions integrated as part of larger corporate financings or transactions are also more common, as IP plays a larger part in the valuation of firms. As a result, loan officers, investment bankers, and venture capitalists are increasing their use of external IP valuation consultants. The head of a leading consulting firm reports that he has been retained by bankers for IP valuation in the liquidation or restructuring of several major bankrupt firms, including a department store chain and a publishing house. Banks traditionally took a very conservative view of IP for use as collateral in financing. There are three recent changes to that attitude. First, banks find that more of their financing business involves firms with significant IP assets. Therefore, they are taking a more sophisticated view of IP valuation and are more willing to accept IP as collateral. Second, changes in the Uniform Commercial Code have standardized the process of "perfecting" IP, under which IP is used as the basis for a security agreement in a financing transaction. Third, with the increase in general licensing activity, IP is now viewed as a more liquid asset than before, so banks have a greater ability to collect money from a foreclosure where the collateral was predominantly IP.

In the venture-capital world, there is substantial recognition of the value that IP contributes to the overall value of a start-up firm. Still, venture capitalists themselves do not depend on formal IP valuations when calculating the value of a start-up firm for investment purposes. According to one industry executive, whose company often solicits venture capital for start-up firms using transferred technology, most venture capitalists will depend first on their knowledge of the industry and their assessment of the start-up's management team when assigning a value to the start-up. As part of the due diligence process to assess the firm's prospects, the venture capitalists will examine its IP portfolio and IP protection, but the IP value is only rarely a major factor in the overall firm valuation.

In preparation for an initial public offering, venture capital firms will occasionally hire IP valuation firms to conduct a discounted cash flow analysis of key IP items. The DCF method is chosen mainly because it is familiar to the investment bankers and investors who attend the start-up's "road show" (the series of presentations marketing the IPO to investors). For complex investments where IP is a major factor, venture capitalists will ask for a hybrid approach or similar sophisticated valuation.

The investment banking community is also using more sophisticated approaches to IP valuation, when necessary. Two different consulting firms report that their business with investment bankers in merger and acquisition transactions has increased significantly in the past three years. As noted earlier, investment bankers in the 1980s and early 1990s preferred using simulations and modeling techniques such as the Monte Carlo method. Today, they are using the same methods as IP valuation experts, focusing on the market approach and the economic approach. However, according to a partner at a technology-focused mergers and acquisition advisory firm in California, the finance community focuses mostly on overall business value and business risk in estimating the value of a merger transaction. While IP can have a large effect on business value, the business issues are of an overriding concern.

One example, cited by an experienced consultant in the IP valuation field, is a recent acquisition by Texas Instruments (TI) of Amati, a digital signal processing semiconductor firm. Amati had annual sales before the merger of $40 million. The final transaction price for the acquisition by TI was $395 million, well above even the market value of Amati. The reason for the high selling price was that Amati's value to TI was contained in the synergy between

Amati's IP portfolio and the IP held by TI, not in its other tangible or intangible assets. Therefore, while another firm would have valued Amati at a much lower level, the combination of TI and Amati had an extremely high value.

Some IP experts criticize investment bankers for their inability to distinguish between business valuation and IP valuation. Representatives of one consulting firm believe that in a merger and acquisition deal, IP valuation only makes sense when it is conducted in the context of the other intangible and tangible assets of the acquiring firm.

CURRENT U.S. PERSPECTIVES ON THE VALUATION OF INTELLECTUAL PROPERTY

While the mainstream of U.S. industry is still not very aware of IP valuation and its related issues, the leading-edge companies and consulting firms in the field continue to push the practice of IP valuation forward. The following are some broad trends mentioned by the interview subjects:

- IP valuation experts continue to refine quantitative methods and reduce the dependence on qualitative and subjective factors in determining values.
- IP valuation is now linked to the new movement focused on valuing "intellectual capital," which is introducing economic theory on the nature and value of knowledge to the practice of IP valuation;
- IP valuation is an active business in the United States, as more consulting firms develop proprietary approaches and software to assist firms in the management, valuation and exploitation of their IP portfolios.

The Refinement of Quantitative Methods

As previously discussed, early attempts to value IP depended almost entirely on qualitative and subjective factors. With the increased financial significance of IP, current practice has shifted more and more to quantitative methods. Where qualitative or subjective judgments are called for, such as estimating future cash flows, experts are attempting to integrate quantitative analysis with those judgments to make them as logically and mathematically sound as possible.

Much of this work involves current efforts by economists to isolate and value other types of intangible assets besides intellectual property. Economists have conducted research into the nature of what is called "Tobin's Q" (named for economist Arthur Tobin), which is the ratio of a firm's market value to its book value. Instead of using the comparable profits method for valuing intangibles, as described earlier, these economists are first trying to determine which intangibles can be valued and which cannot, and looking at ways of valuing some intangibles with nonfinancial but still quantitative measures (such as comparisons of asset strength).

Intellectual Property and Intellectual Capital

The movement to value intellectual property and other intangibles has been given great momentum by recent works on the nature of intellectual capital (IC). Leif Edvinsson, a Swedish business executive who is at the forefront of this movement, defines IC as "intellectual assets which generate new value." IC encompasses the complementary assets which firms use to exploit knowledge and intellectual property, such as human assets and knowledge-sharing processes.

This has increased attention on valuing IP not in isolation, but as part of a system involving other intangibles. For example, some firms are now increasing the valuation of certain IP because they understand that the exploitation of that IP is dependent on the unique human resources in their firms. For example, software firms which acquire new technologies without their inventors find that they are often unable to utilize those technologies effectively. Thus, in one recent transaction, Microsoft Corporation valued its acquisition of Firefly, an artificial intelligence software firm, higher than normal because Firefly's CEO agreed to move to Redmond and join Microsoft.

In another example, a well-known consultant in the biotech valuation field, Dr. Ron Johnson, has put together with his partner, Mr. Peter Allison, a "do-it-yourself" Excel® spreadsheet. This utility is available for free at their website; the address is http://www.biogeneticventures.com. The spreadsheet factors in almost all of the variables for determining valuation in the biotechnology area, including factors such as market data, number of clinical trial subjects, duration of the phase of the clinical trial, patent fees, patient fees, animal studies, FDA approval costs, and manufacturing and marketing costs, among others. Lastly, they figure in common royalty rates, and then add a novel risk-over-time factor, which more accurately shows the reduction in risk as certain milestones are met and achieved. This variant of a risk-adjusted Net Present Value (r-NPV) approach was found to be so striking and novel an approach that it was published in both *Nature Biotechnology* (Sept. 27, 2001, Vol. 19, No. 9, pp. 813–817), and *Red Herring* magazine (Mar. 2002, pp. 92-93).

In the *Nature Biotechnology* article, it lays out the details of some of the factors and how enough knowledge and industry standards have accrued upon which to build a foundation of an accurate valuation. They basically estimate a value based on a combination of risk-adjustment and discounting the anticipated cash flow.

For example, certain markets are fairly well-known and stable and thus are capable of supporting assumptions concerning cost. In clinical testing, they cite data that per patient Phase I testing costs (healthy human toxicity studies) and Phase II testing costs (humans suffering from the disease to be treated) to be about $12,000, respectively. They also cite data from the Pharmaceutical Manufacturing and Research Association (PhMRA) concerning the average number of patients in a trial (Phase I, 20-80; Phase II, 100-300; Phase III, 1000-5000), the average number of years to get FDA approval (9), and the risk mitigation over time as various FDA phases are achieved (Preclinical, 10%;

Phase I, 20%; Phase II 30%; Phase III, 67%; and FDA, 81%). Upon consideration of these and other factors, they built a formula that provides a valuation as soon as variables are entered:

$$rNPV = R_0 \left({}_{npv}P - \sum_{i=0}^{n} {}_{npv}C_i / R_i \right)$$

As stated in the *Red Herring* article, biotech is a $12 billion business in the United States, with well over 300 drugs on the market, and companies have pushed a sufficient number of products through the approval process. These facts provide for the continued development of excellent valuation approaches, such as the example above, and have served to establish the legitimacy of the private and public funding process for these companies. In turn, in means that specialized mechanisms for injecting liquidity into a situation, such as stock for services, can be intelligently undertaken by all players.

THE BUSINESS OF IP VALUATION

IP valuation is now becoming a successful consulting service. All of the IP consultants interviewed for this report stated that their revenues have increased substantially in the past two to five years. These firms are now increasing the usability of their services to reach a broader audience. For example, one consulting firm has developed a software program that guides firms through various IP valuation processes, and includes a license to use that software on an on-going basis. There is also an emerging market for software systems that track and analyze firm IP portfolios. These new products indicate that awareness of IP value is growing into a broad market among U.S. corporations, rather than simply a specialized niche service. The proliferation of "knowledge management" services offered by management consulting firms also shows that the attention to the value of intangible assets goes beyond simple intellectual property, and to other forms of knowledge such as organizational processes and tacit know-how.

Chapter 7

Financial Rules and Regulations Primer: A Brief Overview

For professional service firms to accept equity in their clients, these firms need a solid understanding of the laws and regulations governing financial transactions in privately held companies. In particular, firms should be aware of the investment guidelines promulgated by the Securities and Exchange Commission, as well as the tax considerations for such investments based on Internal Revenue Service rules. Many of the law firms which have engaged in equity-for-services arrangements for many years are specialists in securities law, and have adequate expertise to navigate these rules with little problem. For professional service firms outside the corporate law practice, it is important to ensure a full understanding of all of these rules before entering into an investment or an equity-for-services deal. This chapter provides a very brief and superficial overview of both of these areas; firms, which are considering taking equity in a start-up client, are of course advised to consult with a professional in securities and/or tax law to determine exactly which rules will apply to a given transaction.

OVERVIEW: SECURITIES LAW AND REGULATION FOR PRIVATE OFFERINGS OF STOCK

Professional service firms, which receive equities from nonpublic firms are perhaps at the most risk for running afoul of securities laws. The purpose of the laws governing private equity transactions is to protect both the investor and the entrepreneur from manipulation or outright fraud, as well as to protect future private or public investors. By accepting stock, either through an investment in conjunction with other compensation or directly as payment for services, the professional service provider becomes an outside investor in the client firm. As such, both the client and the service provider must comply with Federal and state securities laws in issuing the stock used in the transaction.

There are essentially two major types of requirements that must be met in providing a private placement of stock. The first is that the emerging firm must obtain an exemption from registration before conducting the transaction. Otherwise, the firm will be treated by regulators as having conducted a public offering of stock, and will then be liable for violating all of the rules associated with such an offering. The common penalty for such violations is that the emerging firm must return all proceeds from the offering, plus attorneys' fees and other considerations. In other words, if a start-up offers a law firm stock in exchange for services, failure to obtain an exemption could require the start-up to pay in cash for those services, plus associated penalties.

To avoid this condition, start-ups can establish an exemption from registration under SEC Rule 506 of Regulation D, identified by the Securities Act of 1933. This rule provides a set of guidelines for a "safe harbor" protecting the start-up from typical registration requirements. A second benefit of using Section 506 exemption, compared to other exemptions contained in the same regulation, is that state securities laws tend to accept Section 506 exemptions as meeting the state's own exemption rules.

To meet the safe harbor requirements, the start-up must maintain records that it has met the conditions of Rule 506. These conditions include:

- That the offering be made without any means of "general solicitation."
- That the offering be made to no more than 35 persons who are not "accredited investors" and that each of those non-accredited investors be financially sophisticated (that is, has such knowledge and experience in financial and business matters that he or she is capable of evaluating the merits and risks of the investment),
- That if the offering is made to any non-accredited investors, the same detailed disclosures required in comparable public offerings be made.
- That a Form D be filed with the Securities and Exchange Commission and the securities administrators of each state with a similar exemption, and in which the offering is made, within 15 days following the first closing of the offering.[99]

---

[99] Michael Liles, Jr., "Securities Law Compliance in Private Offerings by Emerging Companies," accessed October 2001 at http://www.ppmlibrary.com/mikeliles.asp.

The burden of establishing the existence of an exemption from registration under the securities laws is upon the start-up firm. That firm must provide *and* maintain the evidence that it qualifies for the exemption, even in response to later investigation by regulators. If the exemption is challenged by a regulator or investor, or if securities counsel should subsequently be required to render an opinion concerning the offering, the start-up should be in a position to provide a complete file adequately documenting the existence of the exemption. The professional service provider is not without responsibility in this situation. If the services firm has invested in a start-up, and in a later round of financing or in preparation for an IPO the start-up is found to have violated securities law, the professional service provider may be liable for damages from litigation or may be found to have engaged in activities which result in violation of securities law. For example, if the professional service provider e-mailed a large number of contacts that the start-up is soliciting investments, this could be considered a violation of the provision forbidding a "general solicitation" for investment.

In addition, the documentation of the offering should provide for appropriate safeguards, including records and copies of certificates representing the securities and placing a stop-transfer order against the transfer of those certificates pending appropriate assurance of compliance, so that any resales of the securities will be made within the parameters of the private offering or some other exemption from registration.

The "Accredited Investor" Provision

One provision of particular importance to a professional service provider is the "accredited" investor clause of the exemption from registration. An "accredited investor" is someone with a net worth of at least $1 million or has had income of at least $200,000 for the last two years and is expected to have income of at least $200,000 during the current year. Corporations and other entities qualify if all of their owners are accredited or if they have total assets of at least $5 million. An investor entity that has on staff a full-time professional money manager is usually called an "institutional" investor, and is generally considered accredited based on the qualifications of the shareholders in that entity and of the money manager. For this reason, it is very important that a professional service firm positively confirm whether it is considered accredited before making an investment in a start-up or receiving equity from a start-up client. It is also important to consider the nature of the entity to be used in investment activities. As some interview subjects pointed out, this provision also tends to prevent junior-level associates from participating directly in equity-for-services compensation schemes. Instead, a senior partner or senior shareholder in the professional service firm should be designated as investing on behalf of any funds used to supplement the compensation of junior staff.

If a Rule 506 offering is not confined to accredited investors, the company must provide non-accredited investors, and should provide all investors, with disclosure documents that are comparable to what is provided in a public offering of the same general size and type. This can be an expensive and time-consuming requirement, and for this and other reasons, most private offerings are confined to accredited investors.

The Process of Receiving Equity in Start-up Clients

At the outset, the offering must be identified and separated from prior and subsequent offerings, unless the criteria for the safe harbor can be applied to the entire group of offerings as a single "integrated" offering (as when a services firm invests alongside a group of venture capitalists or other qualified investors). The usual way of separating offerings is to allow six months to elapse from the end of the last offering before commencing a new offering, which is the method provided under Regulation D. Note that if one of the criteria for the safe harbor has been violated, the company may have no alternative but to wait out the six month period before commencing a new offering. In limited circumstances the offering may be able to proceed with institutional investors but not with individual ones. Therefore, the services firm or its designated investment entity may still be allowed to complete the transaction with other investors, but individual employees or partners may not be able to participate.

Another common occurrence that may violate securities law is media coverage at or near the time of the offering. If the company becomes the object of media reporting, even if not sought out by the company, a general solicitation may be deemed to be involved. Particularly problematical are news reports or articles that mention the company's possible financial success or the fact that it is or may be seeking financing. Unless the company is actually engaged in product or service marketing efforts, reports by the media should generally be avoided. If product or service marketing efforts are actually in progress, media coverage should be confined to information concerning the company's products or services, and then only to the extent that it might be of interest to potential customers.

This was the situation with the Internet grocery delivery service Webvan, which included among its investors the law firm of Wilson Sonsini. When Webvan entered into registration for its IPO, intense media coverage of the company and its many high-profile investors and executives (including cofounder Louis Borders of Borders Books and chief executive George Sheehan, former head of Andersen Consulting) brought into question whether Webvan had violated the "quiet period" against making a solicitation prior to an IPO. Even though Webvan representatives did not allow themselves to be interviewed, the appearance of potential publicity forced Wilson Sonsini to advise Webvan to delay its initial public offering until well after the media articles had been published. This shows again the potential for conflicts of interest—if Wilson Sonsini had wanted to achieve liquidity of its investment sooner, it might have recommended that Webvan go ahead with its IPO as scheduled. This would have opened the law firm and all Webvan investors to potential accusations of securities fraud.

An issue related to meeting the general solicitation criterion for the Rule 506 safe harbor is the exercise of a measure of oversight and coordination of the selling efforts between the company and the selling agent, if any. This is very important if the selling agent or the investors do not have extensive experience in the securities industry in conducting private offerings. Because a company authorizes its selling agent to represent it in the offering, any errors in the offering by the selling agent are attributable to the company, and if, for example, the selling agent inadvertently engages in a general solicitation or some other prohibited practice, the selling agent's action will cause the exemption to be lost for the company's offering, even if the selling agent is terminated and a new selling agent is subsequently engaged. In this regard, once the exemption is lost for the offering, it cannot be regained, and only an appropriate separation of the offering from a subsequent one will suffice. This usually means waiting for six months without conducting any offering, which is not feasible for many companies in times of cash shortfalls. Of course, if a selling agent causes an exemption to be lost, the company may have a claim against the selling agent, but this is usually small comfort under the circumstances, and any pursuit of the claim at that time is apt to be communicated to any new selling agent that may be engaged, which may make the new selling agent wary of dealing with the company in the subsequent offering.

At a minimum, the engagement agreement with the selling agent should contain a covenant that the selling agent will not engage in any general solicitation in connection with the offering and will so certify to the company's counsel for purposes of counsel's rendering of legal opinions in that or subsequent offerings. Depending upon the circumstances, the company may also wish to screen investor contacts before they are made to confirm that they are eligible to become investors and have not been solicited by means of general solicitation. The engagement agreement should also require the selling agent to provide each investor with all of the disclosure materials then available in the offering before the investor makes an investment decision.

The selling agent, of course will have similar concerns, as any action by the company which would cause a registration exemption to be lost would mean that the selling agent would be liable to all investors who invest through the selling agent, even if all of the sales through the selling agent were properly conducted. The consequences are more severe for the selling agent because the selling agent receives but a fraction of the proceeds of the offering, and if the selling agent is liable to return the proceeds to the investors whom the agent has solicited, there would be no control over the proceeds or ability to return them on their own. Thus, the selling agent will typically insist upon representations and covenants from the company and its management, and perhaps an opinion of its counsel, that provides a measure of assurance that the exemption being relied upon is not destroyed by actions beyond the selling agent's knowledge and control.

Disclosure Issues in Equity-For-Services
The disclosure format for private offerings that include individual accredited investors is typically similar to that for offerings that include non-accredited investors. One reason to use this approach is if one of the investors should turn out not to be accredited as represented, the disclosure requirements

of Rule 506 will still have been met and the safe harbor can be claimed. Essentially the disclosure documents in offerings that include individual investors (sometimes referred to as "retail" offerings) use private placement memoranda that contain extensive risk-factor sections and do not include the business plan, which contains financial forecasts. There is usually a reference in this type of private placement memorandum to the availability of the business plan, and institutional investors routinely request it so they may receive and analyze financial forecasts and the assumptions underlying them. When an offering is confined to institutional investors, no disclosure format is required by Regulation D, and typically a term sheet without risk factors, together with the business plan containing financial statements and forecasts, is used as the principal disclosure document. Although an offering structure and price may be proposed, institutional investors, often acting in concert, may through their professional money managers or the selling agent negotiate a different structure and price, often with a preference in liquidation and distributions over the founders and earlier investors and with a conversion formula that minimizes dilution by subsequent investors.

In order to be able to take advantage of the safe harbor provisions of Rule 506, the company must file a Form D with the Securities and Exchange Commission and with state securities regulators within 15 days following the first closing in the offering. It is important for the company to timely comply with this requirement, despite the existence of the "substantial compliance" provisions applicable to Regulation D and the state counterpart in some states, because some states in apparent reaction to the preemption of the area by recent federal law have seized upon any such noncompliance to deny the exemption under state securities law. This can turn what would otherwise be a simple process into a complex and expensive one. The states also require filing fees that vary from state to state and sometimes can be expensive. In view of the complexities that can creep into the filing process, it is inadvisable to wait until the last minute to prepare and forward the Forms D for filing.

The disclosures to investors should include the following:

Financial Statements and Related Analysis. In start-up and other early-stage companies, the issue of the necessity for inclusion of financial statements in the disclosure document arises. It is often assumed that because the company has no assets to speak of, there is nothing material that would be disclosed by financial statements. This is not necessarily so. The extent of any accrued liabilities, including accrued but unpaid back salaries and other indebtedness to management, can be a material issue that might be appropriately disclosed through financial statements. Also, the company's recent "burn rate" of cash expenditures would generally be disclosed by financial statements, and this can be a material disclosure in the offering. Generally the financial statements should be accompanied by a "management's discussion and analysis" of the company's results of operations and financial condition.

Use of Proceeds. A key issue in any offering is what the proceeds from the offering will be used for and how much of the company's development are those proceeds likely to accomplish. Where the entire amount of the proceeds will not be held in escrow pending the completion of the offering, the order of priority in the use of the proceeds may be important. If the proceeds are going to be used to retire existing obligations that have accrued during the development of the company's products, clear disclosure of this should be made so that investors will understand that not all of the funds that are raised will be used to take the product to the next level of development, but will be used to pay for past development efforts that have brought the company to its current stage of development, as disclosed in connection with the offering.

Capitalization and Dilution. Investors generally wish to know what piece of the company's ownership "pie" will be theirs if they invest in the offering. This information is usually provided by means of a capitalization table showing the company's existing capital structure—that is, the amount of securities currently outstanding, and what if anything was paid for them. For a "retail" offering to individual investors which has a specific structure, there is usually also provided a pro forma presentation showing the effect of investing in the offering as well as a dilution table setting forth in several ways the relative ownership and contributions of the investors as compared with that for the existing owners. Again, the formats for these types of disclosures are often borrowed from those used in public offerings, as these disclosure formats have been accepted by both regulatory and financial communities.

Financial Forecasts. Professional money managers usually spend a significant amount of effort in analyzing a company's financial forecasts and the assumptions underlying those forecasts in determining or recommending whether or not their institution should invest. For offerings directed towards these types of investors, well developed financial forecasts presented in the format prescribed by the accounting profession should provide a measure of credibility to the offering. The accounting principles used in the forecasts should be the same as those that the company has historically used, or at least not contrary to them. There is also certain cautionary wording prescribed by the accounting profession that should be included. For this reason, it is desirable for the company to obtain the guidance of professional public accountants in the preparation and presentation of financial forecasts.

AN ALTERNATIVE FORM OF OFFERING TO PROFESSIONALS SERVICE PROVIDERS: FORM S-8

Form S-8 was created by the SEC to provide a simplified form of registration for securities issued to employees in a compensatory or incentive context. As such, it allows for incorporation of required disclosure information by reference from the public company's reports filed under the Securities Exchange Act of 1934 (the Exchange Act) (such as the company's annual report on Form 10-K and quarterly reports on Form 10-Q). And, unlike SEC Form S-3 (the form used most frequently for incorporating previously registered information by reference in "shelf" registrations), Form S-8 may be used without regard to the length of the issuer's reporting history or the aggregate market value of its securities held by non-affiliates (thus providing a luxury that a client may not otherwise have been afforded). This allows for a much simpler and condensed registration statement.

In addition, a Form S-8 registration statement is not reviewed by the SEC staff and "goes effective" immediately on filing. Furthermore, Form S-8 generally allows for the delivery of regularly prepared materials regarding the benefit plans under which the shares are to be issued in satisfaction of the Securities Act prospectus delivery requirements, eliminating the need to file and deliver a separate prospectus that duplicates this information. All of this results in substantially reduced costs and time savings to the issuer, thus allowing registration of shares that otherwise might have been impractical.

The SEC allows for this limited disclosure and prospectus delivery procedure because employees and other eligible recipients are deemed to have sufficient knowledge of the issuer's business by virtue of their relationship with the company. As the SEC stated in its release revising Form S-8 in February 1999 (Securities Act Release No. 7646), "The compensatory purpose of the offering and employees' familiarity with the issuer's business through the employment relationship justify the use of abbreviated disclosure that would not be adequate in a capital-raising transaction."

Unfortunately, when the SEC expanded Form S-8 to include consultants and advisors, it opened the door for abuse of this simplified registration form. Over the past several years, certain companies have attempted to circumvent the SEC's full-blown registration procedure by masking public stock offerings as S-8 offerings. These companies have, for example, issued S-8 stock to a purported class of "consultants and advisors," who, on the company's instructions, subsequently have sold the stock to the public and either returned the proceeds to the company or used them to pay the company's expenses, including expenses completely unrelated to any service provided by the consultant or advisor. Often, in these cases, the consultants or advisors performed limited or no services for the issuer. The SEC unequivocally has taken the position that the foregoing scenario is capital-raising in nature, and not compensatory, and thus a violation of Section 5 of the Securities Act, as stated in Securities Act Release No. 7646.

More troubling to the services providers who are considering a client's offer to pay them in S-8 stock is the fact that, under the foregoing fact pattern, the SEC will consider the "consultants and advisors" who served as conduits for the unregistered public offering to be "statutory underwriters", as defined in Section 2(a)(11) of the Securities Act, each of them guilty of violating Section 5 of the Securities Act.

The SEC has specifically stated (in Securities Act Release No. 7646):

Attorneys who represent an issuer in matters that are not related to its securities, such as litigation defense, securing U.S. Food and Drug Administration approval of a drug, or obtaining a patent, will be eligible [to receive S-8 stock]. Attorneys who prepare the issuer's Exchange Act reports and proxy statement will be eligible whether or not these documents are incorporated into a Securities Act registration statement. However, any consultant or advisor, including an attorney, who prepares or circulates an Exchange Act report or proxy statement that is part of a promotional scheme that violates federal securities laws will not be eligible. Attorneys serving as counsel to the issuer, its underwriters or any participating broker-dealer in a securities offering will not be eligible. Attorneys and other consultants who assist an issuer in identifying acquisition targets or in structuring mergers or other acquisitions in which securities are issued as consideration, will be eligible, unless the acquisition takes a private company public.

Can S-8 stock be used to reimburse the service providers' expenses and costs? Probably. But which third-party expenses can you pay with the S-8 shares you receive? Of course, even if you qualify to receive shares registered on Form S-8, you will need to deal with the SEC's requirement that the S-8 stock be issued only to individuals (unless, of course, you are a sole practitioner). The consulting contract (that is, engagement letter) can be between the issuer and an entity (such as a law firm), but the securities must be issued to the natural persons (individual lawyers) who actually provide the bona fide services to the issuer. Currently, it is not clear whether individual consultants (lawyers) can either transfer the S-8 registered stock they receive as compensation to his or her firm or sell the stock and remit the proceeds to their firm. The SEC has not spoken officially on this issue.

The SEC currently is considering additional changes to Form S-8 in an attempt to further curb abuses relating to the registration form, including proposals that would require:

- the issuer to be timely in its Exchange Act reports during the 12 calendar months and any portion of a month before the Form S-8 is filed;
- an issuer formed by merger of a nonpublic company into an Exchange Act reporting company with only nominal assets at the time of the merger to wait to file a Form S-8 until it has filed an annual report on Form 10-K containing audited financial statements;
- certification that any consultant or advisor who receives securities registered on the form has not been hired for capital-raising or promotional activities; and
- disclosure of the names of any consultants or advisors receiving securities under Form S-8, the number of securities to be issued and the services that were rendered by each of them.

Finally, once lawyers own the stock of the public company client, they will need to be mindful of SEC prohibitions on insider trading, including those imposed by Rule 10b-5. Generally, Rule 10b-5 prohibits a person from trading "on the basis of" material, non-public information. Subject to the affirmative defenses in Paragraph (c) of Rule 10b5-1, a purchase or sale is "on the basis of" material nonpublic information if the person making the purchase or sale was "aware" of the material nonpublic information when the person made the purchase or sale. To satisfy the affirmative defenses of Paragraph (c) of Rule 10b5-1, a person must establish that:

- before becoming aware of the information, he or she had entered into a binding contract to purchase or sell the security, provided instructions to another person to execute the trade for the instructing person's account, or adopted a written plan for trading securities;
- with respect to the purchase or sale, the contract, instructions or plan either: (1) expressly specified the amount, price and date; (2) provided a written formula or algorithm, or computer program, for determining amounts, prices and dates; or (3) did not permit the person to exercise any subsequent influence over how, when or whether to effect purchases or sales; provided, in addition, that any other person who did exercise such influence was not aware of the material nonpublic information when doing so; and
- the purchase or sale that occurred followed the prior contract, instruction or plan. (A purchase or sale is not pursuant to a contract, instruction or plan if, among other things, the person who entered into it altered or deviated from the contract, instruction or plan or entered into or altered a corresponding or hedging transaction or position with respect to those securities.)

Accordingly, if, through representation of the client, the services provider becomes "aware" of material, nonpublic information, the services firm will either need to comply with the affirmative defense provisions of Paragraph (c) of Rule 10b5-1 or will need to refrain from trading until such time as that information is publicly disclosed.

The use of S-8 stock to compensate professional service providers is a relatively recent development, and is still not fully established in practice or regulation. Any firms looking to engage in such transactions must clearly consult appropriate securities counsel to ensure that all rules are followed.

Chapter 8

Insights from Theory: IPR and the Entrepreneurial Venture

Economics since Adam Smith identifies three major factors that contribute to productivity: land, labor and capital. The industrial age brought new meaning and significance to other factors, according to Joseph Schumpeter (1934): technology and entrepreneurship. Peter Drucker (1985) also added emphasis on the role of innovation. The concept of capital is central to explanations of national and corporate competitiveness and with that we mean not only financial but also human, intellectual, and social capital. The shift in the West from an agrarian economy to one based on manufacturing was marked by the shift from land as the most important factor to physical capital—factories, machinery, and resources which composed these assets—and the financial capital to acquire those assets. The rise of a "postcapitalist" society as described by Drucker suggests that other assets are approaching ascendancy as contributors to economic productivity. The manufacturing-based economy appears to be giving way to a "knowledge-based" economy

In an era of globalized, highly mobile financial capital, multinational corporations can essentially "arbitrage" across national borders to find the best firms to integrate into their mode of production. The increased velocity of commerce (especially electronic commerce) and competition demands multifaceted expertise from a firm. Only through the judicious and experienced application of knowledge can firms hope to outperform their counterparts and achieve sustained competitive advantage.

In postcapitalist economics, wealth flows not to those who control financial capital, but to those who can acquire and direct intellectual capital. The term "intellectual capital" refers to intellectual assets (i.e., skilled workers, scientific knowledge, and business information) which create knowledge into the future through their utilization. Intellectual capital has been defined by analysts at Ernst and Young as "intellectual material that has been formalized, captured and leveraged to produce a higher-value asset." Brooking (1997) views an enterprise as a collection of tangible assets and intellectual capital, with *intellectual capital* composed of market assets, intellectual property assets, human-centered assets, infrastructure assets (see Figure 8.1):

> The postcapitalist knowledge-based economy operates with dynamics which differ radically from those assumed by neoclassical economics. Unlike other forms of capital, intellectual capital is not only unevenly distributed, but it tends to grow without physical limits. A firm which captures and exercises unique knowledge capabilities will tend to attract more expert employees, thus exhibiting "increasing returns to scale." According to Arthur (1996), this dynamic leads to a new form of economics, namely knowledge economics, that is very different from traditional, process-oriented economics. He notes that "they call for different management techniques, strategies, and codes of government regulation." The task of management is then "a series of quests for the next technological winner."

Figure 8.1
Components of Intellectual Capital

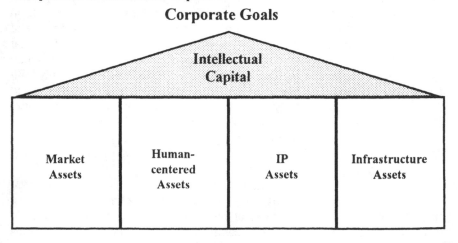

Corporate Goals

Intellectual Capital

| Market Assets | Human-centered Assets | IP Assets | Infrastructure Assets |

Intellectual capital encompasses the intellectual property rights defined under law, but the concepts are very distinct. Intellectual property laws attempt to map traditional systems of diminishing returns onto knowledge. An intellectual property right, like a real property right, is a legal construct which enables an entity to claim ownership of an asset which might otherwise disseminate out of control. In this case, the asset is an invention or other creative act which the firm wishes to use to generate revenues. The value of an intellectual asset is assumed to depend primarily on its ingenuity, but also on its scarcity. An intellectual property right grants the holder of that right sole power to determine who can exploit an intellectual asset.

Due to their nature and the structure of the law, intellectual property is a highly stylized form of knowledge. First, most knowledge is not limited by scarcity. Information and other codified knowledge can be observed, copied, and applied by others without diminishing the knowledge held by the originator. This makes it difficult to detect or prevent the misappropriation or illegal imitation of most knowledge.

Second, intellectual property must be codified in some recordable form so that it can be identified, defined, and protected under law. But knowledge often cannot be recorded for documentation. Following the concepts introduced by Polanyi (1966), many writers categorize knowledge into two types: tacit and explicit. Tacit knowledge is gained through "learning by doing;" it is knowledge which is internalized through practice. This knowledge is not easily depicted in words, diagrams, or other forms of communication, and may in fact not be feasible to articulate at all. In contrast, explicit knowledge can be identified, codified, and isolated more easily. In one conventional view, these two forms of knowledge are distinct and exclusive. Intellectual property rights are capable of protecting explicit knowledge, but not tacit knowledge.

A new view of knowledge proposed by Tsoukas (1996), holds that "tacit and explicit knowledge are mutually constituted...the two are inseparably related." From this perspective, the artificial representation of knowledge in explicit form distorts that knowledge. It ignores the tacit component of knowledge, consisting of intangible elements such as expertise, judgment, and intuition which are necessary for the proper application of the explicit component. More important , tacit knowledge is necessary for understanding the dynamics of knowledge creation. Hence, reverse engineering, which focuses mostly on extracting the explicit knowledge embodied in products, is of limited value in terms of intellectual capital because it does not contribute significantly to the capture or generation of critical tacit knowledge.

If, as Tsoukas (ibid) states, the firm is a "distributed system of knowledge," then firms can exploit individual knowledge only when transformed into organizational knowledge. Organizational knowledge can be classified in three general categories: tacit, rule-based, and background. Tacit knowledge concerns intuitive aspect of knowledge. Rule-based knowledge concerns the behavior and functioning of the organization, and can be both tacit and/or explicit. Finally, background knowledge provides the proper context for understanding other forms of knowledge.

While explicit knowledge may be easily amenable to expropriation, the significant tacit component of organizational knowledge makes transfer difficult. The movement of individual employees among firms allows for the movement of some tacit knowledge. However, since organizational knowledge is the aggregation of individual knowledge, in most cases a single employee will not possess all the tacit knowledge related to the core competence of the firm.

The analysis of intellectual capital produces two immediate implications for firm strategy:

- First, the firm must recognize that explicit knowledge is inherently difficult to protect, even under well-developed regimes of intellectual property law.
- Second, to leverage the full benefits of a firm's IC, it must manage its stock and flow of both explicit knowledge (intellectual property) and tacit knowledge (other intellectual assets).

By controlling and directing the idea migration and the osmosis of knowledge across firms through IPR enforcement and appropriate organizational configurations, one can maximize the wealth of the firm-specific knowledge and know-how that is captured by the firm. The practice of designing mechanisms to improve the generation, intrafirm diffusion, and inter-firm protection of knowledge is the subject of a new field of theory and practice called "knowledge management."

Intellectual property is one kind of intellectual asset which technology-based firms transform into competitive advantage. There are four generally recognized forms of intellectual property in industrialized nations:

- patents, dealing with functional and design inventions;
- trademarks, dealing with commercial origin and identity;
- copyrights, dealing with literary and artistic expressions; and
- trade secrets, which protect the proprietary capabilities of the firm.

Under U.S. law, a patent is granted only by the federal government and lets the patentee exclude others from making, using, selling, importing, or offering an invention for a fixed term, currently 20 years from the date the patent application is filed. A trademark, as defined under the Trademark Act of 1946 (The Lanham Act) is

> any word, name, symbol, or device, or any combination thereof (1) used by a person, or (2) which a person has a bona fide intention to use in commerce...to identify and distinguish his or her goods, including a unique product, from those manufactured or sold by others, and to indicate the source of the goods, even if that source is unknown.

A copyright seeks to promote literary and artistic creativity by protecting, for a limited time, works of original authorship in tangible form. The general rule in the United States for a work created on or after January 1, 1978, whether or not it is published, is that copyright lasts for the author's lifetime plus 70 years after the author's death. The copyright also protects "works made for hire," anonymous, and pseudonymous works for extended periods of time as well (see the Library of Congress web site: http://www.loc.gov).

A trade secret is information that an inventor chooses not to disclose and to which the inventor also controls access, thus providing enduring protection. Trade secrets remain in force only if the holder takes reasonable precautions to prevent them from being revealed to people outside the firm, except through a legal mechanism such as a license.

The integration of knowledge management with the recent work in technology management identifies a new focus for corporate strategy: the creation of a technology IP strategy. This represents a profound shift from previous views of IP in corporations. Historically, intellectual property rights were viewed as a means of maintaining an archive of a firm's creative output, with no value beyond simple record-keeping. As a result, firms' patent portfolios grew through R&D, but the portfolios themselves were not viewed as productive assets.

The first issue to be addressed in developing an IP technology strategy is the formation of a portfolio of intellectual property rights appropriate to the firm's intellectual assets and competitive capabilities. For the technology-based firm, patents and trade secrets are the primary forms of protecting the intellectual property embodied in their most strategic products and services. (For software firms, copyright also protects their products; however, court decisions during the 1980s weakened the protection of software by copyright and in turn made it possible to patent software technologies.) Therefore, it is natural that any IP management system should focus on these two types of intellectual property.

By law, both patents and trade secrets are explicit forms of knowledge in that they must exist in codified form. For patents, the knowledge is embodied in a product or process and is made publicly available in the patent, while trade secrets protect explicit knowledge from public dissemination. If, as Tsoukas (ibid) proposes, all knowledge has a tacit and explicit component, patenting makes more sense for competitive reasons if the explicit knowledge described in the patent has significant accompanying tacit features which complicate its exploitation. The degree of tacitness provides a degree of practical protection against appropriation by competitors, which reinforces the legal protection afforded by the patent. In contrast, trade secret protection should be used for knowledge which is predominantly explicit, since publication would reveal the essentials for using that knowledge.

The need for significant tacit knowledge to utilize a patent also provides a mechanism for maximizing non-licensing revenues. A significant part of value-added to the IP licenser is derived from consulting, training, and other fees by the licensee to the IP owner for utilizing effectively the IP in the context of the licensee's business activities. This creates new business areas for licensers to exploit. For example, a licenser may earn additional revenues by assigning personnel to work with the licensee in using the licensed technology, a practice sometimes called "wet licensing" (derived from the terminology that the licenser is renting out the internalized knowledge or "wetware" or "brainware" of its employees).

To determine when and how to use intellectual property laws to protect knowledge, the firm must consider the importance of the explicit component of that knowledge and the degree to which the invention is important to the firm's competitive advantage. The contrast between knowledge type and competitive status for an invention is illustrated in Figure 8.1.

As illustrated, patents are most effective in protecting technologies which are exploited only with complementary tacit knowledge. Also, since patents provide imperfect protection, they should not be used to protect knowledge which is central to a firm's competitiveness. Technologies suitable for trade secret protection tend to be easily replicated once the core technology has been revealed. Therefore, patenting (which requires public disclosure) is not suitable for such technologies. The relatively greater protection afforded by trade secret laws means that this form of intellectual property can provide a level of security suitable for the core technologies of a firm. This accounts for the increased use of trade secrets rather than patents among U.S. firms as a formal means of intellectual property protection.

Trade secrets carry two potential problems, however. First, companies are not protected in cases where a competitor independently develops and uses the same technology. In the case of patents, the first party to file the patent application (under the prevailing international patenting standards negotiated under the Uruguay Round of the General Agreement on Tariffs and Trade or GATT) would have exclusive use of the technology.

Second, since trade secrets are explicit and codified, they can easily be misappropriated by employees who switch firms. This has led to an increase in trade secret litigation in the U.S. and abroad:

> "Given the increasing value of intangible assets like know-how in the information age, there has been a significant amount of recent litigation where corporations—which are vitally interested in protecting their trade secrets—are willing to take their cases to court," according to a counsel to Dow Chemical in a recent trade secret dispute with General Electric (Carayannis & Alexander, 1998).

An IP technology strategy also encompasses the choice of mechanisms used to protect the company's existing intellectual property portfolio and to defend against competitive actions by other firms. The offensive component of the strategy involves the aggressive pursuit of IP litigation against patent infringers, copyright pirates, and others who seek to devalue the company's IP through imitation or misappropriation. It also addresses the use of increased licensing to generate royalties from previously unused technologies, thus creating new profits. Texas Instruments, for example, has used the offensive IP approach to make its patent litigation and licensing practice the most profitable function in the firm.

Companies must also pursue a defensive IP strategy to prevent disruptive action by competitors. For example, the firm must continually scout out blocking patents held by others in order to avoid potential infringement litigation. If blocking patents are identified, the firm should arrange cross-licensing or other agreements to resolve the conflict. Also, the firm itself can file blocking patents to foreclose the strategic technology options available to competitors.

The key organizational tool used by companies as the foundation of their IP technology strategy is the IP audit. Like the technology audit described by Ford (1988), an IP audit is both a one-time exercise and a periodic routine. It seeks to identify all of the actual or potential intellectual property held by various parts of the firm, including patents, copyrights, trademarks, and trade secrets, and compiles these in a central database. This is accomplished by interviewing company researchers, marketing personnel, and other staff to find out what IP they have generated or used.

This also provides an opportunity to examine the company's IP practices, and to encourage staff to protect all relevant IP through legal tools (patents, trademarks, etc.) and through policy and practices (e.g., ensuring adequate security measures to protect trade secrets). Perhaps the most important goal of the audit is to raise awareness throughout the company, especially among researchers, of the strategic value in identifying, protecting, and exploiting all available intellectual property. It also can be used to encourage the development of the "knowledge-sharing culture" dictated by knowledge management principles.

The IP audit is generally conducted by an IP law firm, which then recommends changes to both procedures and facilities at the company to encourage IP protection. However, law firms may be limited in that they focus primarily on the explicit intellectual property which is protectable by law, and often do not understand the variation in the significance of different pieces of intellectual property or the role of knowledge in competitive strategy. It may be more appropriate to form an internal team to conduct an IP audit, especially one which includes staff trained in the technology management field who can link technology, knowledge and business.

Companies which do not use IP audits often have peripheral inventions which are unprotected or, if protected through a patent filing, are left unexploited by the firm. One consequence of the IP audit is the identification of technologies which should be licensed out. The new awareness of the value of IP fostered by an IP technology strategy will have a reflexive effect on the field of knowledge management, and on corporate approaches to IC. In a static analysis, IP technology strategy dictates that a firm know at any given time what key knowledge it possesses, and how well that knowledge is utilized. However, IP technology strategy also introduces a dynamic aspect to knowledge management, since future revenues can be gained only through the generation of new knowledge. This requires companies to establish more effective learning routines in addition to mechanisms for knowledge sharing and diffusion.

The concept of *strategic technological learning* (Carayannis, 2001a) demands that corporations develop their organizational intelligence, defined as the creation of knowledge in addition to the possession of knowledge. Rather than simply isolating and measuring discrete intellectual assets, true knowledge management must include practices for ensuring that the company continues to produce new knowledge and absorb additional knowledge through external linkages. The organizational intelligence/learning process is a continuous cycle if activities include *environmental sensing/scanning, remembering, perceiving, interpreting, and adapting* and produce tacit and explicit knowledge and know-how as a result of strategic, tactical, and operational technological learning (Carayannis & Alexander, 1998).

The boundaries of the areas where patents and trade secrets are most appropriate reveal that there is also a class of technologies for which strict protection is not clearly advantageous. Several environmental changes are leading firms both to "license out" certain technologies, and to "license in" as an important mode of technology acquisition.

Intellectual capital is created "through two generic processes: combination and exchange....New intellectual capital can be created through incremental or radical change but both involve either combining elements which were previously unconnected or the development of novel ways of combining elements previously associated. When resources are held by different parties, exchange is a pre-requisite for resource combination." The exchange of knowledge assets to create intellectual capital sets the stage for the discussion of licensing and cross-licensing as components of the business and technology strategy of the firm (ibid).

Anecdotal and quantitative data show that over the past decade, U.S. firms have increased their licensing activity. According to data from the U.S. Department of Commerce, international technology licensing between firms has risen by 18 percent per year, and domestic licensing has increased at the rate of 10 percent per year. The decision to license technologies in or out should be guided by the technology strategy of the firm. Ford breaks down technology strategy into three components: technology acquisition, technology management, and technology exploitation. The corporate strategy combined with strategic technology management factors drives the decisions of licensees and licensors to increase their use of licensing.

The firm could use technology licensing in conjunction with strategic objectives, such as to: (a) grow more quickly or increase profitability; (b) maintain or defend its current position; (c) diversify out of its current position by acquiring a technological "foothold" into more promising markets. For example, a firm in a defensive position is less motivated to license out its core technologies. As an example, Apple Computer licensed out the Mac OS in 1995, but in 1997 reversed that decision and acquired the Macintosh operations of its major licensee (Power Computing) when it perceived that licensing had eroded its own share without significantly expanding the market for Mac-compatible machines. Environmental conditions (such as intensity of rivalry, etc.) can also affect strategic technology decisions. This analysis enables a firm to deal more explicitly and effectively with the following strategic technology management questions:

- Is the firm currently falling behind vis-a-vis current and emerging competitors?
- Could licensing allow the firm to play "catch-up" with its competition?
- What is the best licensing strategy given a certain rivarly intensity and market and industry turbulence?

In this context, the key conditions that need to be fulfilled for the productive combination and exchange of knowledge assets through for instance licensing agreements are:

1. accessibility of objectified and collective forms of social knowledge,
2. anticipation of the creation of new valuable knowledge,
3. motivation of the parties to combine and exchange knowledge seen as beneficial to them,
4. capability to execute the knowledge exchange or combination in question, and
5. development of a co-opetitive relationship between the source and acquirer of knowledge.

The management of knowledge as intellectual capital in the context of strategic technology partnerships facilitates the pursuit and achievement of the following strategic corporate objectives of the partners:

1. Maximize the effectiveness and efficiency of higher-order technological learning processes (Carayannis, 2001a; 2002a) with both internal and external foci (with respect to its partners), namely the *organizational intelligence/learning processes* and especially the *rate of technological learning*.
2. Facilitate and foster the development of a current and dynamic evolving portfolio of strategic technological capability options in a more effective and efficient manner from a technology and market risk perspective.

This above discussion yields some important implications of the knowledge management paradigm for the management and development of research collaborations. In any collaboration, and particularly in research involving joint government-university-industry (GUI) research, negotiations over the appropriate division of intellectual property rights (generally focusing on patents) are often cited as the most problematic issue in securing a collaborative agreement. In such negotiations, the parties are generally taking a "zero-sum" approach, competing for exclusive control of the most promising inventions from the collaboration. The knowledge management paradigm suggests three important issues which challenge this perspective.

First, intellectual capital involves knowledge beyond that captured by patents. For many participants in collaboration, the knowledge which is patented may end up being the least valuable product of the partnership. The exchange of tacit knowledge needed to capitalize on the technological opportunities created by collaboration is much more significant. In this sense, disputes over the allocation of patents may be irrelevant and counterproductive to the goals driving the formation of collaborative research ventures.

Second, the knowledge management approach argues strongly for a "co-opetitive" approach to the treatment of intellectual capital in research collaborations. To achieve a "win-win" outcome, a collaboration should produce knowledge of benefit to all participants. In this sense, the practice of knowledge management within a collaboration is the union of the knowledge management policies of all participants, rather than the intersection of those policies. Partners in research should direct their efforts toward ensuring that all other partners receive the knowledge most suitable to their strategies and needs, rather than simply focusing on their own requirements.

Third, economists are now exploring the idea of "social capital" (Carayannis and Alexander, 1998) as enabling people to cooperate towards a common goal beyond purely financial motives: "To form and lead the kinds of hybrid, cooperative organizational forms...companies must command substantial social capital. Clearly, just as knowledge is the lever of intellectual capital, trust is the lever of social capital. Fukuyama (1995) defines trust as "the expectation that arises within a community of regular, honest, and cooperative behavior, based on commonly shared norms, on the part of other members of that community." We argue that building trust in such networks requires the sharing of intellectual capital to build social capital. In other words, knowledge exchange forms the foundation for trust in corporate alliances, linking intellectual capital with social capital.

- Tacit knowledge, which can be manipulated and managed through face-to-face meetings, collaborative work settings, personnel rotation, and mentor-apprentice relationships;
- Rule-based knowledge, which can be transferred as firms directly observe each other's organizational policies and processes and adopt those which lead to improved efficiency and effectiveness;
- Background knowledge, which becomes shared as corporate cultures converge over a term of close interaction and collaboration between organizations, and as a collaborative venture develops its own unique history and identity.

Intellectual property is thus emerging as the essential "currency" for global trade in strategic capabilities for market-based competition, whose use continues to grow (see Figure 8.1). As a result, firms increasingly view their intellectual property as their primary asset or form of capital which can be leveraged into future advantage in technology and products and in this context, the intellectual property audit is becoming an important tool to transforming firms from traditional storekeepers of intellectual capital to firms which strategically utilize and grow their intellectual capital and tap into the wealth of their proprietary and shared knowledge.

Part III:

Insights from Practice and Lessons Learned in IVC

Chapter 9

Insights from Practice:
Case Studies of Equity-for-Service Deals

EQUITY VERSUS FEE FOR SERVICE—CASES IN POINT AND COUNTERPOINT

Many firms barter equity in exchange for everything from salaries to legal services. What are the pitfalls? Companies are using their own stock or promise of stock instead of cash to pay for everything. From rent deposits to legal fees to headhunter fees, these deals have become a standard in the high-tech business. It's long been a practice for companies to use stock options as a means to attract and keep senior employees. And while the odds don't favor the company becoming the next Yahoo!, all it takes is one hit to erase many prior mistakes.[100]

Proceed with Caution

Companies considering the use of equity as payment for services need to be aware of the issues that can result from this practice.   Caution for the giver:

---

[100] This section has been adapted from Jeff Ong-Siong and Steve Cleland, "Examine the Equity Swap Stakes: Many firms barter equity in exchange for everything from salaries to legal services. What are the pitfalls?", *Business Advisor*, November 2000.

Guess who's looking over your shoulder. Are your new partners going to be on your back every time a key decision is made? Are you creating a new group of Monday morning quarterbacks to critique your business decisions? Will they be able to dictate who you use for other services? Will they let you run the company as you see fit?

While most of the people or vendors that receive equity won't be given a sufficient amount to exercise a high degree of control, that doesn't mean these partners will behave accordingly. Address these issues early on in the transaction. Think hard before you give up that board seat. Consider issuing a separate nonvoting series of stock in lieu of voting common. Or conduct your barter with warrants instead of stock.

Whose Side Are You Really On?

If your attorney, consultant, or other party suddenly has a financial interest in your company through the use of equity as payment for services, the reality is that it may be more challenging to be impartial and objective. A consultant's fiduciary responsibility may be impaired by his or her personal involvement.

For example, if you hire a professional advisor to help study a potential merger with another company, the consultant's opinion might be clouded by the immediate gain of the merger offer rather than helping the company grow. A consultant interested in a short-term personal gain could overlook what might be beneficial for your company in the long term.

You Want How Much?

Once out of the realm of dealing with cash, many partners receiving equity may grow fanciful as to what deal they can command. Their argument is that there's risk involved and therefore it should be worth more in equity than in dollars. While smart tech executives know they will become significantly diluted in their ownership as time progresses, there's no reason to hasten this process. There is no rule of thumb to refer to in determining what is a fair transaction–each case stands on its own depending on the level of services bartered.

A good starting point when negotiating an equity-for-services deal with a vendor is to convert the total package into dollars using the most current valuation of the equity. In that way, you know the scope of the deal you may be entering into and can then negotiate how much additional value to assign to things such as risk and minority ownership.

Caution for the receivers: Taxation without monetization–even though you received equity instead of cash for your services, don't think for a second that this was a tax-free transaction. There's a value for that stock and Uncle Sam wants a share of it. And while equity is a valuable commodity, you can't pay your taxes with it (yet). Beware: The government will want even more once you exercise your warrants, and they'll look for one more cut when you sell your shares. An advance call to your tax consultant is definitely in order.

What Do You Mean I Can't Sell My Equity?

Because this isn't legal tender, your equity is worthless as long as the company remains a private company. And even after the company becomes publicly held, there are often restrictions placed on these arrangements as to when shares can be sold. The worst case would be to watch your piece of equity skyrocket on opening day and then crater, knowing you're powerless to reduce your loss. It happens. We know of a well-known tech company that traded its stock for almost every conceivable service known to man. And due to the pre-IPO hype, the willing takers were plentiful.

To avoid real losses, vendors need to take their money off the table. In other words, never enter into deals that are all stock. At least cover your costs and overhead with good old-fashioned cash. Obviously, it's also advisable to research whether the deal is worthwhile. Does the valuation make sense in today's market? Is the company offering a sustainable product? Some old-fashioned due diligence still makes sense in the new market.

As a firm whose practice niches include real estate and law firms, as well as start-up high-tech firms, RBZ has significant experience in dealing with all sides of equity-for-services arrangements. We've seen a number of barter transactions that, in hindsight, were ill-advised, since the tech company no longer had the IPO momentum it may have had nine months previously.

Many of the service providers who have traded stock, such as law firms, have the luxury of licking their wounds and moving on as the loss has already been incurred. However, landlords who took monthly lease "haircuts" in return for stock in what are now troubled companies aren't so lucky. They get to revisit their mistakes monthly until the leases finally terminate. Although such bartering practices have slowed down, they certainly haven't ceased.

Best Practice

Wise vendors are covering the cost of their services with old-fashioned cash, and they view any stock attached to the deal as "gravy." In this way, you can limit and manage any potential losses.

And About Winners and Losers

After several months of a sliding NASDAQ, you'd expect law firms that invest in clients would be taking a bath and some certainly are: for instance, the Venture Law Group, watched its client holdings lose about three-fourths of its value since March 2000.[101] Overall, the seven Bay Area firms that are most aggressive when it comes to taking equity in clients are defying expectations. Case in point: Wilson Sonsini Goodrich & Rosati-Wilson lawyers saw their

---

[101] This section has been adapted from "Stock Market Survivors," Renee Deger, *Recorder* Staff Writer, 7 December, 2000.

holdings skyrocket by 130 percent in the last eight months of 2000. Wilson was the best-performing among the seven equity-taking firms.

"We got lucky," said Mario Rosati, the Wilson partner who manages the firm's stock holdings. Indeed, Wilson was taking Internet infrastructure companies public just as the market fell in love with them.

Joining Wilson among the firms that saw growth were Brobeck, Phleger & Harrison, Cooley Godward, and Gunderson Dettmer Stough Villeneuve Franklin & Hachigian. Along with VLG, Fenwick & West and Gray Cary Ware & Freidenrich saw their portfolios plunge in value. The snapshot of the firms' portfolios was based on stock performance compared to the price at the initial public offering. The companies included went public from December through April. Holding the equity are firm investment funds and individual lawyers. The IPO prices were then compared with what the stock fetched 180 days later when most "lock-ups" that forbid certain shareholders from selling shares expire. After recent years of heady market success, the downturn has reminded firms that stock profits don't come with a guarantee. A senior VLG partner took the sinking stock values in stride. Partner Donald Keller Jr. attributed the decline to a return to a more realistic market. "We all realized that it was too easy over the last year or so and that it would not last," Keller said, referring to the NASDAQ'S steady march upward in recent years.

While the firm counts among its losses its investments in Pets.com Inc., which went out of business in November 2000, the change in overall value of the sample is due primarily to a shift in one company. VLG's holdings in Onvia.com, a Seattle-based online marketplace for business services, were fetching more than $20 million at Onvia's IPO. The stake was worth a quarter of that six months later. Despite the shifts in the market, Keller said that taking equity in start-ups is still a viable long-term strategy.

For Wilson, the soaring portfolio was more happenstance. The firm's stakes in Avanex Corp., a Fremont-based maker of speedier network components, and Viant, a Boston-based Internet consultant, tripled during the six months following the IPOs. When shares became tradeable, Wilson's stake in Avanex was worth $47 million, and its stake in Viant, $2.68 million. However, if the firm didn't sell all of its Viant shares at the lock-up date, it probably should have. The company's stock is now trading at under $5 a share.

Brobeck also seems like a big winner in the market. The firm saw a 96 percent increase in value of newly tradeable stocks held by the firm and individual lawyers. Meanwhile, Cooley Godward saw a modest 10 percent increase in value, and Gunderson Dettmer saw its one holding increase in value by 28 percent. Fenwick and Gray Cary saw their holdings slide in value by 40 and 44 percent, respectively. The gains and losses sometimes reflect just one stock or one lawyer.

At Brobeck, the big winner is partner John Larson. He invested his own money in Richmond-based Sangamo BioSciences, a long-suffering biotechnology company, because his buddy is the CEO. Larson is reticent about the details, but Securities and Exchange Commission filings show he purchased some 142,000 shares for about $300,000 over four years. He's also a board member and received more shares as compensation.

On the day his total 474,460 shares became tradeable, they were worth some $15.27 million. "It's one of those things," said Larson, who did ask his firm to invest as well but was turned down. "Up until about a year ago, it wasn't at all clear it was going to be a wonderful investment."

CASE STUDIES OF EQUITY-FOR-SERVICE DEALS FROM PATENT LAW FIRMS

The following case studies are representative examples of agreements between a patent lawyer and his or her client where legal services were performed in exchange for the corporate stock of the client. The case studies are taken from the actual personal experiences of those interviewed for this book and have been distilled into a generalized and anonymous framework to better analyze the topics developed in this book and to protect the identity of those involved. It should be appreciated that getting people to discuss their successes is easy. However, successes do not provide the same education that failures do and memories of successes may be also prone to inaccuracies. These case studies represent summaries of failures of one sort or another. Some failures are on a personal level. Some are merely failures of luck, timing, location, or execution of a plan. Some may have turned out not to be complete failures, but merely a failure of one component of a project. However, during the interview process it became apparent that memories of failures seem to have left a more lasting footprint on the psyche of those involved. This "failure footprint" has given us a wonderful consequence in the availability of many fine details of the events and that those details are not only rich in number, but in also in their specificity. Of course, the names, places, and times have been changed to protect the innocent, and any resemblance to actual events, persons, or institutions is merely coincidental.

The analytical framework of the case studies assumes a certain level of business, legal, and scientific knowledge in the reader. Specifically, those who have absolutely no knowledge of how a technology business works may not completely understand the context of these case studies. Accordingly, a brief discussion of the factors which were considered, either expressly or inherently, are discussed below before setting off into the case studies themselves.

For context, there were seven open-ended questions that were presented to each interviewee. In order, they were:

1. What were the names of those involved?
2. What is the history or background of the deal?
3. How was the risk of economic loss managed?
4. What was done in terms of screening to avoid getting unintentionally involved?
5. What was the nature of the relationship between the parties and how did it develop through time?
6. What was the ultimate result; did you achieve your goals?

7.   What were the lessons you learned and how would you change your behavior if you had to do it all over again?

In any technology business, it all begins with a "great idea." This great idea is usually a solution to a problem shared by many. Ideally, the solution lends itself to an entrepreneurial solution where the provider of the solution can make a profit by providing the solution. Entrepreneurs understand that the only way to determine if a great idea can make a profit is to start with market research. Market research starts with an evaluation of the competitors and moves through an evaluation of the market size and scope, and ends with some guess about timing and introduction of the product. Suffice it to say that it is well beyond the scope of this book to go into this analysis in detail and there are many fine texts and articles dedicated to these topics. Nonetheless, entrepreneurs have an intuitive grasp of this type of thinking.

The next factor concerns the make-up of the research and development teams. It should be noted that the research team is frequently not the development team. Of course, this parameter is easily quantified on the one hand and impossible on the other. The easy part: do your people have experience conducting research and developing products for start-up businesses in this area? The more years of experience that the team has, the greater your chance of success. The hard part: gauging the skill sets of the various team members and judging whether an effective team can be built from those same individuals. Every business manager, athletic coach, parent, child psychologist, or experienced entrepreneur understands the difficulty of this aspect.

The next factor relates to the existence of a financial plan and to the equity available to the business. Every business eats cash in large quantities and must be fed frequently or else the business dies. The only other fuel source option is "sweat equity". However, this use of a tortured barter system has its limitations. Nonetheless, a financial plan is always part of every start-up, and a delineation of how the business is going to proceed and with what or whose resources is one of the first steps in embarking on a new venture. Accordingly, an evaluation of the level of funding is a critical component in any postmortem analysis.

Patents are also critical to the success of nearly every technology company. In fact, most experienced practitioners will tell you that patents are not suggested, they are required for viability. There are many who try to challenge the paradigm by foregoing patent protection. The first thing that goes missing is any reasonable legal protection for the lead product. Some might rely on confidentiality agreements or employment agreements. Some might try to rely on trade secrets or copyright protection. What is frequently discovered (when it is too late) is that confidentiality agreements and employment agreements can be eviscerated by good lawyers. They are frequently unenforceable. Trade secrets are protectable only under each state's laws and are frequently extremely expensive to pursue in state court and rarely enforceable without a large financial commitment.

It pays to understand the legal reality that an "800-pound gorilla" goes wherever it wants to, subject to very few exceptions. Unless your company is an "800 pound gorilla", financially speaking, you should be careful when relying upon legal tools which require large monetary requirements. Copyrights can be very powerful for loss of an exact copy by an intentional thief. However, protection beyond an exact copy is frequently unavailable and, again, copyright litigation is not inexpensive. The truth is: none of these are as powerful or successful a tool to protect your technology as patents. Patents command a respect that these other legal tools do not. The reasons for this vary according to the circumstance but generally can be pared down to a few well-known reasons, including (1) the presumption of validity of each patent, (2) the expectation of success due to successes by other industry Davids against industry Goliaths, (3) the availability of serious remedies from federal courts including injunctions, triple damages, and having the loser pay attorneys' fees.

The next factor is the proper establishment of the business and the business plan. It goes without saying that a business needs a business plan. The simple fact is, without a business plan, investors will not put money into the business. Identifying and analyzing the robustness of the business plan is an excellent tool to diagnose whether a business got off on the right foot and/or whether failure to execute the plan is a critical factor.

Other factors which are discussed in the case studies and interviews include the quantity and quality of problems with one or more of the following: the actual development of the product, regulatory issues, introduction to the market, care and feeding by an adequate sales force, and management of production and sales to achieve a profit.

It should be noted that out of all of the case studies and interviews conducted, two main factors or principles can be identified which seem to be indicia of final success and which can be used to determine whether to enter into a venture at all: (1) the presence or absence of an inflexible egoist on the research or development team, and (2) the availability of complete information and open dialogue between the team members about the business. With this in mind, each case study is presented below.

From these case studies, there are five preliminary and generic requirements for each start-up to be on the road to success, see Figure 9.1. First, the technology must work. Second, there must be a market for the product which is large and well-defined. Third, there must be sufficient funds to carry the venture until the second round of financing. Fourth, the people involved must have a critical mass of experience with the technology and they must have a track record, preferably a successful track record, in starting up new ventures. Fifth and last, there must be good intellectual property protection of the product, and preferably, enough overlap to provide some level of market defined monopoly.

Figure 9.1
Thematic Topology of Six Case Studies

1. **TECHNOLOGY**
2. **MARKET**
3. **FUNDING**
4. **TRACKRECORD**
5. **IP PORTFOLIO**

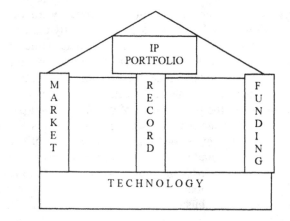

Case Study Number One

This case study involved three main participants: an inventor, a financier, and a patent lawyer. The technology involved the field of biotechnology, specifically the use of a human-derived protein for treating infertility. An important technological point is that the protein was derived from human placental tissue and the administration of this type of human protein imposes a higher level of regulatory risk of nonapproval by the FDA.

During due diligence, a number of critical milestones were successfully accomplished. Namely, the technology was shown to work by way of proof-of-principle experiments in animals. This was an important foundational aspect to going forward. Second, the market analysis showed this area to have a fairly large, well-defined population of motivated, treatable individuals who were known to be able and willing to pay for a product of this type. Third, a relatively large amount of start-up money was raised and available (about $800,000 cash and $350,000 in patent services) to fund the venture. The equity-for-services portion involved the patent attorney investing $350,000 worth of time in exchange for 700,000 shares of the company. Fourth, the people involved had a good amount of scientific experience as well as a track record of success in developing products like this. Fifth, the inventor and financier were able to involve a patent lawyer early in the process so that the technology could be properly searched and positioned. The ability to position technology within a given area–that is, to understand the invention and its variations and compare it to the patentability search results to define both patent claims to protect the product, as well as defining patent claims to clear out and temporarily monopolize an entire market–is critical to the success of technology ventures. The product claims are intended to provide a freedom to sell the invention without competition and the market exclusion claims are intended to provide defensive and licensing opportunities. In this example, good patent protection was obtained. Corporate activity continued, including research and development and a public offering of company shares.

However, a problem developed with the technology. The purification methods available at the time the infertility treatment was developed could not purify protein to ensure that the placental-derived protein was HIV-free. This was not determined to be a major issue by the new venturers. However, this became an issue after an application was made to the FDA for approval and questions were raised. Thus, a crisis situation developed when it appeared that non-approval was imminent. It quickly became apparent that the company needed an FDA lawyer early in process to address the purification issue and avoid a bad first impression with the FDA.

In an attempt to address the issue, management tried to switch to a new product during the approval process. The new product did not have the purification issue of the old product. However, a negative impression of "the product" was already inadvertently created at FDA. Thus, convincing the FDA staffers that they could still approve the product and meet their statutory responsibilities regarding safety, efficacy, and the like became an uphill battle.

During corporate reviews afterward, it became apparent that the project was a total failure. Upon looking into potential causes, it also became apparent that inventor did not communicate effectively to the team concerning the purification requirement. Accordingly, people who were a party to this venture who could have foreseen the problem at the FDA and developed an appropriate solution (e.g., obtained FDA advice and submitted the second product) were kept out of the information loop. This lack of communication within the group of one critical feature brought down the entire project. The result is that the shares of company stock dropped from $6-$8 per share to $0.01 per share upon receipt by the company of the adverse notice from the FDA.

Case Study Number Two

This case study involved four main participants: an inventor, a financier/manager, a second financier/manager, and a patent lawyer. The technology involved biotechnology, specifically a treatment which stimulated the immune cascade and the nitric oxide synthase (NOS) cascade, which resulted in improved wound healing, treatment of erectile dysfunction, treatment of clogged arteries, and increasing the vigor of the patient. The treatment consisted of the intravenous re-administration of 10cc of the patient's own blood which had been pretreated by heating to a specified temperature.

During due diligence, a number of critical milestones were successfully accomplished. The technology was shown to work by way of proof-of-principle experiments in animals. This was an important foundational aspect to going forward. Second, the market analysis showed this area to have a fairly large and well-defined population of motivated, treatable individuals who were known to be able and willing to pay for a product of this type. Third, a relatively large amount of start-up money was raised and available to fund the venture. It should be noted that there were a large number of experienced investors, both domestic and international. The equity-for-services portion involved the patent attorney providing about $400,000 worth of time in exchange for shares of the company. Fourth, the people involved had a good amount of scientific experience as well as a track record of success in developing products like this. Fifth, the inventor and financier were able to involve a patent lawyer early in the process so that the technology could be properly searched and positioned and good patent protection was obtained. Corporate activity continued, including research and development and a public offering of company shares.

However, a couple of minor problems developed with the project. First, the invention of removing a patient's own blood, heating it, and readministering it to the patient had a few drawbacks. The technology, as originally conceived, might be good as a novelty service offered at an old-fashioned spa, especially since the original heating unit consisted of a common heat lamp. However, the problem still existed of how to develop this into a patentable product which can be profitably sold. Another problem involved the machine used to heat the blood, which was quite large and bulky. A last problem involved whether the process had been known or used in a foreign country prior to filing for patent protection. Breaching secrecy of an invention by publishing to the world or offering it for sale can result in an irreversible, albeit unintentional, abandonment of the invention and a loss of patent rights in the United States or Europe or both depending on the particular facts.

A few ideas were floated around to solve these problems. One of them involved creating a smaller heating unit. This could be separately patented and provide value to the portfolio. However, the profit on a $50,000 machine might be $5,000 and the number to be sold would be limited. Another involved creating a line of disposable plastic products and cannisters to be used with the heating unit during the heating process to maintain sterility and to create patentable, marketable products. This idea came from the patent attorney who had some experience with using patent strategies relating to disposables to avoid commoditization of a product.

However, the inventor did not fully appreciate these ideas and objected to the wasteful commercialization of an otherwise simple and effective invention. Aside from debating the merits of a market economy, the inventor's viewpoint won out and highly profitable disposables were not developed.

Another major problem occurred when the company stopped paying the patent attorney's legal bills and the patent attorney had to threaten to file suit to collect. After a settlement where it was agreed that the bills would be paid and it might be in the best interest of the company to use some of the patent attorney's experience, the patent attorney was offered a position on the board of directors to be kept in the information loop.

Although ultimately successful since the product was approved by FDA and the company is now listed on the American Stock Exchange (AMEX), the company conducted a reverse 1:7 stock consolidation in order to go public. As a result, the patent attorney lost valuable stock and received no profit from the venture. The patent attorney also did not receive the type of return commonly received by venture capitalists–namely fivefold return on investment over a five-year period–as was promised although the patent attorney did finally receive all legal fees. Nonetheless, the patent attorney was able to use experience in this particular technical area to leverage expertise in order to address new clients in the same field and to keep the cohesion of and not lose trained attorneys by keeping them engaged. An analogy can be made to a nuclear power station in that there is an opportunity cost of not engaging the horsepower of the plant, and it is better to keep the plant engaged even at less-than-optimum capacity.

An interesting side note: it is important to convert shares received as soon as possible. In this case study, the shares were held too long and sold too late by the patent attorney, resulting in a sale of shares at 10 cents/share, and not at the price available at the IPO or liquidity event, which was $1/share. The idea of "skin in the game" must be balanced to the risk involved. It was important for the company to know that the attorney had "skin in the game" and was sharing in the early-stage risk. However, at the time of the liquidity event, much if not all of the patent work was completed and the marginal value of developing trust through showing loyalty was lost on a corporate entity which had moved past that point.

Case Study Number Three

This case study involved four main participants: an inventor, a financier, a manager, and a patent lawyer. The technology involved biotechnology, specifically a treatment for prostate cancer through the administration of a missing enzyme.

During due diligence, a number of rather critical milestones were not accomplished. Namely, more than seven years after the initial discovery, the technology was not shown to work by way of proof-of-principle experiments in animals. This was an important foundational failure and barrier to going forward. Without proof-of-principle experiments, significant private funding was not available.

Second, although the market analysis showed this area to have a fairly large and well-defined population of motivated, treatable individuals who were known to be able and willing to pay for a product of this type, the delivery of a protein rather than a chemical may have been an underestimated risk factor for some potential investors who stayed out.

Third, a relatively small amount of start-up money was raised and available to fund the venture. In all, there were four original investors who put up $25,000 each. Later, a second round of financing was obtained through an angel investor who enabled the development of a relatively strong patent portfolio.

The original funding was a clear-cut underfunding of a new venture, especially in the biotechnology arena where ventures consume large amounts of capital in research and development. The equity-for-services portion involved the patent attorney providing about $18,000 worth of time: however, despite two offers from the patent attorney to exchange the outstanding balance as well as tack on an additional amount sufficient to enable the development of the patent portfolio, the company declined to provide shares on both occasions. The immediate impact was that the company continued to struggle to fund both research and other commitments including the patent lawyer, which delayed conducting the proof-of-principle experiments. The venture capital funding sources told the company that these experiments were the only thing which were required in order to receive a large funding. Nonetheless, shares were not provided.

Fourth, the people involved had a good amount of scientific experience, but not all of the people had a track record of success in developing products like this. This became apparent when fund-raising was being pursued part-time and a lack of previous contacts in the industry would have been helpful to facilitate deal-making.

Fifth, the inventor and manager were not able to involve a patent lawyer early in the process. Thus, there was a premature publication of the findings which had the net effect of eliminating almost all foreign patent rights. Generally, patent rights in Europe and Japan are completely barred by a publication subject to a very limited exception which did not apply in this scenario anyway. Another complicating factor was the choice of law firm. The original firm, although competent as far as U.S. patent rights were concerned, charged "an arm and a leg." This decision drained precious resources away from the start-up from the very beginning, and upon reacting to this, a transfer to another firm was necessitated. By the time the patent lawyer got involved, it required some clever positioning and strategies to fill out the portfolio within the budget given. Eventually, good patent positions were developed which was important for the following reasons. The original technology, although not being aggressively pursued by the start-up, was being aggressively pursued by a competitor which had developed a related technology during the long period before proof-of-principle in animals was obtained. Thus, the original concept was valuable enough that it was being copied and the patent attorney was able to obtain patent coverage which would allow the larger competitor to feel a threat and seek licensing discussions. Unfortunately, the company felt that the patent position did not have to be shared with anybody and a strategy not to seek a cross-license was pursued while government grants were sought. The good news is that eventually the company brought on some well-connected and experienced management. Soon thereafter, an equity deal was made to alleviate the legal debt and further advance the clinical studies by freeing up capital. It is now expected that success is imminent–better late than never!

Case Study Number Four

This case study involved three main participants: an inventor, a financier, and a patent lawyer. The technology involved the field of pharmaceutical preparations, a topical drug delivery system, (cream), which can be used to administer most any type of drug through the skin, avoiding the need for injections.

During due diligence, a number of critical milestones were successfully accomplished. The technology was shown to work by way of proof-of-principle experiments in animals. This was an important foundational aspect to going forward. Second, the market analysis showed this area to have a fairly large and well-defined population of motivated, treatable individuals who were known to be able and willing to pay for a product of this type. Third, due to a recent failure by the financier only a relatively modest amount of start-up money was raised and available (about $450,000 cash). The way the deal was structured, 35 percent of the shares went to the patent attorney for patent services and other services as needed (e.g., drafting press releases etc.). Another 30 percent went to the financier for the initial cash position as well as for being responsible for future fund-raising; and the remaining 35 percent went to the inventor for providing the laboratory, additional research and development costs, and testing. The equity-for-services portion involved the patent attorney investing $350,000 worth of time in exchange for shares of the company. Fourth, the people involved had a good amount of scientific experience and were well-seasoned in developing products like this, and in developing products in start-up ventures. It is important to note that all of the parties agreed that, this time, the intent would be to conduct R&D with the end goal of licensing the technology. No efforts were taken or expectations raised by the parties that they would end up manufacturing, distributing, or seeking approval of the product. Additionally, the exit strategy (outlined below) was built into the business model and formation of the company. Fifth, the inventor and financier were able to involve a patent lawyer early in the process so that the technology could be properly searched and positioned. In this example, good patent protection was obtained. Corporate activity continued, including research and development and a public offering of company shares.

However, a problem was encountered on the way to going public. In a usual IPO to be listed on the New York Stock Exchange (NYSE), a company must show $25 million in accounts to qualify or the exchange will not list the shares. For the NASDAQ, a similar requirement exists but the amount is only $5 million. Also, the share price must be between about $5 and $50 per share to qualify. Nonetheless, for a start-up to show $5 million in accounts is a lot of money to leave laying around (and not being put to work).

In an interesting side note relevant to this, many people who have been involved with a number of start-up ventures know that when a venture goes south, one of the things that can happen is that the exchange can delist your stock. However, it is not that simple either. The first place you get sent down to when your stock goes below $5 per share is the Bulletin Board. To qualify for the Bulletin Board the share price must be $1 per share. Your shares must also be tradable to investors, you must meet certain accounting and reporting requirements, there must be a broader number of market makers for your stock, and you must have an association with the news services. If you are missing any of these, your stock might listed on the Pink Sheets. The only main requirements to be listed on the Pink Sheets is that the stock trades at 5 cents per share, that the stock is tradable to investors, and that the company attempt to maximize investment for the investors. Of course, this is quite a tumble for certain high-flying stocks, the names of many of which we will all remember for eternity.

However, this stepwise approach, although orderly and fair to companies and investors alike, is not usually seen as a method for stepping up, but rather is seen as the way toward filing Chapter 7 or 11 in bankruptcy. But if a company takes the step-up approach, a start-up can grow and attract investors in a very modest and orderly manner.

Thus, in the above case study, the company started by issuing shares and qualifying for trading on the Pink Sheets. As the company grew, additional testing was performed, additional money was obtained, and the company complied with the accounting and reporting requirements, obtained a broader number of market makers, and became available to the news services. Then the company applied for listing on the Bulletin Board. Soon thereafter, the stock price was steadily above $5 per share and the company applied to be and was successfully listed on the NASDAQ exchange. The company is no longer a start-up, trades publicly today, and the company now has a different set of challenges.

Case Study Number Five

This case study involved three main participants: an inventor, a financier, and a patent lawyer. The technology involved the field of pharmaceuticals, specifically the topical delivery of chemotherapeutics to treat cancer. It should be noted that the inventor was unusually difficult to deal with, the particular character flaw consisted of "being a know-it-all." This is particularly interesting since the type of personality commonly associated with starting a new venture is thought to be quite egotistical or arrogant. In point of fact, that may very well be the case among the younger venturers or those with a spotty track record. However, it is important to note that among the variety of people involved there appears to be an understanding among seasoned veterans that a certain degree of selfless behavior is critical to the success of any new venture.

During due diligence, a number of critical milestones were not accomplished. First, the technology was shown to work by way of proof-of-principle experiments in animals, but there was a problem during clinical testing. Second, the market analysis showed this area to have a fairly large and well-defined population of motivated, treatable individuals who were known to be able and willing to pay for a product of this type. Third, a relatively large amount of start-up money was raised and available to fund the venture. The equity-for-services portion involved the patent attorney initially operating under a straight fee-for-service arrangement and then, as expenses rose, converting to a swap of outstanding accounts receivable of about $50,000 in exchange for stock. However, it was not that simple. As the accounts receivable grew, the patent attorney demanded payment. When it was not forthcoming, legal action was discussed and a settlement of outstanding balances was paid in shares. It should be noted that the same considerations of good investing should apply when evaluating an equity-for-service arrangement when it occurs through default circumstances or when it occurs planned from the beginning. Fourth, the people involved had a good amount of scientific experience as well as a track record of success in developing products like this. Fifth, the patent lawyer was not brought in until later in the company's history, after formation and strategic planning had already been completed. Thus, the technology was not properly searched and positioned but was "shoe-horned" as happens when previously existing facts and circumstances meet the requirements of patent law.

However, a problem developed. Upon testing the product for FDA approval, the inventor did not explain that the product formulation which was tested originally, which data was submitted to the government, was not the same product formulation that was tested later. The inventor did not appreciate that following the rules at the FDA was critical. This lack of identical products prompted a conclusion that the clinical tests did not exhibit efficacy. This means that the FDA didn't think it works and approval is denied. The next mistake was that there was no backup product. The start-up venture was later wrapped and discontinued.

Case Study Number Six

This case study involved three main participants: an inventor, a financier, and a patent lawyer. The technology involved the field of insecticides, specifically the combining of insecticide and paint for applying to the foundations of buildings.

During due diligence, a number of critical milestones were not accomplished. The technology was shown to work by way of proof-of-principle experiments which were confirmed by independent lab results. Second, the market analysis showed this to be a modest but well-defined population of purchasers, who were known to be able and willing to pay for a product of this type. However, the company had no significant amount of funding. The equity-for-services portion involved the patent attorney initially operating under a straight fee-for-service arrangement and then as expenses rose, converting to a swap of outstanding accounts receivable of about $20,000 in exchange for stock. Fourth, the people involved had a good amount of scientific experience as well as a track record of success in developing products like this. Fifth, the patent lawyer was not brought in until later in the company's history, after formation and strategic planning had already been completed. Further, the patent lawyer was not consulted during development or kept in the loop of information. Nonetheless, the patent attorney was able to provide good patent coverage for the product and the market.

However, a problem developed. Unknown to the patent attorney, the company filed for reorganization. All of the insiders knew about it and took care of their affairs. Unfortunately, nobody told the patent lawyer since he did not have a position on the board or access to internal audit reports. Consequently, he continued to provide patent services beyond when he should have and eventually lost his investment. The product is currently sold on the market.

CASE STUDIES FROM OTHER PROFESSIONAL SERVICE FIRMS

Consulting firms have a long history of both working with start-up firms as clients and taking equity stakes in new ventures. Bain & Company, the venerable strategy consulting firm, has long operated an investment unit (Bain Capital) which has applied the company's analytical tools to new investment opportunities. In the 1980s, Andersen Consulting accepted equity from large defense contractors as partial compensation for assisting those clients with restructuring.[102] The Parthenon Group, a mid-sized strategic consulting firm founded in 1991, began using equity as a supplement to regular fees in 1992.[103] For the most part, however, the investing activities of most professional service firms have been kept separate from their actual services. Equity investments are used as a means to earn greater return on capital rather than to receive compensation for services rendered.

Outside the legal industry, the practice of taking equity as compensation began to gain popularity only in the late 1990s, well after the Internet boom erupted. The initial public offering by Netscape in 1996 is widely viewed as the watershed event in the rush to invest in Internet businesses. The significant gains in Netscape's stock price on its first day of trading illustrated the optimism of the Internet era. The rapid rise in the flow of venture capital into the technology sector (particularly into those with Internet-based business models) increased the demand for a range of professional services, including public relations, executive recruiting, graphic design, and management consulting. At the same time, the wild success of many technology IPOs in that time also increased the attractiveness of using equity as a compensation mechanism for professional services. This environment created a "virtuous cycle," whereby the growth in the number of venture-backed businesses expanded both the number of potential clients and potential investment opportunities for all professional service firms.

Firms which began using equity as compensation for professional services did so based on reasons very similar to the development of equity-based compensation in law firms. The challenges of employee recruitment and

---

[102] "Cash? How Old Economy," *The Economist*, 6 May 2000, p. 15-18.
[103] Eric Krell, "A Consultancy of Generalists," *Consulting Magazine*, March 2001, p. 26.

retention was a major factor in the decision of consulting firms to start creating funds using equity from clients. The Big Five consulting and accounting firms began to notice difficulty in recruiting Master of Business Administration (MBA) graduates in the spring of 1999, as more MBA students opted to join entrepreneurial firms rather than large consulting practices.[104] The wake-up call to the major consultancies came in September 1999, when the CEO of Andersen Consulting, George Shaheen, left the firm after more than 30 years of loyal service to head the Internet grocery start-up Webvan.[105] Shortly thereafter, the Big Five firms began making investments in start-up clients. Andersen Consulting took ownership stakes in ChemConnect (a chemical industry business-to-business marketplace), Blue Martini (an electronic commerce software firm), and Shoplink.com (an on-line grocery service). Ernst & Young invested in the Patent & License Exchange and in Intralinks.[106]

To prevent further defections such as that of George Shaheen, Andersen Consulting pooled its equity in these start-ups to create a fund whose returns were distributed to partners.[107] Cambridge Technology Partners, an information technology services and consulting firm, also created an "incubator" program to invest in and nurture start-ups and distribute the returns to employees and shareholders. Investors clearly saw this as a positive development, as the firm's stock price gained 15 percent following the announcement of the new incubator program.[108] By December 1999, all of the Big Five consulting firms were accepting equity investments in start-up clients as at least partial compensation for their services.[109] These firms claimed that the practice was motivated as much by the preferences of their start-up clients as by the consultants' desire for the potential returns from equity-based compensation. According to Richard Polodian, Managing Partner for the Los Angeles office of Arthur Andersen LLP, "The fact of the matter is that the currency that e-business companies want to use to compensate their service providers has changed [from cash fees to equity stakes]."[110]

At the same time, consulting firms also started perceiving equity-for-services compensation as a means to extract greater returns from their own intellectual capital and talent. Bill Achtmeyer, founder of The Parthenon Group, claims that Bain & Company founder Bill Bain was first to promote the idea of charging clients based on the value of the advice given rather than the number of

---

[104] The Big Five accounting consulting firms at that time were Andersen Consulting (now Accenture), Ernst & Young (now Cap Gemini Ernst & Young), KPMG Peat Marwick (now KPMG Consulting), PricewaterhouseCoopers, and Deloitte & Touche.

[105] Tom Rodenhauser, "Shaheen Leaves Andersen," *Inside Consulting*, 9 September 1999.

[106] Kim Girard and Melanie Austria Farmer, "Consulting Firms Shift Gears with Start-up Stakes," *News.Com*, 22 October 1999.

[107] Farmer, Ibid.

[108] Melanie Austria Farmer, "Cambridge Technology to Launch Start-up Incubator Program," *News.Com*, 8 December 1999.

[109] Personal conversation between a manager at Arthur Andersen Consulting and one of the authors, December 1999, New Orleans.

[110] Debora Vrana, "California Dealin'—Financing the State's Emerging Companies," *Los Angeles Times*, 31 January 2000, p. C1.

hours spent giving that advice. Achtmeyer also supports the philosophy that taking equity underscores the consultant's commitment to a client: "My view was that if we really believed that our advice was high-quality and could lead to improvements in value, then we ought to be willing to put our money where our mouth was."[111]

Consulting firms in the late 1990s also began adopting an intellectual venture capital approach as a means of expanding their services to clients. In these programs, consulting firms often "lent out" experienced consultants to spin-off ventures established by their clients. The firm would take partial ownership of the venture in exchange for providing that critical human capital. Again, this strategy was designed in part to improve retention—professionals who were attracted by the excitement and opportunities in Internet start-ups could work in that environment while still maintaining a relationship with the consulting firm. Boston Consulting Group (BCG) in 1999 required clients of its e-commerce consulting services to sign long-term agreements which included a provision that the consulting engagement would result in the formation of a joint venture between BCG and the client, which would then solicit outside investment.

One example of BCG's approach was a consulting project for the appliance manufacturer Whirlpool, where the two firms formed a new venture called Brandwise. The start-up was based around a Website which enabled consumers to compare appliances and other products from multiple manufacturers, supplemented by product testing and reviews from *Good Housekeeping* magazine. The new company began as a joint venture among BCG, Whirlpool, and Hearst Publications (publisher of *Good Housekeeping*), and received tens of millions of dollars in start-up capital from outside investors. BCG helped to recruit Kathy Misunas, then CEO of the SABRE Group, to become head of Brandwise. Fourteen BCG consultants were involved in launching Brandwise. As noted by BCG manager Rob McGill, "In this particular case, we gave BCG consultants the opportunity to really be on the front lines as opposed to behind the scenes."[112]

Many consulting firms created new organizational units to manage these equity-based new ventures, where a consulting firm acted in part as a venture capital firm as well as providing advice to the client. For example, Deloitte Consulting created a $500 million VC fund called Deloitte Consulting Ventures. One venture funded by this unit was a new Website to manage procurement for elementary schools in the United States. The site was developed jointly by Deloitte and Epylon, a provider of hosted e-business solutions for government and public-sector institutions. The two companies did not create a separate entity, but instead set up the venture as a joint project with Epylon, where Deloitte agreed to take a share of the revenues from the new site as partial compensation for its consulting and integration services. These revenues would be generated by transaction fees paid by suppliers who wanted to sell to the 500-

---

[111] Krell, op. cit., p. 30.
[112] Jack Sweeney, "The New Equity Model," *Consulting Magazine*, September 1999.

plus school districts which registered to use the site. Douglas Taylor, global director for the public sector at Deloitte, explained that the use of a joint project structure was "much leaner and more flexible than creating a separate, formal company."[113]

Other consulting firms established special so-called incubator or accelerator programs to help emerging Internet firms to develop and implement strategies, with equity often part of the compensation scheme. Many of these were not traditional incubators, in that they did not provide physical facilities for housing start-ups. Instead, they were "virtual" incubators that provided the supplemental talent and advice needed to help start-up firms to grow into established companies. Andersen Consulting established a series of "launch centers" worldwide to provide services targeted at Internet and technology start-ups.

These clients would be offered the option of paying for those services in part using equity. Start-ups would be screened before participating in the launch centers; they would have to have received $1 to $2 million in initial funding, plus have a core management team in place and a solid business model. Initially, Andersen Consulting expected that it would receive as much as $1.2 billion in equity as payment for services over the period from 2001 to 2004.[114]

Among consulting firms, none has been more aggressive about using equity as a form of compensation for services than the Parthenon Group. As noted above, CEO Bill Achtmeyer believes strongly in the principle that equity ownership aligns the incentives and rewards for both employees and consultants. "Businesspeople make return-on-investment judgments every day, and CEOs are often incented by the rise and fall of the stock price. If we think we can provide good strategic advice, then we ought to take similar risks."[115] He estimates that the firm has historically earned between 10 and 17 percent of total revenues from equity investments in clients.[116] In some cases, such as a consulting engagement for a health-care start-up firm called Bridge Medical, The Parthenon Group took all of its fee as equity. The CEO of Bridge Medical, James Sweeney, agrees that this approach is appealing to both consultants and clients, saying that any consulting firm which does not offer this option for compensation "will become competitively disadvantaged."[117]

Consulting firms also acknowledge some of the limitations and even disadvantages of the equity-for-services model. In one case, Deloitte Consulting entered into such an agreement with one of its clients. Stephen Sprinkle, managing director for service lines and marketing at Deloitte, notes that after that engagement, "the benefits (to Deloitte) ended up being a 240 percent gain of

---

[113] Alan Radding and Mina Landriscina, "Tales of Three Ventures," *Consulting Magazine*, November-December 2000, pp. 58-62.

[114] "Incubators created to exploit Dot-com Fever," *International Accounting Bulletin*, 20 March 2000, p. 4.

[115] Edward Welles, "How to Get Rich in America," *Inc.*, April 1999, p. 40+.

[116] Krell, op. cit., p. 30.

[117] Welles, op. cit.

what was anticipated and the client actually said, 'Gee, I never intended to pay this much money.'"[118]

One limitation encountered in the late 1990s on equity-for-services arrangements in consulting was the potential conflict of interest in using this practice in firms which offer accounting services. The Big Five accounting/consulting firms all maintained very large consulting practices while simultaneously offering traditional public accounting services (such as independent audit services). However, these firms were barred from providing most types of consulting services to firms for which they acted as independent auditors, and clearly should not own equity in those clients. The inherent conflict of interest was quite apparent. Independent auditors provide crucial information to investors about the financial health of public firms. If those auditors, in turn, owned stock in such a client, then they would have an incentive to modify their audit results to hide any facts that might have a negative impact on the client's stock price.

As a result, these large public accounting firms had to maintain very complex networks of relationships with their clients, ensuring that their portfolio of consulting clients (especially those which offered equity for consulting services) did not overlap with their portfolio of audit clients. The situation was one part of an intensive study by the Securities and Exchange Commission on potential business conflicts of large accounting firms. In an interview, Greg Moore (head of the accounting practice for the Los Angeles office of PricewaterhouseCoopers LLP) noted, "The SEC is taking a very hard look at the impartiality of accountants....Accepting stocks could send the wrong impression. We are not doing it."[119]

Other accounting firms decided that as long as they were not acting as an officially designated independent auditor, but instead simply providing financial accounting advice (often called "assurance services" in the accounting industry), there should be no rules barring accountants from owning equity in their clients. In such cases, the accounting firms argued that they were not primarily accountable to shareholders or the public markets, but instead providing managerial accounting expertise to the executives of client firms:

> Arthur Andersen already networks with established companies looking to create an e-business strategy and Internet start-ups through its "100 Days to Market" program, which helps companies get their books in shape before an initial public offering as well as subsequent stock offerings. In that program, Andersen bundles several services, such as tax and financial assistance and Web page design. As part of that program, Andersen will take an equity stake in lieu of fees.[120]

---

[118] Craig Zarley, "Integrators Plot E-business Agenda," *Computer Reseller News*, 25 October 1999.

[119] Jason Booth, "Stock-hungry Firms Trade Services for Equity," *Los Angeles Business Journal*, 14 June 1999.

[120] Debora Vrana, "Arthur Andersen Venture Fund Adds Net Start-ups to Its Equation," *Los Angeles Times*, 31 January 2000, p. C1+.

One strategy adopted by accounting firms to circumvent potential conflict-of-interest rules was to establish the emerging companies practice as a separate legal entity, not designated as an accounting firm. This would give the accounting parent "plausible deniability" that they were not holding stock while acting as an auditor to a client. Grant Thornton, the sixth-largest U.S. public accounting firm in the late 1990s, adopted this approach. In early 2000, the firm announced that its eBusiness Consulting Group would be restructured as a separate entity from Grant Thornton, specifically so that it could take equity as a form of service compensation. In the words of Don Esposito, Grant Thornton CEO, "There are many, many start-ups today in the technology area that are very strapped for cash or capital that have a high degree of need for professional services and the only way they can pay for those services is through an equity participation with the professional services provider."[121]

The practice of taking equity in exchange for consulting services is not limited to U.S. firms. In late 1999, the *Financial Times* of London noted that large European firms were adopting a similar practice, in part as a response to the activities of U.S.-based consultancies in Europe. Both Linklaters and Eversheds, two of the most prominent consulting firms in London, established funds in 1999 to accept equity in return for deferring or even waiving the fees charged to start-ups in the Internet sector. The rise of Internet stocks on European exchanges alerted consulting firms to the potential benefits of this practice. "We decided we had a choice between giving advice away for free and giving it away for free and getting some upside (by taking) a small slug of equity," says Rupert Pearce, head of Linklaters' Internet and e-commerce group. "It was a no-brainer."[122]

The massive falloff in technology stock valuations between 2000 and 2001 is clearly a deterrent to consulting firms expanding their use of equity as compensation. It has not, however, erased the practice entirely. Bain Consulting, for example, reduced the degree to which it accepts equity as compensation. For 2001, it expected that equity would constitute only 5 percent of the firm's annual revenues, compared to 15 percent in the year 2000. The stock market downturn has also made the firm much more selective about the kind of clients who can use equity as payment. "The equity that people try to give you is usually the equity that you least want," according to John Donahoe, worldwide managing director at Bain. "We've tried to be very disciplined."[123]

In general, it appears that smaller consulting firms are still the most aggressive about taking equity as partial compensation. Such firms may be less risk-averse than large consulting firms, which have to satisfy diverse partners or shareholders with their quarterly returns. At the same time, smaller consulting firms may have less choice in the matter—when their consultants are running

---

[121] John Sterlicchi and Elspeth Wales, "Corporate Gamblers Try the Picasso Principle," *The Evening Standard* (London), 15 March 2000, p. 45.

[122] Jean Eaglesham, "All Aboard the E-rocket," *Financial Times*, 15 December 1999, p. 24.d

[123] Thor Valdmanis, "Fewer Firms Taking Equity Option Instead of Cash Payments," *USA Today*, 25 April 2001, Money section, p. 7B.

low on cash, taking equity may be a requirement for retaining that client's business. Bruce Ahern, a San Diego independent consultant to high-technology companies, discussed one situation where he took equity as compensation from a client because there appeared to be no other recourse for getting paid for his time. The client paid part of its fee in cash, but negotiated with Ahern to pay the rest in equity, due to financing problems. "Right now those shares have no value, but who knows down the road? If things work out, it could mean I would end up making more money on this deal. Then again, I could lose it all," Ahern says.[124]

Use of Equity for Compensation in Other Professional Service Firms

Apart from more traditional advisers, such as management consultants, by the year 2000 professional service providers of all types began adopting the equity-for-services model to supplement their conventional compensation and fees. The lure of large gains from clients who could do an IPO within months of founding proved very attractive to a range of service firms. This practice even extended to include other vendors who provided products or services to start-up firms. Jay Whitehead, the founder of an on-line human resources service called EmployeeService.com, told *The Economist* magazine that he received demands for equity from prospective landlords, his equipment leasing firm, and even an inquiry from Cisco Systems, which offered to put him on a priority list for receiving hardware if he gave them equity.[125] Ingrid Rosten, assistant director at the International Business Incubator in San Jose, California, jokes, "I'm waiting for the cleaning lady to start asking [for equity]." Reflecting on the prevalence of stock-for-services payments in Silicon Valley, she explained in an April, 2000 interview, "You can pretty much get anyone to exchange equity-for-services today. All of those lawyers and professional service firms in effect become angel investors."[126]

Several types of professional services firms have become more active in taking equity as partial compensation since the late 1990s. Among the more aggressive firms are executive recruiters and public relations/marketing consultants, as illustrated by the cases below.

Executive Recruiting and Placement

Taking equity as compensation for services is not a very foreign concept in the executive placement industry, since much of their compensation is awarded on a contingency basis. In a typical engagement, a recruiter is paid only after a candidate is hired for the designated position. The recruiter's fee is generally some portion of the executive's starting salary, plus some bonus. Since the nature and experience of the top management team is a major factor in the

---

[124] Michael Allen, "Diverse Firms Feel the Pinch of Dot-com Woes," *San Diego Business Journal*, 24 July 2000, p. 3.

[125] "Cash? How Old Economy," *The Economist*, op. cit.

[126] Rebecca Mowbray, "Professional-Services Firms Accept Shares of Start-ups Rather Than Cash Payments," *The Houston Chronicle*, 23 April 2000, business section, p. 1.

success of a start-up firm, it seems reasonable that recruiters consider their services a very strategic resource for entrepreneurial clients.

Due to the high cost and critical nature of executive placement in start-up formation, recruiters were very eager to accept equity as partial payment for services. Heidrick & Struggles, one of the largest nationwide recruiting firms, created an "equity billing program" for just these situations. Since many dot-com start-ups compensated their executives with generous options packages, Heidrick & Struggles offered a plan where it would receive 33 percent of the first year's cash compensation of a placed executive, plus a third of the executive's first-year vested shares. In 1999, the firm took cash and stock options in 234 clients compared with 18 in 1998. Some start-ups that paid Heidrick & Struggles for its services included Covad Communications, ConvergeNet Technologies, and NetGravity. Lucia Steinhilber, manager of the equity billing program for the firm's Palo Alto office, commented that "Not all the arrangements are going to work out…but over the portfolio, we're hoping to come out better than if we had accepted only cash as payment."[127]

The executive recruiting practice at the consulting firm A.T. Kearney (owned by Electronic Data Systems Corporation) also adopted this same practice. Managing partner Tony Scott justified the move in this way: "If we can add value (with our placement services), then the companies have a higher probability of being successful and we are going to have a higher probability of making a return on those pieces that we take as equity."[128]

Marketing and Public Relations

Marketing firms are also strong believers in equity as compensation for services. Again, with the rush of Internet start-ups flooding the market in 1998 and 1999, public-relations strategy was a key factor in helping new ventures to attract both customers and strategic investors. Michael Terpin, founder, CEO, and chairman of a public-relations firm in Marina del Rey, California, took stock in some 15 Internet start-ups through early 2000. One was Xoom.com, which went public and was subsequently acquired by NBC. Terpin says he is "following the venture-capital model," with the return on Xoom.com covering his total investment.[129]

Pierpoint Communications, a PR firm in Houston, Texas, had made six service-for-stock arrangements with clients by early 2000. Some of the investments were valued at over $100,000. Two such arrangements involved all compensation as equity, which the owner of the firm, Phil Morabito, admitted was risky. "My controller is constantly sitting there telling me there's something called cash flow," Morabito said. "But we're watching it carefully to make sure we don't wake up one day and find out that all our fees are in equity." He also stressed the importance of vetting potential clients. "You've got to make sure

---

[127] Davan Maharaj, "More Firms are Willing to Work for Stock Options," *Los Angeles Times*, 24 January 2000.
[128] Sherry Kuzcynski, "Taking Stock," *HR Magazine*, 1 February 2000, p. 50.
[129] Edward Welles, "The Power of the Multiple: A Sampler," *Inc. Magazine*, April 1999, p. 52.

that things work, because once you have a stake in the company, you're married…God forbid that something goes sour. You have to make sure that the relationship is solid."[130]

As it turns out, Pierpoint ended up taking equity in 11 clients by April 2001, of which at least two became bankrupt and the others seemed unlikely to generate much return. Morabito estimates that he had invested $600,000 in billable hours in those clients, and was clearly discouraged from taking all of his fees as equity in the future. "If someone came in today, I would only take a maximum of 10 percent of our fee in equity," Morabito says. But he was not entirely deterred. "Will my employees and I retire on our equity portfolio? No. But it would take just one of our start-ups to reach the finish line for us to make some money. We may not make money on any of them, but it is fun to be in the game."[131]

Benefits of Equity-based Compensation in Other Professional Services

There are several reasons why a professional service firm would accept equity in place of traditional service fees. These reasons are fairly similar to the justifications for the rise of this practice in law firms. One reason prevalent during the Internet stock boom of 1999 was the tremendous "upside," or potential profits, promised by the availability of equity in pre-IPO start-ups. One managing partner of the executive search firm Heidrick & Struggles stated, "It no longer made any sense for us to accept only cash compensation because that was artificially low….Now, if a prospective client doesn't want to make up the shortfall with stock options, our preference is to avoid doing work for these kinds of companies in favor of others who are aligned with our interests."[132]

Another reason is that an equity stake makes the professional service firm more of a strategic partner in the business than a simple service provider. As noted in one article:

William Drenttele runs a small graphic-design business in Falls Village, Connecticut, doing much of his work for customers in the publishing industry….Drenttele says he asks for equity because he thinks his company's role merits it. "It's a good litmus test. If you get equity, you get treated differently." When you share in the equity, Drenttele explains, the line between being a vendor and a partner is shifted. Discussions with the customer are different. "It really takes finding someone who thinks that what you do enhances the intrinsic worth of what they do."[133]

This sense of tying the fortunes of the service provider to the client runs through many cases of equity-for-service arrangements. In many professional service firms, the professionals prefer to be seen as strategic partners by their

---

[130] Mowbray, op. cit.
[131] Valdmanis, op. cit.
[132] Maharaj, op.cit., p. C1+.
[133] Welles, op. cit.

clients. This may aid in ensuring that the consultant's advice is taken seriously, and gives the professional service provider a more apparent stake in the results of his or her services.

There are also reasons why professional service firms do not take all of their compensation as equity. Certainly risk management is one motivation—putting the entire value of an engagement in an equity arrangement could have serious financial consequences in a down market, as was the case in the year 2000 to 2001. But there are also less tangible reasons why using both a traditional fee structure in conjunction with equity is appropriate. Michael Terpin, the public relations professional quoted earlier, notes "I typically take enough cash to cover my overhead. If your compensation is all in equity, then the client doesn't really value your service, and besides, it's always nice to see how quickly people pay their bills." Terpin also emphasized that equity does have its advantages—the start-ups which he is able to help by taking equity in lieu of fees often have strong relationships to other potential clients in the start-up community, creating a new business development opportunity for his firm.[134]

The use of equity in place of fees also has advantages for the start-up firm, as expressed in the 1998 report "Should You Be Paying Your Consultant in Equity?" by The Parthenon Group, a Boston management consulting firm (The Parthenon Group has taken equity in place of fees in several consulting engagements with start-ups):[135]

1. It encourages consultants to focus on the long-term outlook for the company, rather than on short-term quick fixes.
2. It provides a strong incentive for consultants to give their best performance because they profit when the company profits.
3. It builds relationships and trust between company management and consultants by tying both groups to the same goals.

There are of course more mundane reasons for entrepreneurs to use equity in arrangements with professional service firms, the most obvious being as a means to conserve cash. One cofounder of an Internet technology start-up stated that his firm had issued stock options to certain service providers as an incentive, but that the main reason for issuing equity to consultants was to keep cash on reserve for operating purposes.

In general, professional service firms have just as much interest as law firms in being viewed as "intellectual venture capitalists" in the entrepreneurial sector. For larger firms, using equity in lieu of fees can give their employees the flavor of being engaged in a start-up without the downside risk of tying their careers and total compensation to the financial fortunes of that start-up. For more senior partners or small firms, equity can ensure that the client views the professional as a true partner in the client's future and reassures that client that the interests of the professional and start-up are truly aligned. The professional service

---

[134] Ibid.
[135] Quoted in Kuczynski, op.cit.

industry is perhaps more than any other truly a "knowledge-based" industry. As stated in the recent book, *Developing Knowledge-Based Client Relationships: The Future of Professional Services*, author Russ Dawson states:

> Professional service firms have been aware for decades that they are in the knowledge business have long focused on developing their abilities in leveraging knowledge; they also fully understand that their relationships with clients are the foundation of their current and future success[136]

Equity-based compensation arrangements with entrepreneurial clients help to guarantee that knowledge sharing between professional service providers and start-ups reinforce a long-term, strategic business relationship which ultimately reaps greater rewards for both the consultant and the entrepreneur.

---

[136] Russ Dawson, *Developing Knowledge-Based Client Relationships: The Future of Professional Services* (New York: New York University Press, 1999).

Chapter 10

Equity-for-Service Deals:
Conclusions, Insights, Recommendations

In this book, we have identified the concept of *the intellectual venture capitalist* and studied in practice the way the IVC operates, namely the Equity-for-Service compensation model, in lieu of the traditional fee-for-service compensation model. The equity-for-service approach has been around for some time but it gained significant attention in the late 1990s during the "dot-com" bubble, perhaps for the wrong reasons. We feel that the equity-for-service approach like any powerful idea can be abused and misapplied but that is more, not less, of a reason to try to understand how it works and help educate users and beneficiaries as well as institute more effective legal and financial guidelines for ensuring its benefits are captured and its adverse effects prevented.

With this motivation in mind, we have tried to understand, profile, and critique an alternative to the traditional fee for service approach to bringing together what we call *the idea makers* (the providers of human and intellectual capital: entrepreneurs, inventors, firm cofounders, and early employees) and *the idea brokers* (the providers of financial, intellectual, and social capital: the angel investors, venture capitalists, lawyers, accountants, management and business consultants) who together transform entrepreneurial dreams into business success time and again in the United States and around the world.

Intellectual venture capital is the specialized knowledge, expertise, know-how, networking, and goodwill that each of these stakeholders, including the entrepreneur, brings to the table. Such capital may include but is not limited to financing, ideas, knowledge management, and business or technological processes that facilitate everything from launch to production to marketing and selling. The providers of intellectual venture capital may include but are not limited to angel investors, accountants, patent attorneys, consultants, executive recruiters, and public relations specialists.

In this sense, the intellectual venture capitalist becomes a partner in the new venture, contributing expertise, wisdom, and resources (such as contacts) that are critical to the success of the start-up and not just a supplier of services. Accordingly, the compensation for an intellectual venture capitalist differs substantially from the traditional *fee-for-service model* prevalent in professional services. Instead of simply billing a client for a rough estimate of the time and effort expended, the intellectual VC takes compensation in the form of equity ownership in the new venture (the *equity-for-service model*). This changes the relationship between the professional service provider and the entrepreneur, creating an active partnership towards the success of the new venture in place of the traditional client-provider relationship.

The equity-for-service model compensates the service provider partially in equity, and thus the service provider gains a stake in the *long-term success* of the venture, rather than an individual, short-term task or engagement. The emphasis of this structure is on maintaining a mutually beneficial relationship between the entrepreneur and the professional service firm.

The way the equity-for-service model works, for instance in the case of a law firm providing legal services to an entrepreneur, is similar to the way a stock-option-incentive scheme aims at compensating employees or key company "insiders" (such as founders)—but obviously with the important caveat that the lawyer receiving the equity is an external service provider. The novelty of this approach lies not in the fact that the entrepreneur who provides the lawyer with equity in his firm is also his client, and this as we have seen may raise conflict of interest and other challenges as well as further empower the entrepreneur by providing him access to potentially critically important legal services.

There are a variety of investing arrangements between a law firm and a client entrepreneur:

1. Performing services for stock.
2. Performing services for deferred fees and stock.
3. Performing services for fees with stock as a premium for engagement / expertise.
4. Performing services for fees with a concomitant direct investment in the client in exchange for stock or founders stock.
5. Performing services for fees with a concomitant investment in a venture capital fund which then invests in a client.
6. Performing services for fees and co-investing during a venture capital financing round.

There are a few important caveats we stressed with regards to the equity-based model:

1. Most law firms using this model receive only a small portion of their compensation as equity. The bulk of their compensation is still paid in traditional billings.
2. While start-up firms have limited cash reserves to spend on lawyers, they also cannot issue stock options with impunity. Each option issued dilutes the value of the company, so entrepreneurs must be careful about which outside service providers should be rewarded with options.
3. Much of the interest in the equity-based model of compensation was fueled by the growth of the Internet economy and the "dot-com" stock bubble. Now that many Internet firms have seen their market value collapse post-IPO, interest in this model has clearly waned. Still, the equity-based model was used prior to the emergence of the commercial Internet and is likely to survive the current down-turn in initial public offerings.

The equity-based model of compensation in law firms is normally used in conjunction with traditional fee-for-service billing, and is targeted specifically at addressing the opportunities and pitfalls associated with working for entrepreneurial clients. Earlier, we listed a few key factors which firms consider when establishing an equity investment program:

a. Criteria for deciding to accept equity as payment (under what circumstances will the firm agree to use equity as a form of compensation for services?)
b. Amount of the investment (how should the law firm determine how much equity to accept from the start-up client?)
c. Timing of the investment (when is it appropriate to take equity-for-services?)
d. Format of the investment (how will the legal ownership of equity be established?)
e. Fund sourcing (what sources of funds will be used to take the equity?)
f. Distribution of returns (how and to whom will the profits of the equity investment be distributed?)

From our field research and background study we have painted a complex but we hope insightful picture regarding equity versus fee for service. We have documented diverse and divergent perspectives and opinions from the different groups of stakeholders.

We feel that the equity-for-service approach has real merit and potential, however, it also needs to be matured and adapted to the human, business, legal, market, and technological circumstances at hand.

Moreover, not all cases are amenable to the equity-for-fee approach and it certainly does not represent a panacea. However, when the circumstances are right, the equity-for-service approach may well serve as a catalyst and accelerator of entrepreneurial endeavor and success by providing crucial liquidity to the management, business, and legal services knowledge markets for entrepreneurs.

Our study has shown that there are a number of challenges and possibly needs for legislative reforms and policy interventions as well, aimed at empowering equity-for-service as a catalyst and accelerator of entrepreneurial endeavor and initiative that could help reinvigorate sustainable economic growth and development in the United States and around the world.

The reforms and interventions that may be needed fall in the following categories and we leave these as food for thought with the reader as well as inspiration for our future writings:

1. Legal reforms—there is a need for legislation to enhance transparency and accountability and make dealing with conflicts of interest easier as well as explore ways and means to make the IVC approach more amenable for entrepreneurs while within legal bounds.

2. Business reforms and policies—there is a need to deal with lack of business standards and norms for the IVC approach to make it more of an accessible and user-friendly approach for entrepreneurs.

3. Cultural change and transformation—there is a need to educate and enlighten as well as develop more networking and social capital for both the idea makers and the idea brokers as to the potential that can be unlocked and captured with the IVC approach.

4. Systemic— there is a need for more of an integrative, systems approach leveraging legal, business, and cultural reforms listed above and focusing their impact to bear on catalyzing entrepreneurial endeavor and initiative.

5. Technological—there is a need to make connectivity among idea makers and idea brokers more available, accessible, and affordable both in the United States and certainly around the world to truly empower the IVC approach, and that is where concepts such as global and local, real and virtual incubator networks (Carayannis, 2001a, 2002a) are relevant, timely, and critical.

Appendix

Patents on Intellectual Capital

Patent I: United States Patent 4,838,425
O'Brien et al. June 13, 1989
Tamper indicator for a blister package
Abstract

A tamper indicator for a blister package having a rupturable lid which is attached to a base formed with recesses that hold articles in the recesses between the lid and the base. The indicator comprises an easily ruptured and tearable film that completely covers the exposed surface of the base and is attached to the lid near the juncture of the lid and the base.

Inventors: **O'Brien, Denise M.** (Whippany, NJ); **Croce, Carlo P.** (Leonia, NJ)

Assignee: **Warner-Lambert Company** (Morris Plains, NJ)

Patent II: United States Patent 4,753,790
Silva et al. June 28, 1988
Sorbitol coated comestible and method of preparation
Abstract

A process for producing a sorbitol-coated comestible is disclosed. The process comprises applying to a substantially anhydrous edible core at least two coating solutions comprising sorbitol to coat the edible core, wherein the first coating solution comprises: (a) about 77 to about 81 wt % sorbitol solution comprising about 65 to about 75 wt % sorbitol; (b) about 9.5 to about 12.5 wt % crystalline sorbitol powder; (c) about 0.25 to about 1.5 wt % of at least one film-forming agent; and (d) about 0.1 to about 5.0 wt % of at least one crystallization retardant; and wherein the second coating solution comprises: (a) about 82 to about 92 wt % sorbitol solution comprising about 65 to about 75 wt % sorbitol; (b) about 1.0 to about 2.5 wt % crystalline sorbitol powder; (c) about 0.05 to about 2.0 wt % of at least one film-forming agent; and (d) about 0.1 to about 0.3 wt % of at least one crystallization retardant; and after application of each coating solution, the solution is dried to prepare a final product which is a smooth, hard, and crunchy comestible.

Inventors: **Silva, Jose N.** (Astoria, NY); **Yang, Robert K.** (Randolph, NJ); **Zamudio-Tena, Jose F.** (Morristown, NJ)

Assignee: **Warner-Lambert Company** (Morris Plains, NJ)

Patent III: United States Patent 4,778,640
Braun et al. October 18, 1988
Method of sequentially molding a *razor* cap
Abstract

A lubricating strip having a honeycomb structure of polystyrene and a water-soluble leachable shaving aid of high molecular weight polyethylene oxide is molded in situ on a *razor* cap made of thermoplastic material which has been previously injection molded.

Inventors: **Braun, David B.** (Ridgefield, CT); **Vreeland, William E.** (Shelton, CT); **Motta, Vincent C.** (West Norwalk, CT)

Assignee: **Warner-Lambert Company** (Morris Plains, NJ)

Patent IV: United States Patent 5,796,649

Keum et al. August 18, 1998

Dynamic random access memory capacitor and method for fabricating the same

Abstract

A *DRAM* capacitor and a method for fabricating the same, capable of achieving an increase in surface area and thereby an increase in capacitance while reducing the topology, by simply forming a conduction layer, as a charge storage electrode, comprised of conduction spacers around a double-layer pin-shaped conduction layer pattern or a combination of a central conduction layer pattern and an outer conduction layer pattern having an upwardly-opened dome structure surrounding the central conduction layer pattern, using an etch rate difference between insulating films.

Inventors: **Keum, Dong Yeal** (Kyoungki-do, Korea); **Park, Cheol Soo** (Kyoungki-do); **Ryou, Eui Kyu** (Kyoungki-do)

Assignee: **Hyundai Electronics Industries Co., Ltd.** (Kyoungki-do, Korea)

Patent V: United States Patent 6,447,943

Peled et al. September 10, 2002

Fuel cell **with proton conducting membrane with a pore size less than 30 nm**

Abstract

The present invention provides improved, low-cost fuel cells having reduced fuel crossover, reduced sensitivity to metal ion impurities and ability to operate under a broad range of temperatures. Additionally, new effective organic fuels are described for use in such fuel cells. The invention further provides improved methods for catalyst preparation and a new integrated flow field system for use in H_2 O_2 fuel cells. The *fuel cell* includes a proton conducting membrane having pore diameters which are essentially smaller than 30 nanometers.

Inventors: **Peled, Emanuel** (Even Yehuda, Israel); **Duvdevani, Tair** (Ramat Gan); **Melman; Avi** (Holon); **Aharon, Adi** (Herzliya)

Assignee: **Ramot University Authority for Applied Research & Industrial Development** (Tel Aviv, Israel)

Patent VI: United States Patent 6,414,734
Shigeta et al. July 2, 2002
Liquid crystal display device and liquid crystal projector
Abstract
A liquid crystal display device using a light source having a bright line in a visible region as a light source. On the inner surface of a transparent substrate such as a glass substrate constituting a liquid crystal display device, a laminate structure constituted by a transparent electrode, an alignment layer, and one or more transparent intermediate layers having a refractive index smaller than that of the transparent electrode layer and larger than that of the liquid crystal layer or the transparent substrate is formed. The thicknesses or the like of the layers are determined such that, at the bright line wavelengths of the light source, the sum of reflectances generated on the layer interfaces of the laminate structure is set to be not more than 0.5%.

Inventors: **Shigeta, Masanobu** (Kanagawa-ken, Japan); **Shimizu, Shigeo** (Kanagawa-ken)

Assignee: **Victor Company of Japan, Limited** (Kanagawa-ken, Japan)

Patent VII: United States Patent 6,458,923
Kyle October 1, 2002
Modified position (7) bradykinin antagonist peptides
Abstract
The substitution of the L-Pro at the 7-position of the peptide hormone bradykinin or other substituted analogs of bradykinin with an isoquinoline derivative which converts bradykinin agonists into bradykinin antagonists. The invention further includes the novel 7-position modified bradykinin antagonists which increase enzyme resistance, antagonist potency, and/or specificity of the new bradykinin antagonists. The analogs produced are useful in treating conditions and diseases of a mammal and human in which an excess of bradykinin or related kinins are produced or injected as by insect bites.

Inventors: **Kyle, Donald James** (Abington, MD)

Assignee: **Scios Inc.** (Sunnyvale, CA)

Patent VIII: United States Patent 6,080,753
Lyons et al. June 27, 2000
Stimulating nerve growth with immunophilins
Abstract
Immunophilin ligands act by binding to receptor proteins, immunophilins, which in turn can bind to and regulate the Ca^{2+} dependent phosphatase, calcineurin, and the Ca^{2+} release channel, the ryanodine receptor. Immunophilin ligands have been discovered to enhance neurite outgrowth in neuronal cell systems by increasing sensitivity to neurotrophic factors. The effects of the immunophilin ligands are detected at

subnanomolar concentrations indicating therapeutic application in diseases involving neural degeneration.

Inventors: **Lyons, W. Ernest** (Columbia, MD); **George, Edwin B.** (Baltimore, MD); **Dawson, Ted M.** (Baltimore, MD); **Steiner, Joseph P.** (Hampstead, MD); **Snyder, Solomon H.** (Baltimore, MD)

Assignee: **Johns Hopkins University School of Medicine** (Baltimore, MD)

Patent IX: United States Patent 5,831,572
Damilano November 3, 1998
Method and apparatus for measuring satellite attitude using GPS
Abstract

The apparatus has n non-aligned antennas, where n is at least for receiving radio signals from a plurality of OPS satellites. Radio frequency signals received by the various antennas are processed for measuring their phase differences, and for computing attitude on the basis of said phase differences. The measurement and computing system is repeatedly calibrated on the basis of measurements performed by a star sensor during periods when it provides usable data.

Inventors: **Damilano, Patrice** (Toulouse, France)

Assignee: **Matra Marconi Space France** (France)

Patent X: United States Patent 6,358,220
Langen et al. March 19, 2002
Thermoplastic casting material and method for production thereof
Abstract

The invention relates to a thermoplastic casting material, especially a thermoplastic casting material for orthopedic and other medical applications for immobilization of extremities and/or joints, that comprise a first textile fabric, a thermoplastic polymer applied to the first textile fabric and at least one second textile fabric applied to this composite. Additionally, the invention relates to a method for the production of this thermoplastic casting material that comprises the following steps: (a) application of a thermoplastic polymer on a first textile fabric and (b) application of at least one second textile fabric on the first textile fabric from step (a) provided with the thermoplastic polymer.

Inventors: **Langen, Gunter** (Wolfstein, Germany); **Meister, Marita** (Kaiserslautern); **Burger, Joachim** (Kaiserslautern)

Assignee: **Karl Otto Braun KG** (Wolfstein, Germany)

Patent XI: United States Patent 6,144,542
Ker et al. November 7, 2000
ESD bus lines in CMOS IC's for whole-chip ESD protection
Abstract

In this invention, a new whole-chip ESD protection scheme with the ESD buses has been proposed to solve the ESD protection issue of the CMOS IC having a large number of separated power lines. Multiple ESD buses, which are formed by the wide metal lines, have been added into the CMOS IC having a large number of separated power lines. The bi-directional ESD-connection cells are connected between the separated power lines and the ESD buses, but not between the separated power lines. The ESD current on the CMOS IC with more separated power lines are all conducted into the ESD buses, therefore the ESD current can be conducted by the ESD buses away from the internal circuits and quickly discharged through the designed ESD protection devices to ground. By using this new whole-chip ESD protection scheme with the ESD buses, the CMOS IC having more separated power lines can be still safely protected against ESD damages.

Inventors: **Ker, Ming-Dou** (Hsinchu, Taiwan); **Chang, Hun-Hsien** (Taipei)

Assignee: **Taiwan Semiconductor Manufacturing Co., Ltd.** (Hsinchu, Taiwan)

Patent XII: United States Patent 6,371,199
Gebhart April 16, 2002
Nucleate boiling surfaces for cooling and gas generation
Abstract

This invention provides heat transfer systems and methods of cooling surfaces and heating liquids which employ surfaces including a minimum density of discrete, nucleation sites having a conical cross-section tapering to a minimum predetermined depth. These surfaces are placed in contact with a refrigerant having a preselected boiling point so that the nucleation sites become largely flooded with the refrigerant. The nucleation sites permit nucleate boiling of a refrigerant without a temperature overshoot on the initial ascent. In more preferred variations of this invention, specific site spacing and geometries are employed to contain tiny bubble embryos, which minimize hysteresis and reversal of trend effects.

Inventors: **Gebhart, Benjamin** (Bryn Mawr, PA)

Assignee: **The Trustees of the University of Pennsylvania** (Philadelphia, PA)

Patent XIII: United States Patent 6,007,843
Drizen et al. December 28, 1999
Sustained release delivery system
Abstract

Sustained release compositions comprising a drug dispersed within a polymer matrix, methods of producing the same and treatments with the complex.

Inventors: **Drizen, Alan** (Ontario, CA); **Rothbart, Peter** (Ontario, CA); **Nath, Gary M.** (Bethesda, MD)

Assignee: **LAM Pharmaceuticals Corp.** (Miami, FL)

Patent XIV: United States Patent 6,395,715
Patierno et al. May 28, 2002
Uteroglobin gene therapy for epithelial cell cancer
Abstract

The present invention provides a novel method for inhibiting the growth of tumor cells of epithelial origin, comprising administration of a functional uteroglobin gene in a gene therapy regime, so as to inhibit growth of the tumor cells.

Inventors: **Patierno, Steven R.** (Falls Church, VA); **Manyak, Michael J.** (Chevy Chase, MD)

Assignee: **The George Washington University Medical Center** (Washington, DC)

References

BOOKS

Aoki, Masahiko and Ronald Dore (Editors) (1986). *The Japanese Firm: The Sources of Competitive Strength*. New York: Oxford University Press.

Brandenburger, Adam M. and Barry J. Nalebuff (1996). *Co-opetition*. Cambridge, MA: Harvard Business School Press.

Brooking, A. (1997). *Intellectual Capital*. London: International Thomson Business Press.

Chandler, Alfred D., Jr., (1977). *The Visible Hand: The Managerial Revolution in American Business*. Cambridge, MA: Harvard University Press.

Drucker, P. (1985). *Innovation and Entrepreneurship*. New York: HarperBusiness.

Drucker, P. (1991). *Managing for the Future*. New York: Truman-Talley Dutton.

Fukuyama, F. (1995). *Trust: The Social Virtues and the Creation of Prosperity*. Saratoga, CA: The Free Press.

Grove, Andy S. (1996). *Only the Paranoid Survive*. New York: Currency Doubleday.

Halal, William (1996). *The New Management*. San Francisco: Berret-Koehler Publishers, Inc.

Kay, J. (1995). *Why Firms Succeed*. Oxford: Oxford University Press.

Megantz, Robert C. (1996). *How to License Technology*. New York: John Wiley & Sons, Inc.

Milgrom, P., and J. Roberts (1992). *Economics, Organization, and Management*. Englewood Cliffs, NJ: Prentice-Hall.

Muir, Albert E. (1997). *The Technology Transfer System: Inventions - Marketing - Licensing - Patenting - Setting - Practice - Management - Policy*. New York: Latham Book.

Nonaka, I. and H. Takeuchi. (1995). *The Knowledge-Creating Company*. New York: Oxford University Press.

Parr, Russell L. (1993). *Intellectual Property Infringement Damages: A Litigation Support Handbook*. New York: John Wiley & Sons, Inc.

Parr, Russell L. (1998). *1998 Cumulative Supplement to Intellectual Property Infringement Damages: A Litigation Support Handbook*. New York: John Wiley & Sons, Inc.

Parr, Russell L. and Patrick H. Sullivan (Editors) (1996). *Technology Licensing: Corporate Strategies for Maximizing Value*. New York: John Wiley & Sons, Inc.

Polanyi, M. (1966). *The Tacit Dimension*. London: Routledge & Kegan Paul.

Reich, R. (1991). *The Work of Nations: Preparing Ourselves for 21st Century Capitalism*. New York: Alfred A. Knopf.

Rosenberg, S. and R. Birdzell (1985). *How the West Grew Rich: The Economic Transformation of the Industrial World*. New York: Basic Books.

Schlicher, John W. (1996). *Licensing Intellectual Property: Legal, Business and Market Dynamics*. New York: John Wiley & Sons, Inc.

Schlicher, John W. (1998). *Licensing Intellectual Property 1998: International Regulation, Strategy and Practices*. New York: John Wiley & Sons, Inc.

Schumpeter, J. (1934). *Theory of Economic Development*. New York: HarperCollins.

Simensky, Melvin and Lanning G. Bryer (1994). *The New Role of Intellectual Property in Commercial Transactions*. New York: John Wiley & Sons, Inc.

Simensky, Melvin, Lanning G. Bryer, and Neil J. Wilcof (1998). *1998 Cumulative Supplement to The New Role of Intellectual Property in Commercial Transactions*. New York: John Wiley & Sons, Inc.

Smith, Adam (1776). *An Inquiry into the Nature and Causes of the Wealth of Nations*. Reprinted 1990, New York: Oxford University Press.

Smith, Gordon V. (1997). *Trademark Valuation*. New York: John Wiley & Sons, Inc.

Smith, Gordon V. and Russell L. Parr (1999). *Valuation of Intellectual Property and Intangible Assets*. New York: John Wiley & Sons, Inc.

Williamson, Oliver E. and Scott E. Masten (Editors) (1985). *Transaction Cost Economics*. Aldershot, Hants, England; Brookfield, Vt.: Edward Elgar.

ARTICLES AND PRESENTATIONS

Anson, Weston (1993). "US Intangibles: Big Value, Big Headache." *Managing Intellectual Property*, September, pp. 14-18.

Anson, Weston and Mark Edwards (1996). "A Summary of Current Tax Trends and Issues Affecting Intellectual Property." *Intellectual Property Today*, August.

Arthur, W. B. (1996). "Increasing Returns and the New World of Business." *Harvard Business Review*, July-August, pp. 100-109.

Barney, J. (1991). "Firm Resources and Sustained Competitive Advantage." *Journal of Management*, v. 17, no. 1, pp. 99-120.

Beck, Henry (1995). "The Development, Financing, and Acquisition of Information Age Assets." *The Computer Lawyer*, January, p. 14.

Bertolotti, Nick (1995). "Valuing Intellectual Property." *Managing Intellectual Property*, February, pp. 28-32.

Birkin, Michael (1993). "Placing a Value upon Trademarks and Brand Names." *Managing Intellectual Property*, July/August, pp. 25-31.

Bloom, Christopher A. (1994). "Does the Target's Brainpower Provide a Competitive Edge?" *Mergers and Acquisitions*, January/February, pp. 44-46.

Bransten, Lisa (2001). "Seeking Survival, Start-ups go into Hibernation Mode," *The Wall Street Journal*, December 31.

Brooking, A. and E. Motta (1996). "A Taxonomy of Intellectual Capital and a Methodology for Auditing It." *17th Annual National Business Conference, McMaster University, Ontario, Canada*, 24-26 Jan.

Carayannis, Elias (2001a). "The GloCal Knowledge Manifesto: e-Knowledge for all: Leveraging the Global Digital Divide through Global, Regional and Local (GloCal) Networks of Real and Virtual Incubators and Technical Assistance Centers." *Invited Presentation, InfoDev / IFC, The World Bank Group*, April 12.

Carayannis, Elias (2001b). "Glocal Real, Virtual Incubator Networks (G-RVINs) for Developing and Emerging Economies: Leveraging the Digital Divide to Catalyze Entrepreneurial Growth." *R&D Management Conference*, Dublin, Ireland, September 7-9.

Carayannis Elias (2001c). "Is Higher Order Technological Learning a Firm Core Competence, How, Why, and When: A Longitudinal, Multi-Industry Study of Firm Technological Learning and Market Performance." *International Journal of Technovation*, August.

Carayannis, Elias (2002a). "e-Radicating Poverty: e-Knowledge for all using 'GloCal' Virtual Incubator Networks in Fostering Entrepreneurship for International Development." *International Association for the Management of Technology Conference (IAMOT)*, March 9-15.

Carayannis, Elias et al (2002b). "Measuring Intangibles: Managing Intangibles for Tangible Outcomes." *IAMOT*, Miami, Florida, March 10-14.

Carayannis, Elias et al (2002c). "Intellectual Venture Capitalists: Re-engineering Relationships between Entrepreneurs and Professional Services Firms." *IAMOT*, Miami, Florida, March 10-14.

Carayannis, Elias and Jeffrey Alexander (1998). "Winning by Co-Opeting in Knowledge-Driven, Complex Environments: The Formation of Strategic Technology Government-University-Industry (GUI) Partnerships." *Triple Helix: Government-University-Industry Partnerships*, Westchester, NY, January 7-10.

Carayannis, Elias and Jeffrey Alexander (1999). "Winning by Co-opeting in Knowledge-Driven, Complex Environments: The Formation of Strategic Technology Government-University-Industry (GUI) Partnerships." *Journal of Technology Transfer*, vol. 24, no. 2/3. (*1999 Lang-Rosen Award for Best Paper by the Technology Transfer Society*).

Carayannis, Elias, Alistair Preston, and Marc Awerbuch (1996). "Architectural innovation, technological learning, and the virtual utility concept." *Proceedings of the International Conference on Engineering and Technology Management, IEEE Engineering Management Society*, Vancouver, Canada, August 18-20.

Carayannis, Elias and Samanta Roy (1999). "The Speed and Acceleration of Technological Innovation: A Co-opetitive Dynamics Perspective of the Small Satellites Industry." *Portland International Conference on Management of Engineering and Technology (PICMET 99)*, Portland, Oregon, July (*Best Conference Paper Award*).

Cohen, Laurence (1994). "Brands and Valuations." *Managing Intellectual Property*, June, pp. 23-25.

De Souza, Glenn (1997). "Royalty Methods for Intellectual Property." *Business Economics*, April, pp. 46-57.

Eiblum, Paula and Stephanie C. Ardito (1998). "Royalty Fees Part I: The Copyright Clearance Center and Publishers." *Online*, March/April, pp. 83-86.

Foray, D. (1991). "Repères pour une Économie des Organisations de Recherche-Développement." *Revue d'Économie Politique,* 101 (5).

Gamble, Twila and Jennifer Tanner (1996). "The Strategy of a Licensing Campaign," *Intellectual Property Today,* September, p. 50.

Getzoff, Steven M. (1994). "Brand Valuation and Trade Mark Management." *Managing Intellectual Property,* pp. 27-28.

Ghoshal, S. and P. Moran (1996). "Bad for Practice: a Critique of the Transaction Cost Theory." *Academy of Management Review,* Vol. 21:1, pp. 13-47

Grant, R. (1991). "The Resource-Based Theory of Competitive Advantage: Implications for Strategy Formulation." *California Management Review,* Spring.

Haas, David A., Daniel M. McGavock, and Michael P. Patin (1991). "Licensing Practices, Business Strategy, and Factors Affecting Royalty Rates: Results of a Survey." *Licensing Law and Business Report,* March-April, pp. 205-216.

Kalos, Stephen H. and Jonathan D. Putnam (1997). "On the Incomparability of 'Comparables': An Economic Interpretation of 'Infringer's' Royalties." *The Journal of Proprietary Rights,* April, pp. 2-5.

Killingsworth, Scott (1998a). "Form, Function, and Fairness: Structuring the Technology Joint Venture (Part I)." *The Computer Lawyer,* April, p. 8.

Killingsworth, Scott (1998b). "Form, Function, and Fairness: Structuring the Technology Joint Venture (Part II)." *The Computer Lawyer,* March.

Lerner, Joshua (1994). "The Importance of Patent Scope: An Empirical Analysis." *RAND Journal of Economics,* pp. 319-333.

Misrack, Karyl M. (1997). "Valuing Intellectual Property: The Science and the Art." *The Colorado Lawyer,* August, pp. 85-91.

Mullin, Rick (1996a). "Intellectual Assets." *Chemical Week,* December 11, pp. 26-32.

Mullin, Rick (1996b). "Knowledge Management." *Journal of Business Strategy,* September, pp. 56-59.

Murphy, John M. (1993). "Intangible Assets, Brand Valuations and Changing Industry Attitudes." *Managing Intellectual Property,* June, pp. 7-11.

Nature Biotechnology (2001). "Clinical Trials Costs," vol. 19, September, pp. 813-817.

Neil, D. J. (1988). "The Valuation of Intellectual Property." *Technology Magazine,* March, pp. 31-42.

O'Brien, Chris (1998). "IBM's Patent Penchant." *The Raleigh News and Observer,* 13 January, p. D1.

Reilly, Robert F. (1996). "How Buyers Value Intellectual Properties." *Mergers and Acquisitions,* January-February, pp. 40-44.

Romary, John M. (1998). "Patents for Sale: Evaluating the Value of US Patent Licenses." *European Intellectual Property Review,* June 4, pp. 3-9.

Sager, Ira (1997). "Big Blue Is Out to Collar Software Scofflaws." *Business Week,* 17 March, p. 34.

Schweihs, Robert P. and Robert F. Reilly (1988). "The Valuation of Intellectual Properties." *Licensing Law and Business Report,* May-June, pp. 1-12.

Tsoukas, H. (1996). "The Firm as a Distributed Knowledge System: A Constructionist Approach." *Strategic Management Journal,* 17 (Winter), pp. 11-25.

Udell, Gerald G. and Thomas A. Potter (1989). "Pricing New Technology." *Research-Technology Management,* July-August, pp. 14-18.

Index

About the Authors

ELIAS G. CARAYANNIS is Associate Professor of Management Science at the School of Business and Public Management at George Washington University.

TODD L. JUNEAU is a Partner in Nath & Associates, a law firm in Washington, DC.

CPSIA information can be obtained
at www.ICGtesting.com
Printed in the USA
JSHW041744280822
29673JS00001B/1